A DARK HISTORY OF
CHOCOLATE

A DARK HISTORY OF
CHOCOLATE

EMMA KAY

PEN & SWORD
HISTORY

AN IMPRINT OF PEN & SWORD BOOKS LTD.
YORKSHIRE - PHILADELPHIA

First published in Great Britain in 2021 by
PEN AND SWORD HISTORY
An imprint of
Pen & Sword Books Ltd
Yorkshire – Philadelphia

ISBN 978 1 52676 830 8

A CIP catalogue record for this book is available from the British Library.

Typeset in Times New Roman 11.5/14 by
SJmagic DESIGN SERVICES, India.
Printed and bound by CPI Group (UK) Ltd, Croydon, CR0 4YY

Pen & Sword Books Limited incorporates the imprints of Atlas, Archaeology,
Aviation, Discovery, Family History, Fiction, History, Maritime, Military, Military
Classics, Politics, Select, Transport, True Crime, Air World, Frontline Publishing,
Leo Cooper, Remember When, Seaforth Publishing, The Praetorian Press,
Wharncliffe Local History, Wharncliffe Transport, Wharncliffe True Crime and
White Owl.

For a complete list of Pen & Sword titles please contact
PEN & SWORD BOOKS LIMITED
47 Church Street, Barnsley, South Yorkshire, S70 2AS, England
E-mail: enquiries@pen-and-sword.co.uk
Website: www.pen-and-sword.co.uk

Or
PEN AND SWORD BOOKS
1950 Lawrence Rd, Havertown, PA 19083, USA
E-mail: Uspen-and-sword@casematepublishers.com
Website: www.penandswordbooks.com

Contents

Acknowledgements

I would like to thank a number of staff at Pen & Sword Books for their continued support and for allowing me to write another book for them, which was a joy. In particular, Claire Hopkins, designer Paul Wilkinson for the great book jacket, Lori Jones, Laura Hirst and Karyn Burnham for all their editing skills and the marvellously upbeat Charlie Simpson ever on the treadmill of promotion. And gratitude to Alan Murphy for giving me the ideas.

As always, I must give credit to my long-suffering husband and my gorgeous, patient son: both of them are inspiring, supportive and extremely tolerant when it comes to my work and career. And to friends, family and everyone in my life who continues to encourage me along the way as a food historian.

A special thank you also to The Cockington Chocolate Company in Devon, in particular Tony Fagan and Simon Storey. The angle of the book didn't end up going quite that way, but I learnt a lot from you!

Introduction

While researching this book I discovered a remarkable amount of information about chocolate and its historical connection with the bleaker aspects of global society. I knew, of course, that its origins were Mexican, and that cacao production was intrinsic to the murky world of slavery, but what I hadn't really considered was chocolate's extraordinary capacity to both nurture and adulterate.

Perhaps it is best to start by exploring exactly what the word 'dark' means in the context of the title.

I originally set out with the intention of interviewing chocolatiers and getting some insight into the pitfalls of working with chocolate – politically and economically, as well as planning to investigate the historical impact of plantations, both the human and environmental consequences. What actually happened was a shift towards the scrutiny of stories in which chocolate itself has played a pivotal role, though not in the Valentine's Day, fluffy bunnies and sweet dreams way, obviously, as this was always going to be a dark book: dark, as in the kind that encompasses a grim hopelessness, secretive motives and sinister opportunities. It is a word that has so many definitions it's easy to lose yourself in the potential for exploring all of them. There will be occasions in this book, when you think to yourself, 'well hold on, that's a good thing isn't it?' And yes, there will be the light that emerges from the dark, the hope that chocolate administers in desperate times, its ability to raise the spirits when all else around is chaos. Chocolate has both made men (and women) and broken them too. It has the potential to elevate confidence where inappropriateness prevails and the ability to camouflage death itself. Chocolate is both wondrous and destructive. It is light and dark, just like its different types.

Those of you reading this may already know something of the story of how Europe was introduced to chocolate, but what you might not fully comprehend is the somewhat unscrupulous narrative, from chocolate's medicinal origins to its commercial excesses, with its potential to exploit, kill, drug and abuse in between.

But first I am going to use this bit of the book for its correct purpose, to introduce the reader to the origins of chocolate and its journey towards mainstream stardom throughout the world.

Theobroma Cacao (food of the gods) is a small tree native to the Americas. Growing to around 16-18ft high, with thin, oblong, pointed leaves, its flowers are small and eventually produce pods that can grow up to 10in long. Each one contains around fifty or more seeds, which, when ripe, are dried in the sun, becoming chocolate beans, or nuts. Despite its Greek god-like origins, theobromine is also a close relative of caffeine, both addictive and a stimulant.

Chocolate derives from the Maya words *chacau* and *kaa* – or hot drink. This morphed into *cacauhaltl* and *xocoatl*, eventually becoming cacao. Cacao is the name applied to the plant or beans prior to processing, while chocolate refers to anything made out of the beans. Cocoa is the powdered form of chocolate, where half of the fat or cacao butter is removed from the chocolate liquor. The pods still need to be harvested by hand, which is a time-consuming, intensive and laborious process, undertaken with a machete. Each pod contains around forty beans and most cacao trees take at least three years to produce beans. These beans are fermented, dried, roasted and crushed. This separates the nib from the hull. The nibs are then ground, before being ready to make into a variety of chocolate products.

Cacao is believed to have originated in the Amazon some 4,000 years ago. The Maya worshipped an ancient fertility goddess of chocolate, flowers and fruit, who they named Ixcacao. She blessed the annual harvests and protected the people. The Popol Vuh, or the 'Book of the Community', was a narrative passed down orally by the Maya peoples, which was eventually recorded in writing in the 1500s. A more concise manuscript of these stories was transcribed later in the eighteenth century. It provides early accounts, myths and legends of the ancient indigenous communities of what we now know as Mexico, Belize, Guatemala, El Salvador, Nicaragua, Honduras and Costa Rica among others, sometimes referred to as Mesoamerica. This is where some of the earliest historical accounts of cacao originate. The Mayan god, Ekchuah, was the god of merchants and cacao planters. Those who owned cacao plantations held sacrificial rituals, offering up dogs unlucky enough to have cacao-coloured markings in Ekchuah's honour.

During human sacrifices such as the Aztec annual festival of Huitzilopochtli, (god of war and sun) honouring Yacatecuhtli, patron to the god of commerce and travellers, the individual was often given a thick cup of cacao to drink before the event, to lull them into a state of euphoria, open their minds to the spirit world and presumably make the whole process a little less distressing. The Aztecs believed cacao was a gift from their god, Quetzalcoatl, who was supposed to have discovered it inside a mountain. As well as drinking it as a thick, unsweetened liquid, the cacao bean was a valuable currency. The English translation of Pietro Martire d'Anghiera's *The decades of the newe worlde or west India conteynyng the nauigations and conquestes of the Spanyardes,* published in 1555, notes that the people of new Spain, or Mexico as we now know it 'haue not the use of golde and syluer money, but use in the steade therof the halfe shelles of almonds, whiche kynde of Bararous money they caule Cacao.'[1]

It is interesting to note that cacao fruit was often compared to almonds in early literary references. There is a physical similarity, and almonds and cacao have often traditionally been paired together in recipes. Both nuts can also help with reducing cholesterol. It was also popular for a time to mould chocolate into the shape of almonds, which Britain had been importing since at least the 1400s but which may have become an expensive commodity.

The recipe below is from Mary Eales's book *Mrs Mary Eales's Receipts,* originally written in 1711, before being published at the time of her supposed death in 1718. Gum Dragon is a bit like an early gelatine, once used in a lot of confectionery. The 'spoonful's of Ben' mentioned here could refer to ben-nuts, from which oil was extracted, and which were a bit similar to horseradish in taste.

Interestingly, Eales claimed to be the confectioner to Queen Anne. There are no formal records of her listed in the royal household at this time, so she may have made a one-off product for the queen and exploited her claims, though her book of receipts was published by the Royal Bookbinders, J.Brindley. Incidentally, Mary Eales is also cited with some frequency as publishing the first recipe for ice cream in English. However, there are other earlier references for this, including the manuscript recipe book of Grace Carteret, 1st Countess of Granville.

Mary Eales's recipe for chocolate almonds
Take two Pound of fine sifted Sugar, half a Pound of
Chocolate grated, and sifted thro' an Hair Sieve, a Grain
of Musk, a Grain of Amber, and two Spoonful's of Ben;
make this up to a stiff Paste with Gum-Dragon steep'd well
in Orange-Flower-Water; beat it well in a Mortar; make it in
a Mould like Almonds; lay them to dry on Papers, but not
in a Stove.

Some historians argue that it was Christopher Columbus, who, on
intercepting a ship carrying cacao beans in 1502, was the one to introduce
Europe to its riches, while Guatemalan Mayans were believed to have
presented Prince Philip of Spain with clay gourds filled with chocolate
in the mid-sixteenth century, instantly making it the drink of choice in
the Spanish court.

The catalyst is more likely to have been the result of early
Conquistadors usurping the Aztec kingdoms prevailed over by
Montezuma.

In the 1400s the Aztecs ruled an empire in central Mexico, one that
included some 400 cities. Moctezuma II, or Montezuma (translating as
'he who frowns like a lord') acquired the throne in 1502 as the ninth and
final emperor of the Aztec people. He received a broad education and
became skilled in mathematics and military strategy.

Montezuma led numerous successful conquests and was attentive
towards the welfare of his people. Personal details about the man himself
remain scarce and contradictory.

Spanish explorers arrived in Tenochtitlan, what is now known as
Mexico City, in 1518 to resupply and carry out repairs. Dissatisfied with
their tardiness, Captain Hernán Cortés, who was leading the expedition,
caught up with the crew and soon became acquainted with the Aztecs.

Desperate for a meeting with Montezuma, Cortés attempted
contact several times, but to no avail, with Montezuma being reluctant
to host foreign visitors at a time when the Aztec calendar predicted
bad omens for the year ahead. A battle ensued, and with the Spanish
having the advantage of horse and fire power over the Aztecs, who
had never even seen a horse, Montezuma had no choice but to receive
Cortés and his Conquistadors. The emperor provided them with a
great deal of freedom, which would be to his disadvantage. As soon

as the Spanish overthrew Montezuma, he lost all authority, leaving his people vulnerable.

An officer from Cortés' crew, Bernal Diaz del Castillo, wrote accounts of the Mexican conquest and the initial arrival of the Spanish, describing cacao beans that were being sold in the market place, in what today is a suburb of Mexico City.

> On reaching the market-place [at Tlatelolco] … we were astounded at the great number of people and the quantities of merchandise, and at the orderliness and good arrangements that prevailed, for we had never seen such a thing before. Let us begin with the dealers in gold, silver, and precious stones, feathers, cloaks, and embroidered goods, and male and female slaves … there were those who sold coarser cloth, and cotton goods and fabrics made of twisted thread, and there were chocolate merchants with the chocolate. In this way you could see every kind of merchandise to be found anywhere in New Spain.

Castillo also recorded one of the many elaborate feasts held by Montezuma, noting:

> At another time he would have jesters to enliven him with their witticisms. Others again danced and sung before him. Motecusuma took great delight in these entertainments, and ordered the broken victuals and pitchers of cacao liquor to be distributed among these performers. As soon as he had finished his dinner the four women cleared the cloths and brought him water to wash his hands. During this interval he discoursed a little with the four old men, and then left table to enjoy his afternoon's nap.[2]

A victim of his own downfall, Montezuma's people allegedly turned against him and he was pelted to death with stones in 1520.[3] There is, however, another theory claiming Montezuma was murdered by the Spanish when he became surplus to their requirements. He is depicted in a fairly recently discovered manuscript of illustrations as shackled and hung by a rope.

Bernal Diaz Del Castillo suggested Montezuma was a noble and well-respected leader:

> Cortés and all of us captains and soldiers wept for him, and there was no one among us that knew him and had dealings with him who did not mourn him as if he were our father, which was not surprising, since he was so good ... The Great Montezuma, was about forty years old, of good height, well proportioned, spare and slight, and not very dark, though of the usual Indian complexion. He did not wear his hair long but just over his ears, and he had a short black beard, well-shaped and thin ... His face was rather long and cheerful, he had fine eyes, and in his appearance and manner could express geniality or, when necessary, a serious composure. He was neat and clean, and took a bath every afternoon ... He had many women as his mistresses, the daughters of chieftains, but two legitimate wives ... The clothes he wore one day he did not wear again until three or four days later. He had a guard of two hundred chieftains lodged in rooms beside his own, only some of whom were permitted to speak to him.[4]

Montezuma's reputation remains a contentious one, but undoubtedly his hospitality towards the Spanish was eventually warm and welcoming, extending to offerings of native food and drink, including *xocoatl*, or chocolate. It was originally thought to have been discovered by the first Mexican civilization, the Olmecs, who then passed it down to the Maya, before the Aztecs coveted it more than gold.

Cortés returned to Spain in 1528 with cocoa beans from Mexico and from there its popularity spread throughout Europe. Cacao was imported from Spain's colonies in large quantities from the first half of the seventeenth century and the Dutch in particular shipped a great deal of cacao, enabling it to be sold in chocolate houses as early as the 1660s.

Colonists of 'New Spain' forced local communities into slavery on freshly planted cacao plantations. Several centuries of misrule, disease and epidemics meant that only a very small percentage of the original enslaved native population remained by the end of the seventeenth century. By the 1800s cacao had migrated to Africa, with cuttings from

South America finding their way into various colonies of West Africa, including Ghana, Nigeria, French Cameroun and the Ivory Coast. Africa now provides most of the world's cacao for chocolate production.

When the British captured Jamaica from the Spanish in 1655, they discovered flourishing 'cacao walks', which they soon took advantage of, securing Jamaica as England's main supplier for a time. The price of cacao began to fall after Spain lost its monopoly and French, English and Dutch producers started to cultivate it throughout their own colonies.

It is thought that the Carletti family, either father or son, were the first to introduce chocolate into Italy following their travels in the West Indies and Spain sometime in the early 1600s. The Italians originally drank their chocolate cold, with ice cubes or snow. The first town to receive cocoa was, allegedly, Perugia, a legend that extends today with its annual chocolate festival, the largest in Europe, together with the town's iconic chocolate '*baci*', or kiss, established in 1922, but now owned by Nestlé.[5] The Germans were one of the first countries to adopt the fashion for drinking chocolate before retiring to bed and Switzerland started manufacturing chocolate in 1792, but it wasn't until the 1800s that it really became popular and mass-produced. The presence of chocolate in Belgium can be traced back to around 1635 when Emmanuel Swares de Rinero granted exclusivity on its manufacture in the Brabant region around thirty years later.

Chocolate first arrived in Norway sometime during the eighteenth century, when a merchant in Trondheim placed a newspaper advertisement for 'a kind of medicinal chocolate, which will help your stomach, chest, is good for healing coughs, gets rid of dizziness, clears phlegm and encourages fulfilment of marital duties': it was seen as both healthy and 'sinful'.[6]

The overall growth in popularity of chocolate throughout Europe can be attributed to its evolution from a simple drink mixed with water or milk to the main component of confectionery and other culinary items. The Oxford English Dictionary suggests that the earliest accounts of chocolate being consumed as a beverage in England were in 1604 and as a paste or cake in 1659. Chocolate also became subject to strict government control, to raise revenue from customs and excise, as well as to protect English chocolate-makers from overseas rivals. A list of 'Goods Imported to London' from 25 to 28 February 1721 confirms that 35 cwt. (about 1.7 tons) of chocolate came to the UK via Holland.[7]

By 1723 all imports of 'ready-made' chocolate were banned. New taxes were introduced, with the announcement that: 'every Druggist, Grocer, Chandler, Coffeehouse-keeper, Chocolatehouse-keeper, and all other Persons who shall become a Seller or Sellers, Dealer or Dealers in Coffee, Tea, Cocoa Nuts or Chocolate, either Wholesale or Retail, or Maker of Chocolate [were requested to register the exact origins of their products].'

After 1723 regulations in England regarding the making of chocolate in the home and allocation of cacao nuts for personal use, re-established the importation of solid chocolate 'cakes' of ground and bound cacao beans. In fact, this made little difference to the trade of chocolate in this form, as it was frequently exposed to insect decay and unpleasant odours, tainting its overall quality.[8]

John Nott's *Cooks and Confectioners Dictionary* of 1723 directs the reader on how chocolate was prepared with both water and milk at this time (Nott was cook to The Duke of Bolton). It is interesting to see that flour was originally used to thicken the drink, which must have made it very dense.

> **To make Chocolate with Water**
> To a Quart of Water, put a quarter of Pound of Chocolate without Sugar, fine Sugar a quarter of a Pound, good Brandy a quarter of a Pound, fine Flour half a quarter of an Ounce and a little Salt; mix them, dissolve them and boil them, which will be done in ten or twelve Minutes.

> **To make Chocolate with Milk**
> Take a Quart of Milk, Chocolate without Sugar four Ounces, fine Sugar as much; fine Flour or Starch half a quarter of an Ounce, a little Salt; mix them, dissolve them and boil them as before.[9]

In this book you will discover stories of how pirates, murderers and seducers have exploited chocolate for financial, personal and emotional gain. It has led to the destruction, not only of individual souls, but of whole communities. Chocolate also has the potential to hide the wickedest of intentions and most despicable acts.

Writing in 1714, the church officer Paul Lorrain declared: 'Nothing in the World so nastily made for the Body of Mankind, as Chocolate upon a Stone, not to mention the many nasty Adulteries, or what is sold about Streets, little better than Poyson.'[10]

Chocolate was frequently adulterated with noxious ingredients including vanilla and Castile soap, a hard, vegetable oil-based soap originating in Syria and introduced to Europe by the Crusaders. The vanilla gave it an odour, while the soap made it froth up when dissolved in liquid. Flour was also used to bulk up the chocolate in the absence of cocoa beans.

The 1899 book *Practical Confectionery Recipes for Household and Manufacturers* indicates that there were two main ways at the time to identify chocolate that had been adulterated – that it crumbled when broken and it felt warm on the tongue, as opposed to being cool. Chocolate, however, can also mask poisonous substances and disguise the deadliest of enemies. Its potential to become addictive as both stimulant and mood enhancer also makes it a powerful drug. The French eighteenth-century writer Voltaire is alleged to have drunk in excess of forty cups a day of coffee mixed with chocolate, to keep his writing inspired and prolific, while in 1995 a humble Mars Bar was used to smuggle heroin and cannabis into a prison.[11]

The human brain produces a chemical called phenylethylamine, which occurs when lovers become aroused. It is also found in chocolate, so, perhaps it's no surprise that, historically, chocolate has been abused for its seductive powers, arousing those desires that may otherwise have been quelled. It's interesting to note here how there remains a propensity for regarding some historic characters as charming and romantic, dashing and adventurous, when perhaps we should be re-evaluating them, exposing their faults and acknowledging their unseemly natures. For example, was Giacomo Casanova an irresistible and debonair wooer of women, or was he a debauched, immoral and promiscuous abuser, with chocolate at the heart of his entrapments. This book will take you through a journey of some of these histories, which is not always for the fainthearted. There are gruesome tales and challenging narratives, as well as some difficult and distasteful insights into the wider study of cacao production and manufacture.

There are also some sad stories related to chocolate. Take, for example, the traditional model of the nineteenth-century workhouse, built for those who were unable to support themselves financially, and which later evolved into other forms of social care, including 'cottage homes', where children of the poorest in society lived, along with a house 'parent' of some kind. Isabel Green, one of the residents of these 'homes' in Dewsbury in the 1950s, recalled Christmases spent there, when her biological mother would send her annual box of Black Magic chocolates (Black Magic was a popular and affordable luxury brand created in the 1930s by Rowntree's and is now owned by Nestlé). Sadly, Isabel never got to taste any of the chocolate, as each year it was taken by the staff and blatantly eaten in front of her and her sister, Sylvia.[12]

In the 1990s, prisoners in the Soviet Union were forbidden food packages containing chocolate. These restrictions were enforced to prevent the inmates hoarding high-calorie products that could fuel them with the strength needed to escape.[13] Perhaps this was a theory shared by the staff at Isabel Green's cottage home. In fact, this rule remained a restriction in Russian prisons until at least 2006, according to Human Rights Watch interviews, and may well still be enforced today. Interestingly, a similar act of 1822 sanctioned across some American prisons called for the prohibition of the following foods: crackers, milk, onions, chocolate, tobacco, snuff, tea, coffee, rice, pepper, flour, apples and cider.[14] Presumably because they were considered luxury items.

Our book focuses on a range of areas reflecting on chocolate's controversial past. Some are inadvertently sinister, like the establishment of the nationwide Cocoa Rooms of the late-1800s, with a remit to curb the evils of alcohol in society, or the presence of chocolate in moments of extreme hardship. Others, however, such as the growth of the salacious chocolate houses of the eighteenth-century, and the grim repercussions of over-farmed cocoa plantations, retain chocolate right at the heart of their depravity.

As Europeans continued to modify chocolate to suit their tastes – adding sugar, heating and grinding the cocoa solids to make them smoother and less bitter, creating solid bars of chocolate, which eventually became chocolate puddings and desserts – the world inevitably became more reliant on it.

One of the earliest examples of chocolate actually being used in the culinary sense is in 1723, when a recipe for 'chocolate biskets' was published in John Nott's *The Cook's and Confectioner's Dictionary:*

To make Chocolate Biskets
Scrape a little Chocolate upon the Whites of Eggs, so much
as will give it the Taste and Colour of the Chocolate. Then
mingle with it powder Sugar, till it becomes a pliable Paste.
Then dress your Biskets upon Sheets of Paper, in what Form
you please and set them into the Oven to be bak'd with a
gentle Fire, both at top and underneath.[15]

While this demand increased, slavery, including child labour and the
profiteering of overseas lands by wealthier nations, intensified. The
world's reliance on chocolate is visible in the archives of trade and
empire, adventurers and explorers, during war and finally as a global
commercial enterprise which threatens to implode at any moment.

As the planet continues to deplete its cacao resources, scientists
working with major chocolate manufacturers have begun to study the
genetic properties of the cacao tree in the hope of creating some sort
of genetically modified replica, which is both immune to disease and
environmental impacts. The consequences of this are formidable – the
daunting ramifications of genetic modification versus losing chocolate
as we know it forever could probably fill a book of its own. While it is
imperative that a solution is found to safeguard the future of chocolate,
it is of equal importance that the outstanding legacies of child labour,
and other unethical practices that prevail, are eradicated and that the
integrity of the environment is maintained.

The book does include some shocking content, but where I have
linked recipes to dreadful examples of depravity I have been conscious
of trying not to diminish or sensationalise the importance of the story
itself: rather I have attempted to emphasise the juxtaposition between
the narrative and the recipe.

I hope that after reading this book you will gain a broader understanding
of the astonishing historic contribution that chocolate has made to the
world, as well as appreciating some its more shadowy aspects. A world
without chocolate seems unfathomable, but imminent change is also
essential to its survival.

Early recipes using chocolate in cooking, as opposed to drinking,
are rare and usually limited to chocolate cream 'biskets' or puffs. In
1737 T. Reed/Read put together a compilation of recipes in *The Whole
Duty of a Woman,* clearly contributed by others. Recipe plagiary was

rife throughout the eighteenth and nineteenth centuries, with many authors simply rewriting whole books and putting their name to it, which sometimes makes it difficult to attribute the correct author to the recipe. Reed's book unusually lists all the contributors at the start. This recipe for chocolate tart is a nice way to introduce the book as an example of how chocolate was being incorporated in a culinary capacity, beyond drinking, very early on in European society.

A Chocolate Tart

We take two Spoonful's of Rice-Flour, some salt, with the yolk of four Eggs, and a little Milk; mix all these together, but don't let them curdle; then grate some chocolate and dry it before the fire, and when your Cream is boiled, mix the Chocolate well in it; and so set it to cool; make your Tart of good fine Flour, put in the Cream and bake it: When it is enough, glaze it with powder Sugar with a red hot Fire-shovel; then serve it.

Chapter 1

Killers, Cargo and Cajolery: Chocolate at its Darkest

Throughout history, characters like Casanova and Madame du Barry procured chocolate to seduce their partners while early Mexican communities were reliant on its hallucinogenic properties, evidence of which has been uncovered in ancient cave drawings.

From poisonous potions concealed with cocoa, to the heinous acts of slavery and piracy, the archives are littered with evidence linking chocolate to a myriad of dirty deeds and sullied tales of the trade and consumption of chocolate.

Chocolate also features at the heart of many tragic and perilous endeavours, as if the ancient Aztec communities themselves had cursed cacao the very day it left their shores.

Trade and slavery

Formed in 1600 by a group of merchants granted a Royal Charter by Queen Elizabeth I, which then expanded into an entire naval system, commanding armies and controlling nations, the East India Company managed all trading activities from the 'East Indies' to England up until 1833. British colonies in the West Indies were regulated in a very different way. The first colonies of the British Empire were those of Virginia in North America and Barbados in the West Indies. African slaves were transported to these colonies to work on the plantations from the early 1600s. This trade increased after 1700 when slaves were also transported to Spanish South America. It has been estimated that some twelve million Africans were captured and transported to the Americas over a 200-year period. Jamaica was earmarked for cacao cultivation by the English early on, following the lucrative spoils of cotton, sugar and the highly coveted natural blue dye, indigo.

By 1688 the Dutch were importing large quantities of cacao from the Spanish controlled West Indies into Holland, which raised the price considerably for the English, who were finding Jamaican cacao difficult to acquire, while trade relations with Spain remained difficult.[1] Bahia in Brazil was also the location for small experimental cacao plantations in the 1600s. These expanded and became some of the most significant cacao producing regions in the world.

The South Sea Company, the company granted monopoly to trade with the islands of the south seas and south America from 1711, documented an estimated 5,000 slaves being imported into Spanish American ports including Porto Bello, Panama, Cartagena, Havana, Guatemala and many others between 1727 and 1739.

The peak of the French slave trade in Africa was between 1783-92, and cocoa, along with sugar, coffee and cotton, poured into the nation at an estimated value of 160 million livres in 1785.[2] São Tomé, one of Africa's oldest colonial cities, and its neighbouring island, Principe, were the world's third largest exporters of cocoa after Ecuador and Brazil by the early 1900s. Despite its abolition some half a century before, slaves were still being used to harvest the fruit.[3]

By the eighteenth century the world had become bewitched by chocolate, with nations competing with one another for control of its production and distribution, regardless of the cost to lives. Countless ships were intercepted by the Spanish and plundered for their cargoes of cacao beans. This letter from Governor Pulleine to The Council of Trade and Plantations, offers one example of this:

> The Spaniards, from several of ye ports, here in ye North Seas, arm out sloops with commissions to seize all English vessels in which they find, any Spanish money (even to ye value of but ten peices of eight), any salt, cacao, or hides, for wch. reasons any vessels that trade in these parts, from port to port, are certainly prizes, if they can overpower them, having one or other of these commodities always aboard 'em. This Island has already had three vessels thus taken, since ye Peace, and they even apprehend their total ruin, if your Ldships Do't interfere, by our Embassadour, at ye Court of Spain, to gain them reparation, and that, very suddenly: For, we know not what remedy to apply against

people, that make daily captures of us, in ye midst of a Peace newly concluded; for which reason, we might hope, it wou'd have been better observ'd. I most humbly entreat your Lordships to let me hear something encourageing from you on this head, to keep this poor Island from desponding; for they are in ye uttmost consternation. *Refers to enclusure,* the rest haveing not given in their complaints: but I expect it from them daily. I hear likewise, of several other vessels taken belonging to other collonys; but that being no business of mine, shall say nothing further to it, *etc.* P.S. Since my concludeing this letter, one Mr. Jones has brought the enclosed complaint, *etc.* I am afraid if some speedy care be not taken; your Lships will have frequent occasions of being teaz'd with things of this kind, to ye great sorrow of H.M. subjects here.

Signed, Henry Pulleine. *Endorsed*, Recd. 22nd, Read 23rd Feb. 1713/14. 2 *pp. Enclosed*,[4]

The following deposition made by mariner George Graves from 1671 is also indicative of the marauding actions of the Spanish at this time.

He was a prisoner at Carthagena in the West Indies last December, and there saw and was on board the *Thomas and Richard*, and spoke with the mate, boatswain, and others of her company, who told him that the said ship being laden with cacao, sugar, elephants' teeth, gold, and divers other goods, and some passengers bound from Jamaica to London, was, last September, taken by a Spanish ship in latitude 29° 30' about three days' sail this side the Gulf of Florida, and brought in there as prize, and that the said mate and others are made prisoners and slaves there, and that when he made his escape thence about the end of March last, they were detained there as prisoners, and that when he made his escape there were several Englishmen kept there as slaves and very barbarously used, being forced to work with irons on with the King's slaves all day, and put into prison at night, having only the allowance of half a royal a day, and that two of them told him they had been slaves there these five years

3

past, and that about last February, when news was brought of a peace concluded between the English and Spanish, some of the said Englishmen made slaves there went to the Governor and demanded their liberty, and begged that their irons might be taken off, and that he answered, "Ye dogs and cuckolds, go to work," and thereupon one of the Spaniards in company of the Governor drew his sword and cut one or two of the said Englishmen in the head.[5]

Even after its so-called abolition, the production of both coffee and cocoa continued to increase, along with the import and export of slave labour. At the beginning of the twentieth century Henry Nevinson wrote a damning new book affirming the continued practice of slavery, despite abolition. He recounted his time spent in São Tomé, one of the oldest African colonial cities founded by the Portuguese to cultivate sugar cane in the 1400s.

By 1909, together with neighbouring Angola and Principe, these countries were recognised as areas practising forced labour on a massive scale. Individuals, listed as 'servicaes' (signed documents agreeing to willingly work for a contracted number of years) – or, as Nevinson wrote, 'the free will of sheep going to the butcher's' – were brought from Angola to work on the islands of São Tomé and Principe, which had become the world's leading source of cacao at this time. It was also primarily where Cadbury acquired at least fifty per cent of its cocoa during the early 1900s. An estimated 67,000 'servicaes' were shipped there between 1888 and 1908.[6] Americans and English at this time were benefitting significantly from the cheap chocolate and cocoa from this region.

These islands were once famed for their coffee production, but the trade decreased significantly between 1891 and 1901, whereas the cocoa trade boomed, increasing from 3597 tons to 14, 914 in the same period.[7] Nevinson's 1906 description of a cocoa plantation located about six miles or so from the port at São Tomé makes for disturbing reading. The plantation owner's house had separate buildings attached for the overseers, or 'gangers', to live, together with quarters for domestic slaves and possibly coerced concubines. Opposite stood the slave quarters for the plantation labourers. These were long sheds, some two stories high, arranged like army barracks. Some dwellings were isolated, while some were partitioned off like stables. Other buildings stored the cocoa and work equipment, while a large barn served as a kitchen for the slaves. Each family had their own space here to light a fire for cooking on the ground. The other end of the quadrangle served as a hospital. The centre was paved and occupied with large flat pans to dry the cocoa beans. And here the slaves would gather two or three times a week to receive their rations of meal or dried fish. At 6.00 pm those designated with the task of feeding the cattle and horses brought large bundles of grass. On a Sunday at this same time slaves were 'treated' to a sup of wine, and tobacco leaves for the adults, surrounded by intimidating overseers with whips or long sticks and growling dogs. The distribution of rations was all completed in silence, moving around a circle in single file, reminiscent of a military exercise.

Once a month wages were paid. The minimum for a man was fixed at the equivalent of under ten shillings. Women received considerably less.[8] In 1910 this would have the purchasing power of around £39, or the average daily wage for a skilled tradesman. The money could only be spent in the plantation store, which meant any profits just went straight back into the pockets of the plantation owners. Nevinson conversed with a visiting doctor who confirmed that on one of the plantations the death rate was between twelve and fourteen-per cent annually. He attributed these dramatic figures to unhappiness. To live for three or four years as a cocoa plantation slave in São Tomé would be considered an achievement. There was also a high mortality rate among children, with a quarter of them dying each year, making the price of slaves high.[9] As a direct consequence of Nevinson's observations, and a great deal of negative press generated by a considerable British abolitionist campaign, Portugal suspended all its shipments of 'servicaes' to the islands in 1909. What followed were years of complex legislation and attempts to reform national Portuguese attitudes on forced labor.[10]

But the problem of slavery and the processing of cacao was much greater than any legislation can reform. It was embedded in the culture of its production. With plantations often located in remote areas, where vulnerable local communities became fodder for exploitation, the land was controlled by criminal bribery and corruption.

Today the Ivory Coast produces a third of the world's cocoa and a study conducted in 2002 revealed that over 284,000 children were working as slaves on cocoa farms located in Ghana, Nigeria, Cameroon and the Ivory Coast.[11]

Pirates and Privateers

Pirates or privateers (an authorised pirate), frequently raided ships carrying cacao. Privateer Captain Fowler of St. Kitts took down a French brigantine on the coast of Caracas in 1746, her cargo chiefly consisting of cacao.[12]

Sir Thomas Cavendish, an English explorer and privateer who enjoyed raiding Spanish towns and ships in the manner of Francis Drake, took control of the defenceless port of Guatulco (Huatulco), Mexico, in 1586. It had a few hundred inhabitants and good local trade networks. On arrival, Cavendish and his crew raided a fifty-tonne ship anchored in the port, loaded with cacao. The area was described as 'having a hundred brush and wattle huts, a church and a large custom house filled with cacao and indigo.' Cavendish and his men torched the whole town and desecrated the church. All the remaining inhabitants fled into the jungle to safety. What became of them is anyone's guess.[13]

François L'Olonnais, or Jean-David Nau, was a French pirate operating in the Caribbean in the 1660s. His reputation reads like the stuff of nightmares. He raped, pillaged, tortured, burned people alive, forced the eyes out of the sockets of his victims, and, in one instance, ripped the heart of a man out before eating it in front of his crew. He went on a bloodthirsty spree off the coast of Mexico and destroyed so many towns that the governor of Havana sent a party of soldiers to protect local communities from his cruelty. L'Olonnais beheaded them all, except one whom he returned to Havana, sending the message that he would never be deterred. Not long after this incident L'Olonnais ransacked the city of Maracaibo in Venezuela, along the way attacking a Spanish galleon that was loaded with cacao. In Maracaibo he mercilessly tortured the citizens until they yielded all their precious belongings.[14]

Caribbean pirates and privateers were a constant source of trouble for early colonial planters. Trinidad was significantly raided at least five times between 1594 and 1674, and in 1716 the pirate Blackbeard, also known as Captain Edward Thatch (Teach), plundered a huge ship carrying a vast cargo of cacao bound for Cadiz, before setting it alight.[15] Two years later Blackbeard's crew captured two French ships carrying cacao near Bermuda, asserting one vessel as abandoned, thus enabling Blackbeard to claim its contents legally. Unlike L'Olonnais, Blackbeard was thought to be all bark and no bite. He carefully constructed his legendary fearsome reputation despite allegedly disliking violence, and relied mostly on his frightening appearance to instil fear in others.

William Kidd was the most infamous pirate to be executed in London. Robert Culliford and William Mason mutinied and stole Kidd's ship, the *Blessed William*, leaving him stranded ashore in Antigua. After commandeering the ship, William Mason attacked and looted several Spanish ships, before deciding to attack the Spanish island of Banquilla. On arrival they rounded up men, women and children, demanding money and goods, before resorting to burning their houses down, forcing them to comply and leading to the locals handing over cacao nuts and sweets to the value of two-thousand pieces of eight, (around two thousand Spanish dollars).[16]

Chocolate buccaneer William Hughes wrote *The American Physitian* in 1672. An English botanist, Hughes set out for the New World in a privateered ship making its way around the Caribbean in the 1640s. He documented his travels, most notably writing about the sugar trade and cacao. He described cacao in detail and watched it being harvested twice a year, in January and then again in May. He confirmed the different varieties produced and the unique qualities of chocolate, depending on the tree, the country it was grown in and the climate. Hughes focused on Jamaican plantations, and claimed the beans were a better variety compared to Mexican cacao. Hughes includes a method for making chocolate, which he observed on many occasions:

> They take the cacao's, when they are well cured and dried in the sun, or by some other moderate artificial heat, in a convenient vessel, placed over a gentle fire; and peel off the film or crusty skins of them and then beat them in a stone mortar to very small particles into a kind of paste which will be almost like unto almond paste, by its natural oiliness, and maybe made up alone (or at least by adding thereto an egg and a little flower of maize) into lumps, rowls, cakes, balls, lozanges, etc. or put into boxes of what bigness the makers up of it please and then set or laid in the shade (for the sun it melteth) upon clean and smooth boards, with a leaf or some white paper under it, and in a short time it becometh hard; which may be kept a fortnight, a month, a quarter or half a year: nay, it may be indifferently kept a whole year, if need so require for daily use.

Hughes notes other variations of cacao preparation and lists some of its medicinal benefits, including the addition of saffron to treat fluxes like diarrhoea, or almonds and sugar or cloves to aid upset stomachs. He also recommended consuming scalding hot chocolate to alleviate 'pustules, tumours or swellings', typical ailments of the average sailor.[17]

Murders, mishaps and miasma

For centuries chocolate has provided the means to kill, lure and deceive. There are many rehashed tales, like that of the seventeenth-century Mexican bishop who had a disagreement with the local ladies of his congregation, denying them the right to drink chocolate during services. Their revenge was to poison his chocolate. In more recent years Frenchman Ghislain Beaumont was convicted of murdering both his parents by spiking their chocolate mousse with insecticide, before watching them both die across the dinner table. An action he undertook for resenting their refusal to allow him to leave home and marry: he was aged forty-five.[18] There's the tale of the confectioner who died in Philadelphia in 2002, his body discovered submerged in a vat of 1,200 gallons of liquid chocolate. Yoni Cordon had been working on a platform near the opening of the vat, used for mixing the chocolate, when he must have slipped and fallen in, but there were no witnesses.[19]

There's also an abundance of lesser-known, older tales, including the labourer from Birmingham who died in 1890 after a great fondness for chocolate creams led to his ultimate demise. An inquest determined that his stomach was so inflamed that it must have resulted from an unsanitary copper mould, which was used to shape the chocolate.[20] While in Buckie, Scotland, in 1898, a Miss C. Melville, the daughter of Captain Melville, the town's Harbourmaster, received a box of chocolates late one evening. Immediately after eating one of the treats, her mother, who shared the box with her, began to vomit, and died about an hour later.[21]

Poisoned chocolate remains one of the most common methods of murder throughout history. In 1913, in Atlantic City, New Jersey, a man was witnessed acting strangely, laying an open box of chocolates on the pavement. He was said to have looked 'excited' before running away. Nearby, children came out of a house to eat the chocolates, but were stopped just in time by the servants. When the police were called it was discovered that enough bichloride of mercury had been added to the chocolates to kill two people.[22] Perhaps one of the saddest cases of murder by chocolate in early twentieth-century America was in 1911, when a five-year-old boy's frozen body was discovered in a swamp on the outskirts of New York. He had acid burns around his mouth, an empty bottle of poison underneath him and a chocolate bar nearby. The police concluded that the boy was lured away from his home, bribed by chocolate, and then had poison forced down his throat. The child was dressed in very expensive clothes and it was suspected that he was part of a kidnapping plot from out of town that had gone horribly wrong.[23]

Newly married Miss Agnes Price of Gloucestershire received a box of chocolates in the post on the 8 September 1925, with the simple message, 'From Harry'. Knowing a Harry and therefore not being suspicious, she bit into one of the chocolates and immediately tasted a great bitterness, spitting it out before swallowing it. Her husband, Mr Smith, cut into one of the chocolates and noticed a blue substance, later identified as strychnine. It transpired that before his marriage to Agnes, Smith had had a relationship with a lady named Annie Davenport, who, on finding herself pregnant, allegedly sent the poisoned chocolates to Miss Price in a jealous rage.[24]

In 1920 a farmer from East Yorkshire, Thomas Liddle, was charged with attempting to murder nine different individuals by sending them poisoned chocolates in the post. The nine victims were all recipients in the final will of Liddle's sister, Annie Holmes.[25] He was sentenced to ten years of penal servitude.

Christina Edmunds, known as the chocolate cream killer, was found guilty of three charges of administering poison with intent to murder and one charge of actual murder of a boy, in Brighton in December 1871.[26] During the trial at the Central Criminal Court in London, she was declared insane and committed to Broadmoor lunatic asylum. She was thirty-four years old and of no occupation. Edmunds had laced numerous chocolate creams with strychnine and distributed them around Brighton by purchasing them from the confectioner, John Maynard, before poisoning the chocolates and returning them unknowingly to Maynard who resold them onto the public.

Jules Gouffe was a renowned French chef and brother of Alphonse Gouffe, pastry cook to Queen Victoria. His recipe for chocolate creams would have been read widely by literate English society in translated versions for the British market.

Chocolate creams

Boil ¼ lb of sugar with one stick of vanilla, until it registers 40° on the syrup gauge; Add 2 tablespoonfuls of double cream and pour the whole into a basin;

When partly cold, take out the vanilla and work the sugar with a wooden spoon until it forms a paste and divide this in portions of the size of a small nut.

Melt some chocolate in a sugar-boiler, adding sufficient syrup at 20° to bring it to the consistence of thick *bouillie*. (a bit like porridge)

Dip each ball of cream in the chocolate; take it out with a fork and put them on a baking sheet till cold; then take them off and put them on a sieve to dry.

Observation – These Chocolate Creams may be flavoured with Coffee Caramel, Kirshwasser, Pistachios &c.; instead of the Vanilla.[27]

***

Madeleine Smith, the twenty-one-year-old daughter of a respectable upper-middle-class family in Glasgow, became one of the century's most publicised female criminals when she was accused of poisoning her lower-ranking lover, Emile L'Angelier, in order to pursue a more financially advantageous coupling. It was the vast exchange of letters between the two lovers that placed Madeleine, and in particular her reputation, on trial. The public at the time would have been shocked by the frankness with which she wrote to L'Angelier about their pre-marital sexual encounters.

In 1855 she wrote from Helensburgh on a Wednesday morning around 5.00 am:

> Thank you, my love, for coming so far to see your Mimi. It is truly a pleasure to see my Emile. If we did wrong last night, it must have been in the excitement of our love. I suppose we ought to have waited till we were married.
>
> Yes, beloved, I did truly love you with my soul. I was happy. It was a pleasure to be with you. Oh, if we could have remained never more to have parted. But we must hope the

time shall come. I must have been very stupid to you last night, but everything goes out of my head when I see you my darling love ... Tell me pet, were you angry at me for allowing you to do what you did? Was it very bad of me? I shall always remember last night.[28]

Madeleine Smith came from an affluent family, who divided their time between their Glasgow townhouse and country retreat 'Rowaleyn'. She fell in love with a lowly paid clerk from Jersey, ten years her senior, who initially deceived her into thinking he was French aristocracy. Disapproved of by her family, Madeleine continued to court Pierre Emile L'Angelier in secret. He would wait outside the house at night and Madeleine would bring him cups of cocoa. The two exchanged a great deal of written correspondence for about a year until she was introduced to Billy Minnoch, a wealthy bachelor, who moved in the same social circles as her family and was approved of by her father. It was not long after this that Madeleine decided to start cooling the relationship with L'Angelier. She became engaged to Minnoch and wrote to her old lover, informing him that she no longer desired his attentions and demanding he return all her letters. L'Angelier began to blackmail Madeleine, using the letters as ammunition.

Not long after, L'Angelier started to meet up again with Madeleine following his initial threats, then he fell ill. His close friend, Mary Arthur Perry, testified in court that, after drinking chocolate with Madeleine on several occasions, L'Angelier had been sick, saying, 'I can't think why I was so unwell after getting that coffee and chocolate from her.'[29] Meanwhile, Madeleine was busy purchasing arsenic from a nearby druggist, which she stipulated was for use in the garden. By March 1857, Pierre Emile L'Angelier was dead, found with a letter in his pocket from Madeleine. Not long after, an autopsy confirmed that L'Angelier's body contained fatal doses of arsenic. Madeleine was arrested and went on trial in Edinburgh for his murder. When the question of disguising arsenic in chocolate was raised, Frederick Penny, Professor of Chemistry at the University of Glasgow, was called to testify. He stated:

Cocoa or coffee is a vehicle in which a large dose might be given. There is a great difference between giving rise to suspicion and actual detection. I have found by actual experiment, that when thirty or forty grains of arsenic are put into a cup of warm chocolate, a large portion of the arsenic settles down in the bottom of the cup; and I think a person drinking such poisonous chocolate would suspect something when the gritty particles came into his mouth. But if the same quantity, and even a larger quantity, was boiled with the chocolate, instead of merely being stirred or mixed, none of it settles down, and so might be gulped over.[30]

Amazingly, Madeleine Smith was acquitted, based on the fact that there was not enough hard evidence to suggest that she and L'Angelier were ever actually seen together in public during the weeks leading up to his death. The case has become one of the most famous criminal stories in British history. Smith left Scotland and her fiancé, Minnoch, despite his gracious attempts to support her throughout the trial. She went on to marry twice, first to the artist George J. Wardle, with whom she spent many years socialising with the Bloomsbury set, her identity largely going undetected. Later in life she moved to New York where she married again, before returning to England and dying at the age of ninety-two.

In 1919 the diaries of writer Somerset Maugham revealed a strange reference to Smith, whose surname at that time would have been Wardle. It was 1907 and she would have been seventy-two. It stated:

H.B (the stage actor H.B. Irving) went down to stay in the country. His next-door neighbour was a very quiet, prim old lady; becoming acquainted with her, he gradually connected her with the heroine of a celebrated murder case which had excited the world fifty years before. She had been tried and found not guilty but the evidence was so damning that, notwithstanding the verdict, the general opinion was that she had in point of fact committed the crime. She discovered that he had found out her identity, taxed him with it, and presently said to him: "I suppose you want to know whether I did it or not. I did, and what's more, if it were all to happen again, I'd do it again."

This story did not appear in print until after Madeleine's death and Maugham admitted that the woman in question was indeed Madeleine Smith.[31]

Here is a recipe for hot chocolate, published the same year that L'Angelier died. Maybe it was even the one Madeleine used to poison him:

> **To make Chocolate (French receipt)**
> An ounce of chocolate, if good will be sufficient for one person. Rasp and then boil it from 5 to 10 minutes, with about 4 tablespoonsful of water. When it is extremely smooth, add nearly a pint of new milk, give it another boil stir it well or mill it and serve it directly.
>
> For water chocolate use three quarters of a pint of water instead of the milk and send rich hot cream to table with it. The taste must decide whether it shall be made thicker or thinner.[32]

In Britain, from the nineteenth century onwards, there are literally hundreds of cases of poisoned chocolates being sent to silence, scare and eradicate individuals altogether. It wasn't just in Britain either. In the 1700s the Turkish Pasha of Rhodes planned to massacre the Knights of Malta by poisoning the water supply that was specifically used to make the coffee and chocolate prepared regularly for the knights.[33]

***

Perhaps one of the most outlandish cases of mass poisoning is that which took place in Rome during the seventeenth century. Numerous women, who admitted to killing their husbands in this way during confessionals, were reported to the Catholic clergy at the time. No names were ever disclosed, as is the sacred discretional code of the church, but the problem became significant when unusually high numbers of women started living on their own, left suddenly and unexpectedly by their husbands. Widows in seventeenth-century Rome became a customary occurrence.

The papal authorities launched an investigation and discovered a syndicate of young women who were meeting regularly at the house of a known witch and fortune teller, Hieronyma Spara, who was teaching these young wives the art of poisoning. The church craftily placed a female spy at the heart of the action. She was made to appear

13

as wealthy as possible in order to gain favour with the group of women and provided a convincing story about her husband's infidelities and beatings. Following an audience with Hieronyma, the women sold her a slow-acting poison, which was both clear and tasteless.

Once the group had been exposed, the authorities moved in and tortured them into admitting their crimes. Some thirty women were publicly whipped through the streets. Others, including Spara, were hanged, or banished from the country if they held high-ranking positions in society. Several months later more women were whipped and dragged through the streets naked, and there were further hangings as increasing numbers of poisoners and members of the group were exposed. It then came to light that there were also specialist vendors using the same poison, acquired from the syndicate. This was administered in small doses, enabling the killers to choose how long they wanted their victims to take to die, whether it was several days, a week, six months or more.

Throughout the ongoing investigations there was one name repeatedly mentioned, that of Giulia Tofana, or 'Tophania', a woman who is now thought to have been responsible for the murder of over 600 people, and who went undetected for some two decades. She distributed the poison throughout Italy in small vials marked 'Manna of St Nicholas of Barri', a saint associated with miraculous oils. This oil was then typically added to … you guessed it … chocolate, or sometimes tea or soup.

Tophania was clever. She never lived in one place long enough to get caught, constantly changed her name and even took refuge in a monastery, despite the Viceroy of Naples's widespread campaign to flush her out. All the time she continued with her villainous work. She was eventually discovered in a nunnery, where she was shielded from the viceroy. His patience ran out and he sent troops in to arrest her. After a lengthy internal battle of the clergy, in which the viceroy was threatened with excommunication and a surge of public support for the killer hampered her capture, infiltrators were carefully placed among local people to spread a story about Tophania and her plans to poison the walls and fountains of the city. This soon shifted public opinion and she was swiftly arrested, tortured, strangled, and her body thrown over the wall into the garden of the nunnery which had once shielded her.[34] It is understood that some of her accomplices were bricked into dungeons while still alive. There are also accounts citing Hieronyma Spara, or Girolama Spera, as Tophania's daughter.

This fascinating story left me with so many unanswered questions about the infidelities of men in seventeenth-century Italy, men who were clearly cruel enough to be found so dispensable to their wives. Were Italian women so repressed? Certainly, many marriages then would have been pre-arranged, leaving women no recourse to escape. And what rage or injustices drove Tophania to such extremes? Or was it just a way to earn money in economically challenging times? Was she more psychopath than avenging angel? We do know that her mother was executed for murdering the man she married, which provides some clarity to the overall story. I also cannot help but marvel at the antics of the late medieval Italian clergy, who had all the acumen of a central intelligence agency and the tenacity of a dung beetle.

I say this so many times when I'm researching – but, surely this is a tale worthy of a film script.

***

Another twisted narrative fuelled by retribution, hatred and greed occurred in seventeenth-century France, when Captain Godin de Sainte-Croix, also known as the Chevalier de Sainte-Croix, sought revenge against the d'Aubrays, a noble family who had imprisoned him for a time. The Chevalier was also consumed by avarice and living well beyond his means. Marie-Madeleine d'Aubray, Marquise de Brinvilliers, conspired with her lover, Sainte-Croix, to kill three members of her own family. It was decided that he would manufacture the poison and she would administer it.

At first Marie-Madeleine practised administering the poisons to dogs, rabbits and birds, before moving on to hospitals, where she poisoned the sick and elderly by lacing their soup. When she was ready to carry out the act of killing her father and two brothers, she began by poisoning her father's chocolate, after which he immediately fell ill and soon after died. For some reason, a third party was brought in to finish off Brinvilliers' brothers, who were dead in less than six weeks.

To their despair, a long-lost sister emerged after the deaths. She vacated to Paris before Sainte-Croix could do his worst. In a final twist to the tale, which I have somewhat shortened, Sainte-Croix was ironically found dead in his laboratory, struck down by noxious fumes while in the process of mixing his poisons. The authorities retrieved a box for which he left instructions specifically to be handed to Marie-Madeleine on his death. Unfortunately for Brinvilliers, the instructions were ignored and the box searched. It contained enough damning information against Chevalier's lover to warrant her arrest. Brinvilliers escaped to England, where she remained for three years, before attempting to re-enter France in 1676. She sought sanctity in a convent, but the authorities sent in a spy disguised as a priest and well-wisher. Fuelled by narcissistic flattery, she agreed to meet him again outside the convent walls, where she was greeted, not by an intriguing new admirer, but by law-enforcers ready to take her away.

After a lengthy trial where all was revealed, she was condemned to be drawn on a hurdle with her feet bare, a rope around her neck and a burning torch in her hand. She was dragged in front of the on-looking crowds, from outside Notre Dame to the Place de Grève, where she was beheaded and finally burnt, her ashes scattered to the wind.[35] The poison that Marie-Madeleine had used was Aqua Tofana, the legendary recipe of Giulia Tophania, which Sainte-Croix had remastered in his laboratory.

***

It isn't just poisoned chocolate that has the capacity to inflict suffering. A Berlin confectionery company dropped chocolate 'bombs' from aeroplanes in 1926 as a marketing device, but so many people were badly bruised they had to stop the campaign. These were hard chocolates 'wrapped in heavy foil'.[36] Individuals have also historically been drugged with chocolate for all manner of ominous reasons, such as the passenger travelling from Rolleston to Derby in 1911 who accepted a piece of chocolate from a fellow passenger in first-class. The recipient of the chocolate lost consciousness only to wake and find all his money had been stolen.[37] In 1918 there was a spree of cases on London buses and trams where female conductors were offered drugged chocolates by a passenger, though there was no clear determined motive.[38] In 1986 police cracked a crime ring which aimed drug-impregnated chocolate at children. Chocolate bars containing cannabis, which looked like standard Cadbury's Dairy Milk bars, were seized from a factory in Bristol.[39]

Dial is a benzodiazepine, often used to assist with anxiety. It was administered to Miss Annie Tomlinson in 1935 by her close friend, William Deakin, who, on discovering she was pregnant agreed to help her with inducing a miscarriage. He assured her that whatever he gave her would be disguised in chocolate form. Sometime later he produced some chocolates in a white paper bag, which were slightly crushed and rewrapped. They also tasted bitter. Annie ate the chocolates, went home and passed out. The next thing she remembered was waking up in the hospital. Here she was later informed that Deakin had also been admitted to the same hospital, where he died of gunshot wounds from a suspected suicide.

This is a very intriguing case riddled with gaps and few explanations. The coroner pronounced Deakin's death as suicide under the influence of dial, the same drug administered to Annie in the chocolates to stimulate an abortion. Why Deakin had used dial at all is confusing, as there is no medical evidence of it being capable of triggering a miscarriage. And why did he also ingest the drug himself? Was he a candidate for the unborn child's father, or rather just the 'good friend' whom Annie claimed him to be?[40]

A follow-up report published in the *Sheffield Independent* on Saturday, 19 January 1935, provides some answers to this mystery. It transpired that William Deakin left a suicide note, written in a drugged state just before he shot himself. It talked about his great love, not for Annie but Betty, to whom he had formerly been engaged. It also mentioned his 'suspicions' about Annie. The report confirmed that police had visited Deakin as soon as Annie was submitted with suspected poisoning. He denied any responsibility towards the child she was carrying and just a few hours later shot himself.

The poisoned confections were chocolate creams, the most popular variety of the time, a smooth inside coated in chocolate. The chocolates had been cut in two, the grains of dial added, and reassembled. It remains unclear as to whether Deakin was the father of the unborn child, or whether he killed himself out of fear of mistakenly killing Annie, who he knew was in the hospital. Perhaps he was still grieving the break-up of his engagement, or perhaps his intention was to murder Annie. These things we will never know, but it is yet another of the many examples of the sinister association between chocolate and human tragedy.

***

On occasion poisons fail and there is no better example of this than with the bleak tale of Rasputin (the Mad Monk), a man who continues to fascinate historians and cultural exponents. Rasputin was both a controversial and enigmatic figure, a mystic accused of charlatan practices who managed to ingratiate himself into the Russian emperors' household, on the premise of healing the Tsar's haemophiliac son, and adopting the role of holy man and shaman.

The significant influence he held at the royal palace was met with contempt by many, and with increasing reports of rape, fraud and inappropriate behaviour, Rasputin began to be scrutinized widely as a threat to the empire. A group of noblemen led by Felix Yusupov devised a plan to murder Rasputin in December 1916. In addition to Yusupov's own memoirs, there have been numerous accounts of the assassination, including that of Countess Marianna Erlkovna von Pistohlkor, who observed:

> Yusupov had often invited Rasputin to come to see his house. On the day in question he demurred, as he had been warned by the police that he should not go out. He was, however, persuaded. There were present the Grand Duke Dimitri Pavlovich the Duma member [Vladimir] Purishevich [a right-wing politician and outspoken critic both of Rasputin and the manner in which the tsar was conducting affairs], an officer named [Sergei] Sukotin [a guards officer recuperating from wounds and friend of Yusupov's mother], a doctor [Stanislaus de Lazovert] and Yusupov. They had prepared port, a poisoned bottle on a side table, and an unpoisoned bottle, poisoned pink cakes and unpoisoned chocolate cakes.[41]

Yusupov offered Rasputin the port and cakes, which had been laced with cyanide, the effects of which took some time to prevail. In the early hours of the morning Yusupov must have given up on the poison, took himself upstairs to retrieve a gun from his fellow conspirators and shot Rasputin in the chest. This time he went down. What followed was a complicated ruse, where one of the men disguised himself as the enigmatic monk, to make it look as if Rasputin had travelled home that night.

When they returned to check on Rasputin, he miraculously leapt up and attacked Yusupov, before a chase ensued and Rasputin was shot again, straight through the forehead, killing him.

Recipe for Ptichye Moloko

Ptichye Moloko, or Birds' Milk Cake (not literally), was initially a type of confection introduced into Soviet Russia in the 1960s, which evolved into a cake, developed by a group of confectioners under the guidance of famed Moscow based Russian pastry chef Vladimir Guralnik. The cake, more of a torte really, became so popular that customers began queuing outside delicatessens to get a slice at extortionate prices, during a time of a black-market economy and a shortage of basic goods.

The recipe began to be widely recreated and is now available in various different guises throughout most of Russia. Topped with a rich chocolate ganache glaze, the cake gets its name from the delicate and decadent soufflé-like layers between the sponge. The following recipe is challenging for a novice, but I'm certain would be worth the efforts.

Ingredients for the sponge
2 eggs
100g sugar
100g plain flour
1/3 teaspoon baking powder
a pinch of salt

Ingredients for the soufflé
20g gelatine
100ml milk
5 eggs
100g sugar
150g butter
1 tablespoon plain flour

Ingredients for the glaze
100g dark chocolate
100g cream
50g butter

Method

First, make your basic sponge: beat the eggs with sugar until grains dissolve, add sifted flour with salt and baking powder, and mix everything together carefully. Bake for about 30 minutes at 180°C and cool completely. Then, cut your sponge in two layers and set aside.

Before starting with the cream cover the gelatine with 100ml water and leave for about 20 minutes to swell.

The soufflé consists of custard cream and meringue, so begin with the custard. Separate the yolks from the whites and leave the whites in the fridge. In a clear bowl stir the yolks with sugar. Pour in milk, add some flour and mix properly. Put the bowl on a bain-marie and bring the mixture to a boil – constantly stir the cream with a whisk to prevent lumps from forming.

When the cream is thick enough, remove it from the heat and let cool a bit. Meanwhile, in a clear bowl beat the butter for a couple of minutes.

While the custard cream is still slightly warm, start adding it tablespoon by tablespoon into the soft butter and whisk with a mixer on low speed.

Leave the cream in the fridge for 20-30 minutes so that it thickens.

Next, back to gelatine: warm it on low heat until fully dissolved.

Beat egg whites with sugar until it acquires stiff peaks and glossy texture.

Next is very important: carefully drip liquid gelatine into the meringue and whisk the mixture.

Now you have to work fast: prepare your sponge layers and cooking ring in advance. Carefully add gelatine meringue to the custard cream and stir with a spatula – here is your airy soufflé base for *ptichye moloko*.

The soufflé thickens very quickly so do not miss the moment. Place one sponge on the bottom of the ring, layer with half of the soufflé, then place another sponge and cover it with the remaining soufflé.

To prepare the glaze bring cream almost to a boil, remove from heat and add chopped dark chocolate. Wait for a couple of minutes, and stir the mixture until the chocolate dissolves and the glaze is nice and smooth. Add butter and give the glaze a final stir.

Pour the glaze on top of the cake, and leave in the refrigerator. Chill the cake for at least 5 hours, better overnight.

Carefully remove *ptichye moloko* from the cooking ring and enjoy your masterpiece.[42]

Seduction

Studies suggest that chocolate releases phenylethylamine and serotonin, which when consumed can induce aphrodisiac and mood-lifting effects. It also has the capacity to activate cannabinoid receptors in the brain, resulting in feelings of euphoria and acute sensitivity.[43] The Aztec leader Montezuma was said to drink fifty cups of chocolate daily to satisfy his harem of wives, while Aztecs and Mayans indulged in ritual orgies during the cocoa bean harvests.[44]

In its European infancy, chocolate received a lot of bad press for its known abilities to enhance the mood. In 1624 the German Joan Fran Rauch wrote a pamphlet condemning the use of chocolate, calling it 'a violent inflamer of the passions' and suggesting that monks should be forbidden to drink it.[45] The famous eighteenth-century naturalist Carl von Linné noted that chocolate acted as an aphrodisiac, as did the Spanish scientist and writer Pedro Felipe Monlau in his *Higiene de Matrimonio: El Libro de los Casados* (The Book of Marriage Hygiene), written in 1881, claiming that cacao paste and cocoa butter enhanced sexual desire.

A rumour circulated in the English and American media during the 1800s that Napoleon Bonaparte was party to a rather unpleasant incident involving a previous lover. Allegedly the French military leader took a customary daily cup of chocolate every morning, which would not have been unusual. Pauline Riotti was a member of the Corsican court, seduced by Napoleon from an early age, before being abandoned when she became pregnant. Riotti took revenge on him by infiltrating the kitchens and preparing his morning chocolate with poison. Pauline was witnessed in the act by one of the cooks and word was sent to Bonaparte warning him not to drink the chocolate, which he then forced Pauline to drink in front of him. She fell into convulsions and died. The cook who reported her was made a legion of honour, while Pauline was publicly declared insane on her death.[46] Whether this story was merely a crafted piece of propaganda, or whether it was actually true is unclear.

It is understood that Anna of Austria, who was born and raised in Madrid in the early 1600s, introduced the French court to chocolate on her marriage to Louis XIII. It was, however, her son Louis XIV, who would make it famous throughout Paris.[47] When Marie-Antoinette married Louis XVI in 1770 (aged fourteen), her personal chocolate-maker apparently accompanied her to the court.

Many biographers of Marie-Antoinette argue about her demands for creating a new position of 'Charge of Chocolate Maker to the Queen'. French archives, however, reveal that a Jean de Herrera was appointed the same title at least a century before to the wife of Louis XIV, Maria Theresa of Spain, who is alleged to have greatly influenced the drinking of chocolate in France. The Marquise de Montespan also wrote about the queen's young Spanish soubrette, the Señora Molina, who was 'well furnished with silver kitchen utensils, has a sort of private kitchen or scullery reserved for her own use and there it is that the manufacture takes place of clove-scented chocolate, brown soups and gravies, stews redolent with garlic, capsicums and nutmeg and all that nauseous pastry in which the young infanta revels.' Marie-Theresa was also alleged to have black and rotting teeth – a consequence of all the chocolate she consumed.[48]

Marie-Antoinette's chocolate-maker (not the one she allegedly brought with her to Versailles), Sulpice Debauve, who was also pharmacist to King Louis XVI, created new recipes combining orchid bulbs to enhance strength, orange blossom to calm the nerves and almond milk to restore good digestion.[49] He was an advocate for high cocoa content and as a chemist he had the knowledge to marry the right flavours in order to create the best tasting combinations. Debauve created a medallion-shaped chocolate that was both rich in texture and sweet from the honey that he added, designed to act as a headache remedy for the queen. Marie-Antoinette enjoyed them so much that he named them Pistoles (pastilles) de Marie-Antoinette. You can still find these for sale today in the original shop of 1807, Debauve & Gallais, which the famed chemist opened in Paris, together with his nephew, Antoine

Gallais. Marie-Antoinette started each morning with chocolate and a roll when she was awaiting trial in the prison of the Conciergerie prior to her execution during the Revolution.[50] Perhaps her ongoing headaches were an omen for darker events to come.

***

Versailles was undoubtedly witness to a great deal of activity centred around chocolate, particularly among the courtesans. Madame de Pompadour, the former chief mistress of Louis XV, was, according to Jeanne Du Barry's biographer, Stanley Loomis, lacking in sensuality. Adopting a variety of aphrodisiacs to kick-start her libido, she is said to have started each morning with truffle and celery soup washed down with hot chocolate laced with vanilla and ambergris (from the intestine of sperm whales).[51] Louis XV himself was often ill, his weaknesses attributed to his excessive consumption of chocolate.[52]

The story of Madame du Barry, King Louis XV's courtesan, and one of the most remarkable beauties of her generation, makes for fascinating reading. At the start of their relationship, before going public, it was said that du Barry would sweeten Louis' chocolate with honey while he prepared her coffee.[53]

But it is her relationship with the enslaved Louis-Benoit Zamor which is one of the most interesting aspects of Madame du Barry's narrative. Zamor was just eleven years-old when he was taken from what we recognise today as Bangladesh (or possibly Sidi, in East Africa), and trafficked and sold onto the court of Louis XV. Presented as a 'gift' to Countess du Barry, she lavished him with trinkets, a broad education and a constant supply of luxury chocolates. Despite their bizarre maternal relationship, it was Zamor who betrayed his mistress as an informant to the Committee of Public Safety, taking the side of the insurgents during the French Revolution, which eventually deposed the monarchy and sent du Barry to the guillotine. Predicting the consequences of the ensuing revolution, du Barry smuggled a range of jewels, luxury objects and treasures out of France to England and also within the grounds of her house. Following her arrest, and in an attempt to save her own life, du Barry revealed the location of this swag to the administrators of the new French Republic. Among the items buried opposite the ice-house in a gold dressing case was a 'chafing-dish with spirits of wine, a milk jug [and] a large chocolate pot'.[54] Needless to say, this made no difference to her case and her execution prevailed.

***

From female courtesans to ardent and intrepid men of the seventeen-hundreds. In his memoirs, the Venetian adventurer and the man who had many complex female relationships, Giacomo Casanova, makes numerous references to chocolate, including presenting the niece of a Madame Morin with a dozen pounds of chocolate that he purchased in Genoa.[55] These chocolates may well have come from Genoa's oldest and most prestigious of confectioners, Pietro Romanengo, established in 1780 and still trading today, using many of the original techniques and manufacturing methods of the time. Genoa was one of the first ports to import sugar into Europe, so it was ideally placed to manufacture confection.

Casanova also indulged in chocolate every morning and occasionally around supper time, using a recipe which was of 'a peculiar kind,' which he made himself. It was perhaps similar to the chocolate he once requested at the Palais Royal, to be made with water, which he wrote about in his memories as being 'very bad'. He also frequented chocolate houses with great regularity wherever he was in Europe.[56] While in Switzerland, Casanova stayed at the house of a duke, whose two daughters were charged with looking after him during his stay. Casanova's memoirs talk brazenly about sexually assaulting one of these girls, Rose, on a regular basis, particularly when she brought him chocolate in his rooms, chastising her when she denied his propositions, but insinuating she also reciprocated these advances.[57] It is very difficult to distinguish from memoirs and journals of the past whether some sexual encounters were consensual or not, as the male ego often suggests a reciprocal response. I think it is important to refrain from romanticising these encounters, which can perpetuate confusing cultural norms of what constitutes abuse.

***

Chocolate was frequently embraced as a love potion in early Spanish societies, to attract a lover, repel a rival or change the behaviour of an existing lover. With its strong flavour it could readily mask the addition

24

of other ingredients used in witchcraft, like human flesh, worms to tame a partner, or menstrual blood, which was commonly added to potions designed to attract the object of a person's affection. Being of a thick consistency it was also possible to disguise powders in a chocolate drink, which has always been a beverage commonly offered in mixed convivial social situations.

The Spanish Inquisition was one of the longest reigns of terror and persecution in history. Heretics, including Jews and Protestants, who did not manage to escape were forced to confess their sins to the Catholic hierarchy. Frequently found guilty, they were imprisoned or executed publicly, unless they willingly confessed. A confession could earn an alternative penance of various degrees of severity.

As chocolate in Spain during the 1600s was a luxury commodity, limited to those in power, royalty, the priesthood and the rich, its consumption outside of these circles was considered sinful and questionable, with some chocolate merchants being accused of witchcraft and inducement. It was basically a non-Christian activity, which could find those accused guilty of blasphemy against the church. There are numerous Inquisition transcripts detailing those individuals who were put on trial for manipulating chocolate in this way – particularly in the art of seduction.

In 1626 in the town of Teotitlan, in Mexico, thirty-year-old Maria Bravo acquired a recipe from a local indigenous woman, in order to secure the affections of a man she desired, feelings which were not reciprocated. The spell involved mixing her menstrual blood together with chocolate and then feeding it to her intended. After carrying out this task, Maria was disillusioned when it became apparent that the man remained disinterested and decided to confess her 'sin' to the Inquisition Tribunal. Similarly, Ana Perdomo from Tepeaca, in south east Mexico, admitted to mixing her own menstrual blood with chocolate in an attempt to regain the love of her husband whose affections had strayed elsewhere.

Six years earlier, in the city of Guadalajara, in western Mexico, Juana de Bracamonte, who was said to be around twenty-three years of age, declared that while living in the house of a Doña Francisca Sezor, Francisca had prepared a large bowl of cacao for Don Antonio de Figueroa, a man with whom Juana de Bracamonte was in love. According to Doña Francisca Sezor, her cousin had given her 'magical powders' which she added to the cacao to persuade Don Antonio de Figueroa to fall in love with her: powders which she added in front of Juana de Bracamonte. Doña Francisca had already died, according to the testimonial, so it is unclear as to why Juana de Bracamonte was confessing, but the document also noted that she was not speaking out of hatred or malevolence. It is possible that her accuser was Don Antonio de Figueroa, or she simply confessed out of fear rather than face persecution.

In the same city that year, Don Baltasar Peña declared that he had found a sample of flesh, allegedly taken from a man who had not long been hung, drawn and quartered, under the bed of one of his household staff. The woman who had acquired the flesh had roasted it and then mixed it with chocolate, though for what purpose remains unclear. Given that this bizarre concoction was under the bed, it might suggest there was some sort of sexual element.

It wasn't only women who used chocolate as a seduction tool, Simon Hernan of Mexico City found himself in 1690 under pressure to denounce his sins and declared to the Inquisition that he had dissolved 'some powders' into the church chocolate cup during mass, then gave the concoction to a Spanish woman called Micaela in order to 'enjoy her favours'.[58]

European cultures generally viewed chocolate as a decadent and seductive beverage. It was an aristocratic drink, often indulged in the morning and in chocolate houses with questionable morals. Right up until the middle of the nineteenth century it was viewed as a lewd and louche beverage. Part of this derives from its heritage as a drink symbolic of diabolical Mexican rituals and one that took some time to become conventional and affordable throughout Europe.

Chocolate and mass murderers

It is perhaps unsurprising that chocolate's historic association with death and morbidity extends to the disturbing world of serial killers.

Jeffrey Dahmer, or 'The Milwaukee Cannibal', held down a commonplace job at the Ambrosia chocolate factory. Following his arrest he was said to have informed detectives that he kept the skull of one of his murder victims as a token in his work locker. Dahmer's victims were young and middle-aged, and he enticed them back to his apartment before drugging and killing them, usually by strangulation.

He also performed terrible experiments on his victims, drilling holes in their heads, injecting acids, removing parts of their brains, sometimes when they were still merely unconscious. His motivation was sexual control, and his final act was to dismember them and then either dissolve their body parts in acid or retain other parts as trophies.[59]

The Ambrosia chocolate factory had to relocate to avoid all the unwanted attention they received after Dahmer was convicted. For decades before the Dahmer circus, the old factory, founded by local German businessman Otto Schoenleber in 1894, was notorious for the sweet smell it emitted across several streets in downtown Milwaukee. The Cargill Cocoa & Chocolate Company acquired the Ambrosia name and the new factory several years ago.

The Ambrosia Chocolate Company ran a contest in 1983, presumably for local people to come up with some innovative ways of cooking with chocolate. The winning entry for Chocolate Brickle Bars was by Kris Kittleson. Unfortunately, the method for preparing the chocolate-almond topping was omitted from the recipe.

Chocolate Brickle Bars
2/3 cup miniature semisweet chocolate pieces
½ cup crushed chow Mein noodles
2/3 cup peanut butter
1 package (6oz) brickle chips (little toffee pieces)
½ cup powdered sugar
¼ cup instant non-fat dry milk powder
2 tablespoons water
¼ cup honey

Chocolate-almond topping
In mixing bowl, combine chocolate pieces, chow Mein noodles, peanut butter, ½ cup of the brickle chips, powdered sugar, dry milk, water and honey. Mix well.

Press mixture into 8-in by 8-in baking pan. Refrigerate until firm.

Meanwhile, prepare chocolate almond topping. Spread mixture over firm bars. Sprinkle with remaining ¼ cup brickle chips. Cut into 1-in by 2-in bars. Makes 32 cookies.[60]

Over a twenty-year period, librarians working at Milwaukee Public Library retained hundreds of recipes from both the *Milwaukee Journal* and *Sentinel* which provide a fascinating insight into the diversity of local food from the 1960s to the 1980s and reflects the city's considerable German heritage, of which Dahmer was a part.

The European torte most associated with Germany and the Austrian *sachertorte* is a heavily iced and glazed multi-layered extravagance, often containing chocolate.

A 1963 recipe for apricot-chocolate torte was published in the *Milwaukee Journal* and promises all the richness associated with this decadent cake.

Apricot-Chocolate Torte
1 cup butter
1½ cups sugar
3 eggs
1 teaspoon vanilla
3 cups sifted cake flour
2½ teaspoons baking powder
1 teaspoon salt
1 cup milk

Butter and flour the cake pans; set aside. Cream butter and sugar. Add eggs and beat until light and fluffy. Blend in vanilla. Sift dry ingredients; add to creamed mixture alternately with the milk, starting and ending with dry ingredients. Divide batter equally between three round 9-in cake pans and bake for 25 minutes in a preheated 350 °C oven. Cool for 10 minutes. Remove from pans onto cake racks. Cool completely. With a sharp knife split each layer in half. Spread chocolate custard filling between layers and top with apricot glaze. Lightly frost sides with chocolate custard filling.

Chocolate Custard Filling
½ cup sugar
4 eggs
1 cup butter

4 squares semi-sweet chocolate, melted and cooled
1 teaspoon vanilla

Combine sugar and eggs in top of double boiler and heat, stirring constantly, until thick and amber coloured. Cool. Cream butter; blend in chocolate and vanilla. Add butter mixture to eggs, beating until well mixed and sufficient to fill five thin layers and frost sides of torte. If filling becomes too thick, beat vigorously to proper consistency for spreading.

Apricot Glaze
½ cup apricot jam
1 tablespoon corn-starch
¼ cup cold water
1 tablespoon lemon juice
¼ teaspoon salt

Combine ingredients in saucepan and heat, stirring constantly until thick. Cool.

Bohemia, which now encompasses all the territories of the Czech Republic, once comprised a German-speaking border, which later became the Sudetenland. German-Bohemians living in the Sudetenland were forced to resettle throughout Germany after the Second World War.

Undoubtedly, with its German ancestry, this recipe for chocolate Bohemian Balls, published in the *Milwaukee Journal* in 1964, pays homage to this historical region.

It is more or less an alcohol-free version of the popular Christmas German treat, *Rumkugeln* – chocolate rum balls.

Bohemian Balls
¾ cup vegetable shortening
1 cup and 4 tablespoons powdered sugar
9oz sweet chocolate, grated
1 cup ground nuts
1 teaspoon vanilla
1¼ cups of flour

Mix ingredients together with wooden spoon. Roll in balls size of hickory nut. Bake at 350°C for 8 minutes. Roll in powdered sugar while warm and cool. Makes about five dozen.[61]

***

Given chocolate's propensity for both comfort and stimulation, it is perhaps to be expected that there have been so many requests on death row for chocolate to feature as part of a final meal. It conceivably offers the condemned a little nostalgic solace and reassurance at a time of inevitable finality.

Timothy McVeigh, christened the Oklahoma City Bomber, who killed 168 people and injured just under 700, in 1995, requested two pints of mint chocolate chip ice cream for his final meal before execution, while John Martin Scripps, an English serial killer whose crimes were committed in multiple countries, requested pizza and hot chocolate for his final meal, prior to being hanged for his crimes in Singapore in 1996.[62]

Here's a recipe from the 1990s for mint chocolate chip ice cream, taken from *The Trellis Cookbook* by Marcel Desaulniers. The Trellis was, until very recently, an iconic restaurant in the heart of Colonial Williamsburg in Virginia, and was made famous for Desaulniers' 'Death by Chocolate' dessert. The Trellis changed ownership in 2020 and is now trading as La Piazza.

Mint Chocolate-Chip Ice Cream
2 cups heavy cream
¾ cup chopped fresh mint
1 cup granulated sugar
1½ cups half-and-half (half milk and half cream)
½ cup egg yolks
1 cup chocolate chips
½ teaspoon salt
1 cup tightly packed light brown sugar
¼ lb unsalted butter – cut into 8 pieces
2 eggs
2 teaspoons pure vanilla extract
1 cup water
1 cup sour cream

Twelve hours in advance of preparing the ice-cream, combine 1 cup heavy cream, ¼ cup chopped mint and ¼ cup sugar in a stainless-steel bowl. Tightly cover with film wrap and refrigerate.

Strain the cream and mint mixture through a fine strainer into a 2½ quart saucepan. Use a ladle to gently press down on the mint leaves to extract as much flavour as possible. Add the remaining cup heavy cream and 1½ cups half-and-half and heat over medium high heat. When hot add ¼ cup sugar and stir to dissolve. Bring the mixture to a boil.

While the cream is heating, place ½ cup egg yolks and the remaining ½ cup sugar in the bowl of an electric mixer fitted with a paddle. Beat the eggs on high for 2-2½ minutes. Scrape down the sides of the bowl. Beat on high until slightly thickened and lemon coloured, an additional 2½-3 minutes (at this point the cream should be boiling. If not adjust the mixer speed to low and continue to mix until the cream boils. If this is not done, the egg yolks will develop undesirable lumps).

Pour the boiling cream into the beaten egg yolks and whisk to combine. Return to the saucepan and heat over medium high heat, stirring constantly. Bring to a temperature of 185°C for 2-4 minutes.

Remove from the heat and transfer to a stainless-steel bowl. Cool in an ice water bath to a temperature of 40-45°C for about 15 minutes.

When cold, fold in the chocolate chips and freeze in an ice cream freezer, following the manufacturer's instructions. Transfer the semi-frozen ice cream to a 2-quart plastic container. Securely cover the container, then place in the freezer for at least 4 hours.[63]

Joseph Cannon, who shot and killed a woman when carrying out a robbery, was served chocolate cake, chocolate ice cream and a chocolate milkshake before receiving a lethal injection in Texas. Andrew Six, who raped a young girl before murdering her sister during a robbery, requested a chocolate pie as part of his last meal before being administered a lethal injection in Missouri.

A pint of chocolate ice cream was on the requested menu for Michael Durocher before he was electrocuted for murdering his girlfriend, her two children and two other victims.

Judy Buenoana, aka 'The Black Widow', who murdered her son and husband, before attempting to murder her lovers for their insurance premiums, was granted permission to spend her last day on death row eating chocolates while watching television programmes. John Ashley Brown Jr, who stabbed a man during a robbery, requested two chocolate malts before his lethal injection in Louisiana, and Roger Dale Stafford, who shot a family before murdering six employees of a steakhouse, asked for two chocolate milkshakes to wash down his hot dogs and French fries in Oklahoma before a lethal injection was administered.

Here is an easy recipe for Chocolate Malted Milkshake found in Brenda Van Niekerk's *50 Decadent Milkshake Recipes:*

Chocolate Malted Milkshake
500ml chocolate ice cream
187ml milk
25ml malted milk powder
Whipped cream for garnish
Grated chocolate for garnish

Method
Place all ingredients into a blender.

Blend on high until smooth.

Add more ice cream if you want a thicker milkshake and more milk if you want a thinner milkshake.

Top with whipped cream and grated chocolate.[64]

Chocolate and disasters

The German *Hindenburg* passenger airship was the biggest commercial airship to ever be built. As it was attempting to land at the naval base in Lakehurst, New Jersey, on 6 May 6 1937, an electrostatic discharge, or spark, ignited leaking hydrogen, causing a massive explosion. Of the ninety-seven passengers, sixty-two miraculously survived by jumping dozens of feet to safety. It was the first significant transport disaster to be captured on film.

On the day the airship crashed, pears in chocolate sauce was served from the menu. The following recipe was written by Arthur Wyman, who trained as a chef and baker in Europe, Asia and Egypt before testing recipes for the *Los Angeles Times* throughout the 1920s and including them in his regular Saturday column 'Practical Recipes'. Wyman was particularly well known for incorporating Californian fruit into his recipes.

Pears with Chocolate Sauce

Pare four Bartlett pears, cut in quarters, lengthways and sauté in butter until browned. Arrange in serving dish and pour over the following sauce. Chill thoroughly before serving. For the sauce put 2oz of sweet chocolate, one tablespoonful sugar, 1¼ cupfuls cold milk in double boiler, and let cook for 5 minutes, then add one teaspoon arrowroot, mixed with ¼ cupful thin cream and a few grains salt, and cook 10 minutes, stirring constantly. Melt 1½ tablespoons butter, add ¼ cupful powdered sugar, and cook until well caramelised, stirring constantly. Add to first mixture and flavour with ½ teaspoonful vanilla.[65]

***

Thanks to Hollywood and a wealth of written accounts, almost everyone knows something of the legacy of RMS *Titanic*, the majestic British passenger liner, thought to be unsinkable, which hit an iceberg in the early hours of 15 April 1912. The last menu for first-class passengers served on that fateful night included chocolate and vanilla eclairs.

Maria Parloa was a prolific cookery writer and culinary pioneer, she died just a couple of years before the *Titanic* embarked on its fateful voyage. I have included her recipes for chocolate and vanilla éclairs here, for no other reason other than that she travelled widely across America and Europe, learning her art and teaching others, and she was a product of the pioneering *Titanic* generation.

Eclairs

Put one cupful of boiling water and half a cupful of butter in a large saucepan, and when it boils up, turn in one pint of flour. Beat well with the vegetable masher. When perfectly smooth, and velvety to the touch, remove from the fire. Break five eggs into a bowl. When the paste is nearly cold, beat the eggs into it with the hand. Only a small part of the eggs should be added at a time. When the mixture is thoroughly beaten (it will take about 20 minutes), spread on buttered sheets in oblong pieces about 4in long and 1½ in wide. These must be about 2in apart. Bake in a rather quick oven for about 25 minutes. As soon as they are done, ice with either chocolate or vanilla frosting. When the icing is cold, cut the éclairs on one side and fill them.

Chocolate éclairs
Put 1½ cupfuls of milk in the double boiler. Beat together 2/3 cupful of sugar, ¼ cupful of flour, two eggs, and ¼ teaspoonful of salt. Stir the mixture into the boiling milk. Cook 15 minutes, stirring often. When cold, flavor with one teaspoonful of vanilla extract. Put two squares of scraped chocolate with five tablespoonfuls of powdered sugar and three of boiling water. Stir over the fire until smooth and glossy. Dip the tops of the éclairs in this as they come from the oven. When the chocolate icing is dry, cut open, and fill with the cream, which should be cold. If a chocolate flavour is liked with the cream, one tablespoonful of the dissolved chocolate may be added to it.

Vanilla éclairs
Make an icing with the whites of two eggs and 1½ cupfuls of powdered sugar. Flavour with one teaspoonful of vanilla extract. Frost the éclairs; and when dry, open, and fill with a cream, the same as chocolate éclairs. They may be filled with cream sweetened, flavoured with vanilla and whipped to a stiff froth. Strawberry and raspberry preserves are sometimes used to fill éclairs. They are then named after the fruit with which they are filled.[66]

***

There are few places more mysterious as space itself. Russian cosmonaut Yuri Gagarin was the first person to orbit the earth in 1961, his 'space food' consisted of stuffed tubes, a little like toothpaste containing 'juices, liquid chocolate and soup'.[67] Chocolate was also a staple food on all the Apollo missions, including dehydrated chocolate puddings and vacuum-packed brownies.[68]

Today, astronauts enjoy anything from chocolate-covered cookies to chocolate mints and a variety of specialist chocolates. There's one little chocolate in particular that has accompanied at least 130 of NASA's space missions and that's Mars' M&M's. Those little multi-coloured buttons of joy continue to feature on the menu for most astronauts, placed in small clear plastic bags, which are eaten and also frequently juggled for entertainment in challenging environments with little gravity.

Given their historic presence on so many missions, M&M's would almost certainly have been stored on board the space shuttle *Challenger* on its tragic mission in 1986, when all seven astronauts on board lost their lives.

***

In 1972 a plane crashed into the Andes on its way to Chile for an amateur rugby match. Sixteen of the forty-five passengers, including the rugby team, their friends and family members, survived. They lasted seventy-two days in sub-zero conditions, eventually relying on the frozen meat of their dead companions to stay alive. A successful book and subsequent film, *Alive*, told the story. It has been well documented that among the food available to the survivors were eight chocolate bars. A square was issued to each person during the evening until rations ran out.

To pass the time and keep their minds working the survivors would regularly talk about their favourite home-cooked dish or a dish that they cooked themselves, the most exotic food they had eaten, the oddest food, their favourite puddings and so on. During one of these many discussions, Roy Harley, an electronics student from Uruguay, who also managed to get a transistor radio to work, described a dish of peanuts and *dulce de leche* coated with chocolate.[69]

Harley may have been referring to a very well-known Latin-American dessert called *alfajor*, which are particularly favoured among children. They come in a variety of flavours – almond, hazelnut, coconut, peanut and so on – all filled with *dulce de leche* and often coated in chocolate. (Queen Isabela II of Spain was an alleged obsessive of sweets and sweet desserts. Her 'pastrycook museum' was said to have extended into almost every room of the palace from *tortas*, to *panes pintados* (painted buns), turrones (nuts covered in sugar and honey), jellies, blancmanges, barley sugars, sugared rice and of course *alfajor*.)[70]

Several members of the survival group went in desperate search of help, walking for days before encountering a lone shepherd who rode some eight hours to reach police and begin the rescue process.

***

In 1988 students at Hirosaki University, Japan, detected high levels of radioactive substances in sixteen of the twenty-two brands of chocolate sold in the country. The research team attributed this to contaminated milk, possibly a consequence of the Chernobyl nuclear plant disaster of 1986, considered to be the worst nuclear disaster in history. Hundreds of people died in the explosion itself, while potentially thousands of radiation-induced deaths have occurred since.[71]

The Japanese have a particular fondness for chocolate covered bananas, a widespread tradition in which the fruit is covered in all manner of different types of chocolate, often colourful, sometimes elaborately decorated and always attached to a stick. Perhaps due to their shape, they are particularly popular at the Kanamara Matsuri Festival (Festival of the Steel Phallus) held annually in Kawasaki in April. Given the Japanese association with decorum and politeness, this festival, which symbolises everything that is the opposite of sexual repression and reservation, brings marginalised communities including LGBTQ groups all together.

The narrative behind the origins of the festival are rather more sinister, however. In a nutshell, according to ancient Japanese legend, a jealous demon with sharp teeth inhabited the vagina of a young woman he had fallen in love with and bit off the penises of all her lovers. The woman lived in fear and despair until one day she had a blacksmith craft an iron dildo which broke the teeth of the demon and the metal phallus became a shrine to sexual protection and fertility. From the sixteenth-century, prostitutes would gather outside the shrine of Kanamara seeking prosperity and protection from venereal diseases by worshipping

Kanayama Hiko no Kami and Kanayama Hime no Kami, deities that are associated with Blacksmiths.[72]

Choco-Bananas
Ingredients (for four people)
2 big green bananas
2 pairs of disposable chopsticks or 4 popsicle sticks
Chocolate sprinkles or your choice of toppings
70g chocolate
hot water

Method
Cut bananas into half or the size that you favour and put a stick on each banana.

Put bananas in the fridge while tempering chocolate.

Put a bowl of chocolate on hot water (around 60°C).

Once chocolate is all melted, check the temperature. If it is under 35°C it's perfect, so take it off the heat. (If it goes over 35°C be careful as chocolate doesn't harden).

Take out bananas from the fridge, and cover bananas with chocolate as quickly as you can.

Quickly decorate and sprinkle to chocolate covered bananas, and let it dry.[73]

***

Another annual event where chocolate is central to commemorating dark subject matter is the Great Chocolate Train Wreck Festival which marks an event in the village of Hamilton, Madison County, New York, on 27 September. On this day in 1955 a train travelling from Oswego to Norwich derailed and crashed into a coal shed. The contents of the carriages included hundreds of units of Nestlé chocolate drinks, thousands of Nestlé crunch bars and dozens of boxes of chocolate chips. Thankfully no one was seriously injured, but the village was blessed with stockpiles of goodies and ever since they have honoured the crash with a variety of chocolate-themed activities.[74] The residents of Hamilton could have enjoyed making chocolate chip cookies similar to these, in an attempt not to waste all that stock.

Chocolate Chippers
1 cup butter or margarine
1½ cups brown sugar
2 eggs
1 teaspoon vanilla
2 cups plain flour
¼ cup cornflour
1 teaspoon bicarbonate of soda
2 cups chocolate chips
1 cup chopped walnuts (optional)

Cream butter and sugar together. Beat in eggs one at a time. Add vanilla. Stir flour, cornflour, salt and bicarbonate of soda together. Stir in chocolate chips and nuts if using. Drop spoonfuls onto a greased baking sheet. Bake at 350°F (180°C) for 10-15 minutes.[75]

Chapter 2

Potions, Perilous Passages and Political Conflict: The Milkier Elements of Chocolate

Over the centuries, chocolate has been promoted as everything from a cure for deadly infections and disease, health supplement and stimulant, laxative and slimming aid. In Christian terms it has been referred to as sinful and aligned with sorcery, a reputation gained by its esoteric Aztec roots.

It has also played a significant role in situations where adversity requires a level of endurance, from exploration to war. During the Second World War in Britain contraband goods were rife, and though cocoa powder was not rationed, solid chocolate was. The black-market chocolate that was in circulation was often very hard and bitter. Despite chocolate manufacturers and the government reaching an agreement on the necessary amount of cocoa required to continue production, sugar rationing significantly limited the manufacture of chocolate.

Some manufacturers like Rowntree's of York added saccharin to their products, but the artificial flavour was not popular with buyers. The following wartime chocolate recipes were published in the *Taunton Courier and Western Advertiser* on Saturday, 20 November 1943:

Chocolate fingers

Ingredients: 3oz sugar, 2½ oz margarine, 1 egg (reconstituted), 5oz flour, ½ oz cocoa, ¼g ill milk, ½ teaspoonful vanilla essence.

Sieve the flour and cocoa. Beat the margarine to a cream with a wooden spoon. Beat the sugar, and then the egg. Stir in the dry ingredients alternately with the milk. Lastly add the vanilla essence. When well blended, put into a well-greased shallow tin measuring approximately 20in by 6in. Put in a moderate oven for 15 minutes. Turn out and cool on a wire cake tray. When cold cut into neat fingers.

Baked Chocolate Custard Tart
Ingredients: 4oz shortcrust pastry, ½ pint milk, 2 eggs (reconstituted), a little sugar to sweeten, 2 teaspoonfuls cocoa. Blend the cocoa with a very little cold milk, put the remainder on to boil and when almost boiling stir in the blended cocoa, and allow to simmer for a few minutes. Meanwhile beat the two eggs. Then pour on the hot milk, continuing to whisk or beat meanwhile. Pour the custard into pastry-lined tin and bake in a moderate oven for 20 minutes to half an hour until the custard set. If liked, the tart tin can be lined with pastry and baked before the custard is added.

War and political conflict

Chocolate has been an essential staple for the military since its discovery. From the cacao tablets consumed by Aztec warriors to Napoleon's faith in its abilities to bolster stamina.

The strategic use of methamphetamine, also known as meth or crystal meth, by German armed forces during the Second World War was commonplace. If you've ever watched the multi-award-winning television series *Breaking Bad* you will know all about methamphetamine, a highly addictive drug which acts as a stimulant on the nervous system. In addition to significantly elevating a person's mood, it can cause brain bleeding, psychosis and extreme levels of violent behaviour.

A pharmaceutical company, Temmler began mass producing methamphetamine tablets in Berlin during the 1930s under the brand name of Pervitin, a trend that the chocolate manufacturers, Hildebrand adopted. They produced chocolates laced with methamphetamine which were marketed to German homemakers, along with the strap line 'Hildebrand chocolates are always a delight'. Two to three chocolates a day were recommended to make housework more fun![1]

The history of chocolate in Germany is similar to the rest of Europe: it was originally consumed as a luxury or medicinal drink in the seventeenth century, and then became a refined solid product by the 1800s. Today, the most popular manufacturers in Germany are probably Milka and Ritter Sport, founded in 1901 and 1912 respectively.

Originating in Austria, but very much associated with Central European and in particular German cuisine, the strudel becomes an even more enticing pastry when paired with chocolate as it is here in this recipe.

German Chocolate Strudeln (Chocolate Strudels)
To make the strudel paste
Beat two eggs and the yolks of two others. Warm a piece of butter the size of an egg and add it to the eggs with a little salt. Work in by degrees as much fine flour as will form a dough, knead this till quite smooth. Divide the paste into small balls and roll them round in the hands. Then with a smooth rolling pin, roll them out as thinly as possible. They should be the size of a saucer but rather oval.

To make the filling
Grate vanilla chocolate and mix it with some pounded almonds and the yolks of two or three eggs, with the whites beaten to a snow. Spread hot butter over the strudels and then the chocolate as thin as a knife blade. Roll them up, sprinkle sugar and chocolate over and bake them. Pour some cream or milk over when they are nearly done. They must be kept a pale brown.[2]

***

During the South African Boer War, Queen Victoria sent special edition boxed chocolates out to British troops. They came in tins, weighing half a pound each and every effort was made in December 1899 to ensure each consignment reached the soldiers as close enough to the festive period as possible.[3] This is quite possibly one of the reasons why gifting chocolate at Christmas became so popular.

The Boer War was a conflict over empire and British rule in South Africa. It was tactically a harsh and brutal war in which British troops subjected Boers (descendants of original Dutch settlers) to extreme forms of coercion, including the use of concentration camps and the extensive burning of land and property. After two and a half years of violent combat, Britain emerged victorious, but failed to provide any enfranchisement for indigenous black communities, resulting in years of Boer oppression and inequality, contributing to the broader long-standing issues of apartheid.

41

There is a very popular treat in South Africa called the chocolate pepper cookie, which I assume must derive from both the ancient Dutch/German *Pfefferkuchen* (a spiced cookie) originally created for children and to be used as cattle feed, and the Viennese *Wienerstube* cookie. The recipe I found for Viennese cookies in a 1952 *Journal of Home Economics* calls for Nestlé chocolate, though other chocolate manufacturers are available.

Chocolate Viennese Cookies
1 packet (around 300g) of Nestlé semi-sweet chocolate chips, melted over hot (not boiling) water.

Sift together and set aside
2 cups sifted flour
¼ tsp cloves
1 tsp cinnamon

Combine and beat until smooth
½ cup butter
½ cup lard or vegetable fat

Add one at a time and mix well with the fats
1 cup sugar
1 egg
1 cup unblanched almonds, ground finely
1 tablespoon of grated lemon rind
The sifted flour mix

Divide the dough in half. Roll each half between waxed paper to about 35cm x 25cm. Chill.

Place one half onto a baking sheet and spread with the melted chocolate. Top with the remaining dough. With a knife or pastry wheel cut into 5cm squares and seal all the outside edges. Bake for 15 minutes at 375°F/190°C. While still hot recut the squares. Yields approximately 26 cookies.[4]

***

Chocolate was historically used as a currency for bartering in Prisoner of War Camps. R.A. Radford's 1945 publication *The Economic Organization of a P.O.W. Camp* is an observation of his time spent as a prisoner during the Second World War, when Radford was captured in Libya in 1942. Prisoners frequently exchanged goods and services ranging from jam to razor blades in an environment where supplies were often reliant on Red Cross donations. These contained items like tinned milk, jam, butter, biscuits, chocolate, bully beef, sugar and cigarettes. At a transit camp in Italy, Radford described the simple barter of a non-smoking friend giving their cigarette ration in exchange for the others' chocolate ration. Similarly, Sikh prisoners, who refused beef in their diet would exchange this for jam or margarine. As the economies shifted and trade grew in this way, a specific worth for each item began to emerge. For example, while one tin of jam was equal to half a pound of margarine, several rations of chocolate would be equal to one ration of cigarettes. Towards the end of the war in Germany, Radford specified the reduction in supplies, with some rations halving. One loaf of bread could be exchanged for one bar of chocolate in 1945 and there was a subsequent rush of prisoners selling bread and buying chocolate.[5]

During the Second World War, a subsidiary company of Nestlé, called Maggi, allegedly employed prisoners of war and Jewish slave labour in its factory in Germany near the Swiss border.[6] In August 2000 Nestlé paid a staggering twenty-five million Swiss francs into a settlement for Holocaust survivors and other Jewish organisations as reparation for its commercial activity in countries under the Nazi regime during the war.[7]

The German military also resorted to dirty tactics in First World War British trenches, when disguised German infiltrators, acting as chocolate vendors, doled out sweet treats, winning the trust of British soldiers who welcomed the comfort that a little bit of chocolate provided. Two able seamen of the Royal Naval Volunteer Reserve who fought in the trenches, told journalists in 1914 that these chocolate bearers were often dressed in Belgian uniforms, or posed as civilian guides 'plying us with chocolates, [while] ascertaining our every movement and were finding out all they possibly could about the disposal of our forces, their strength and their equipment.'[8]

This is a recipe for chocolate caramels, published not long after the end of the First World War:

> Take 3oz of finely grated vanilla chocolate, 1lb of best sugar loaf, ½ pint cream, ½ pint milk. Dissolve the sugar in the milk, add the cream and bring slowly to boiling point. Dissolve the chocolate in the smallest possible quantity of hot water, stir it into the syrup and boil very gently until a little dropped into cold water at once hardens and crisps easily. Pour it onto an oiled slab into a square formed by bars, or failing this, into an old tin. When cold cut into squares with a caramel cutter or a buttered knife and wrap each piece in wax paper.[9]

The reality is that all participants of war resort to covert activities, including British secret agents who were sent on missions to Spain during the Second World War. Their assumed identities had to remain as convincing and authentic as possible and one of the ways they could achieve this was to smell of garlic, like the Spanish, who infused so many of their dishes with it.

Britain of the 1930s had a bit of an aversion to garlic, so to sweeten the bitter pill – or garlic in this instance – British spies were issued with chocolate bars laced with garlic.[10]

Garlic is also a terrific natural aid for high blood pressure – which must have been a common danger for secret service personnel – so garlic chocolate potentially solved two issues at the same time.

The Oxford Symposium on Food and Cookery published a method for chocolate-coated candied garlic in the 1980s. Whether this is something M15 had adopted some fifty years previously, I have no idea, but it makes for a great recipe, with the added suggestion for serving it alongside an espresso coffee.

Chocolate Coated Candied Garlic
1 cup water
4 tablespoons syrup
½ cup rosewater
1 cup peeled garlic cloves
Rind of half a lemon
Semi-sweet chocolate

Combine water, syrup, rosewater and lemon peel in a skillet. Bring to a boil and boil until a syrup is obtained. Add garlic and simmer until garlic is tender and candied.

Remove garlic from syrup and cool on a rack. Dip candied garlic in melted semi-sweet chocolate. Let cool.[11]

There are also some moving stories that emerged from the hell of war which relate to chocolate. American military operations in North-Eastern France during the First World War led to soldiers fighting on the frontline in the village of Xammes. Diaries from infantrymen at this time describe the intensity of shelling, making it impossible for anything to get through to the troops. Private Elmer P. Richards was wounded by shrapnel. On learning of the plight of his company, he managed to procure a significant quantity of chocolate, then walked two miles through the shell fire in agony to ensure that each and every man received a portion to keep themselves sustained.[12] Also in France, Gaston Menier, the then Chief Operating Manager of the famous family-run French chocolate company, turned his chateau into a hospital, maintaining a team of highly organised surgeons and nurses at his own expense to care for wounded French.[13]

Across the Atlantic, chocolate was just as important in times of conflict to the Americans, who had consumed it as a hot beverage in the new colonies since at least 1765. In the Southern states chocolate was unavailable during the Civil War, so a substitute was invented from peanuts, which were roasted, skinned and ground down in a mortar. This mix was then blended with milk that had been boiled and sugar was added. According to the memoirs of Virginia Clay-Clopton, the drink proved to be 'delightful to our palates'.[14]

In 1937 Captain Paul Logan commissioned the US chocolate giant Hershey to create a 4-oz bar of chocolate for troops to access in emergencies. These 600-calorie Ration D bars could provide all the sustenance a soldier required for one day. Most importantly, the components of the bar itself meant that it was able to withstand extreme temperatures and possessed very little flavour. Thus discouraging any temptation to consume the snack at any other time than in an emergency. The D Ration bar contained chocolate liquor, sugar, skim milk powder, cocoa butter, oat flour and vanillin. It was successfully manufactured for United States troops throughout the Second World War.[15] Rationed chocolate has also historically been integral to the Swiss army, which even has its own brand name that continues today.

There was a period when Hershey's collaborated with American company Durkee Famous Foods, who were particularly well-known for their margarine and shredded coconut. Durkee went through a series of mergers and takeovers in the 1980s and were most recently acquired by B&G Foods. In the 1950s you could find the Hershey and Durkee brands entwined together in numerous projects, such as this 'exclusive' fudge recipe created by the two food giants.

10 Minute Wonder Fudge
Melt together 1 packet (6oz) Hershey's semi-sweet 'Chocolate Dainties' (chocolate chips) with 4 level tablespoons Durkee's Margarine (half of ¼ lb stick) in a double boiler.

Add 3 tablespoons warm water and 1 teaspoon vanilla to the mix.

Sift 3 level cups confectioners' sugar (icing sugar) and a dash of salt into a large mixing bowl.

Mix 1 cup Durkee's 'Stayfresh Coconut' or 1 x 5-oz can of Durkee's 'Dixie Cut Coconut' (shredded coconut should do) with the sugar.

Stir the melted mixture into the bowl of dry ingredients.

Press into an 8-in pan.

If desired top with coconut. Chill in refrigerator until set. Remove from refrigerator, cut into squares and serve. (Makes about 1½ lb).[16]

***

Twentieth-century American and European consumerism wasn't something that the Russian people would have been familiar with. Following the Revolution, Communists condemned chocolate until Stalin began promoting it as a positive economic symbol during the 1920s and 30s. When the Bolsheviks seized power in 1917 they viewed chocolate suspiciously and with disdain. This was undoubtedly a legacy of the strict doctrines of the Russian Orthodox Church, which for centuries had been obsessed with fasting, believing that the physical pleasures of food hindered a person's spiritual and moral well-being. The sudden rise in chocolate consumption across Russia in the late nineteenth century was viewed as a reflection of the growth of the bourgeoisie.

The October Revolution led by Vladimir Lenin, which kick-started the Russian Revolution, was a time of events and activities organised with the intention of bringing down the existing government. Writer Alexander Blok, who at first embraced the Revolution, before denouncing it in later life, wrote a symbolic poem about the October Revolution in 1917, *The Twelve*. This poem captures the feelings and mood of the Russian people at the time. It also highlights the overriding contempt for chocolate throughout this period.[17]

In the poem, a soldier of the Red Guard shoots his girlfriend, Katya, for abandoning the revolutionary cause. Katya was also promiscuous with members of bourgeoise society, accepting gifts for sex. Blok describes her thus:

> She wore lacy underwear,
> Wear it now, yes, wear it now!
> With officers she fornicated
> Fornicate, now, fornicate!
>
> Oh, yeah, fornicate!
> Feel the heart just skip a beat!
>
> Remember, Katya, that officer –
> He did not escape the knife ...
> Left your memory already?
> Is your memory stale, you broad?
> Well, then, freshen it, Take it off to bed with you!
>
> Kat'ka always wore gray gaiters,
> Devoured chocolat "Mignon",
> Used to date the young cadets,
> But now with soldiers off she's gone.[18]

The Mignon chocolate that Blok mentions here was quite possibly the same Mignon established in 1912 in Ukraine, initially as a bakery which began retailing sweets and chocolates. Its founder, Hovsep Ter-Poghossain Sr, was arrested during the Communist regime, accused of being a capitalist. His family fled to Iran. On his release four years later Hovsep Sr was reunited with his family and re-established his business successfully in Tehran. By the 1960s, under the ownership of his children, the business began to specialise in chocolate. Today, as third-generation chocolatiers, Mignon now has shops across the United States. Communism was never going to beat them.[19]

Continuing with the Russian theme, Michelle Polzine's outrageously decadent Russian honey cake is a descendant of the historic Medovik Tort, allegedly created by the head chef to Russian Tsar, Alexander I. The most authentic Russian honey cakes are those simply made with sponge and a cream filling, but numerous varieties have emerged over the years. Famous for her San Francisco-based '20th Century Café', Polzine spent a great deal of time researching and developing her own intricate version and in 2017 she finally shared it with chef and *New York Times* journalist Samin Nosrat. It has become one of the most sought-after Russian honey cakes on the planet. However, there is another specific layered chocolate and honey cream cake from the Ukraine, which is incredibly similar to the Russian honey cake, but contains chocolate and is traditionally known as a Spartak cake (Spartacus). I am curious as to whether this cake has any relationship to the historic chocolate and confectionery factory 'Spartak', which based in Gomel, in Belarus, on the Russian border.

The following recipe is from Nadejda Reilly's *Ukrainian Cuisine*. Be aware that this is a complex recipe, but can yield impressive results.

Spartak Cake (chocolate honey cream cake)
Cake Pastry
2¼ cups plain flour, sifted
¼ cup unsweetened cocoa powder
1 teaspoon bicarbonate of soda
1 tablespoon white wine vinegar
½ cup whole milk
¼ cup honey
1 large egg, beaten
¼ stick unsalted butter, soft (about 2 tablespoons)

Cream Filling
2 cups whole milk
1½-2 tablespoons potato starch

2 sticks unsalted butter, soft (1 cup)
1½ cups granulated sugar
6oz dark chocolate, chopped
1 teaspoon vanilla extract

Preparing and Baking Cake Pastry
Preheat oven to 350°F/180°C. Grease and line 4 x 9-in round cake tins. In a small saucepan, combine milk, honey, bicarbonate, vinegar, beaten egg and butter. Stirring constantly, cook the mixture on medium-low heat for 2-3 minutes. Cool the mixture completely. In a standard mixer, combine milk-honey mixture, sifted flour and cocoa powder. Mix on a low speed until the dough is mixed. Rest the dough for 30 minutes. Evenly divide it into four pieces. Transfer the dough pieces into the prepared cake tins. Bake them for 20-30 minutes or until a stick comes out clean. Cool completely in the tins.

Preparing Cream Filling
In a small saucepan, combine 1½ cups of milk and ½ cup of sugar. Bring it to a boil. Mix together the remaining half cup of milk and potato starch until dissolved. Add to the boiling milk. Stirring constantly, cook it for 3-5 minutes until the mixture thickens. Cool the mixture completely. Beat together butter and the remaining 1 cup sugar and vanilla extract until creamy and fluffy. Add milk cream, ¼ cup at a time. Mix it well until the cream is creamy and all the ingredients are incorporated. Coarsely chop the chocolate. Do not mix it with the cream.

Assembling Spartak Cake
Divide the cream filling among four cake layers, leaving more cream for the top layer and cake sides. Assemble cake as follows: first, second, third and fourth layers: cake pastry, cream filling and sprinkled chopped chocolate. Use a large spatula to evenly spread the cream filling all over the layers, cake top and sides, as well as evenly sprinkle the chopped chocolate all over the layers. Pack the sides of the cake with

chopped chocolate. Refrigerate the cake after assembling. Take it out 20-30 minutes before serving.

To make a chocolate filling, simply add melted chocolate or cocoa to either cooking milk mixture or to the butter.[20]

***

From one revolution, to another, it would seem chocolate has featured in more than one. Louis Constant Wairy was head valet to Napoleon and his memoirs reveal a great deal about the emperor and court life.

Danzig, now known as Gdansk in Poland, was a strategically important city during the Napoleonic Wars. As such, it was besieged and captured by French troops under the leadership of Napoleon's military commander, Marshall François Lefebvre, in 1807. For his efforts Lefebvre was awarded the title of Duc (Duke).

Napoleon summoned Lefebvre very early one morning to take breakfast and to impart the news about his new title. The Marshall was confused by the emperor addressing him as 'Duc' throughout their meeting, and he was even more perplexed when Napoleon announced that he wanted to give him a pound of chocolate from the city of Danzig, as a souvenir of his triumphs.

Napoleon made a show of moving to a casket and taking out a long, square packet which he handed to Lefebvre, saying something along the lines of 'Duc de Danzig, accept this chocolate; little presents nourish friendship.' Then Napoleon, Lefebvre and a third companion sat down to breakfast, which was said to be a large pasty, designed to represent the city of Danzig, which they all 'attacked' and ate symbolically.

On returning home Lefebvre hastily opened the package to find the equivalent in banknotes of 100,000 écu's (French currency of the time). From then on it became customary in the French army to call money 'Danzig chocolate', which was also a generic reference to any treat issued to a soldier.[21]

Wuzetka is a delightful cake from Poland, the origins of which are ambivalent. Some say the name derives from the street in Warsaw where the bakery that invented it was located in the early 1940s. Others believe it is named after the iconic W-Z route, a major thoroughfare in Warsaw, and one of the city's first post-war building projects.

It's basically a chocolate sponge cake filled with cream and a thin layer of jam/fruit, topped off with a dollop of cream and a single cherry.

Having visited Poland, I can vouch for the fact that they make very good chocolate indeed. Sourcing a recipe for Wuzetka from a book proved to be extremely difficult, so I turned to the next best thing in this age of technological accessibility – a Polish cookery blog, specifically *Beata's Pastries*. Beata's recipes are popular and traditional to Poland and hopefully little will be lost in the translation of it into English.

Wuzetka cake
8 eggs
250g of sugar
8 tablespoons of flour
1 teaspoon of soda,
3 tablespoons of cocoa

Cream and filling
750ml of cream
3 teaspoons of gelatine
5 tablespoons of powdered sugar
3 tbsp thick apricot marmalade (I think cherry will be just as good)

Icing
250ml of cream
200g of dark chocolate

Method
Beat eggs with sugar until fluffy and thick.

Then add the flour mixed with soda and cocoa in portions (it's best to mix the mass now with a spoon rather than a mixer).

Pour the dough into a mould (25 x 25 cm) lined with paper or greased with butter and sprinkled with breadcrumbs.

Bake for 25 minutes at 180°C. Once it has cooled down, cut the dough in half into two pancakes.

Make a cream: steam the gelatine in 5-6 tablespoons of water and cool.

Beat chilled fondant stiff with powdered sugar.

Add cooled gelatine to it and stir all the time. Set aside 4 tablespoons of cream for decoration.

Put the top of the cake into a mould (it can now be soaked – which in my opinion is very useful for this sponge cake), put all the remaining mass on it, cover with the other top (I also suggest soaking it a little).

Brush the top with marmalade and refrigerate for an hour.

Make the topping: heat the cream (do not boil it), add the broken chocolate to it.

Stir until it dissolves. When it is slightly cool, pour it over the cake.

On top, squeeze the rosettes from the cream that has been left behind.

Put everything back in the fridge for an hour.[22]

Incidentally, Polish society initially met chocolate with scorn. Its dark, sticky qualities were thought to be satanic, while its effects on the nervous system were rousing. They were reluctant for this reason to consume it during Lent. Polish people also found the taste bitter and repugnant until it began to be served hot. Chocolate's abilities to provide an uplifting beverage eventually increased its popularity, particularly when King John III Sobieski declared his passion for '*ciokolata*'. Writing to his wife in 1665, he requested chocolate, a chocolate pot and a stick to stir and whisk it with.

Chocolate as medicine

The Badianus Manuscript is an early book of Aztec medicinal herbal remedies, compiled in the 1500s. It contains instructions for a remedy using cacao flowers to sooth sore feet and alleviate fatigue, while the Florentine Codex – a research study, also from the 1500s, held at the Laurentian library in Florence, documenting early Mesoamerican cultures – suggests a prescription of maize, cacao and the herb *tlacoxochitl* (*Calliandra anomala*), to quell fevers and breathlessness, as well as helping with heart conditions.[23]

Aztec tribes equated chocolate with blood, as both were powerful life-giving fluids. Chocolate was sometimes reddened with achiote, before being used as a treatment for haemorrhages.[24] During the early modern period, European missionaries and colonial authorities in South America considered cacao to have great medicinal properties. Jesuits working in Paraguay in the 1580s documented the 'Virtues of Cacao' in a weighty manuscript, which documented treatments for everything from stomach and liver complaints to asthma.[25]

Juan de Cárdenas' published account of 'New Spain' in 1591 translate as *Wonderful problems and secrets of the Indies*. It offers a comprehensive list of all the ingredients in Mexico that were added to chocolate to achieve a variety of outcomes:

> the first spice added to said drink is called *gueyncaztle* by the Indians and ear-flower by the Spanish … because of its good aroma … it gives the pleasure of its fragrance to this drink … Therefore, this drink strengthens and comforts the vital virtues, helping to engender life spirits.
>
> It likewise has a very pleasant taste, which makes what is drunk even more beneficial … *Gueyncaztle* is followed second by *mecasuchil*, which is nothing more than some sticks or threads, brown and thin, which because they have this shape of thin threads, are called by this name, which means 'rose in the form of a thread'… The third in order, and the first in soft and delicate aromas, is the so-called *tlixochil*, which in our language is called aromatic vanilla, because they are really long and brown vanilla pods with insides full of black seeds, but fewer than those of mustard … they compete with musk and amber … They add to said chocolate a very soft and mild odour and therefore have an advantage over all other spices in being cordial and friendly to the heart.
>
> Achiote is also counted as a spice, since it is no less valued in this drink than cardamom in medicinal and aromatic compounds … Achiote [is added] to this drink in order to give it pretty red colour and in order to give sustenance and to fatten the person who drinks it … Some people tend to add a little of everything [to chocolate] if they feel cold in

the stomach, or the belly, and also add some toasted chilies to the chocolate and some large seeds of dry cilantro, called pepper.[26]

Incidentally, *Gueyncaztle*, ear-flower, or its scientific name *cymbopetalum*, is still cultivated as a spice from the dried petals of the plant in numerous regions of Guatemala.

***

The first known text in English specifically concerning chocolate was *A Curious Treatsie of the Nature and Quality of Chocolate,* translated from a Spanish book written by Antonio Colmenero de Ledesma. A second book was published in 1652, translated by Captain James Wadsworth, titled *Chocolate: or, An Indian Drink* (Indians being Natives of the Americas).

The book was sold by John Dakins in Holborn, who also traded in medicines, a common combination of retailing apparently in the seventeenth century. Dakins and Wadsworth marketed the book along with chocolate, which they sold on the pretext of its medicinal qualities.[27] This started a popular trend amongst booksellers – buy a book and get your chocolate at the same time.

The physician Henry Stubbe, writing in 1662, goes as far as recommending chocolate as a remedy for cognitive issues, one that is effective at curing 'hot distempers and madness of the brain in young unmarried folks'. Stubbe claimed to have seen 'maniacs' and those suffering from melancholy cured with properly administered chocolate.[28] His book, *The Indian Nectar: A Discourse Concerning Chcocolata,* also claimed that English land soldiers based in Jamaica benefitted significantly from chocolate: 'the help of the cacao nut made into paste with sugar and dissolved in water, neither having, nor wanting other food, they usually sustain themselves sometimes for a long season and I have been assure that the Indian woman do feed on it, (eating it often) that they scarce eat any solid meat twice in a week; yet feel no decay of heat or strength'.

Stubbe provided documented evidence from other physicians working in the New World on the curative benefits of chocolate. From a 'learned' Doctor Roblez working in Peru, he gauged that people in this country would hang the cacao, then boil it until the oil, which resembled a white butter, dispersed. This was then toasted in a clay oven, then mixed with cinnamon, cloves and aniseeds, before several pounds of cacao was added. The infusion was then ground down into a paste, before being formed into cakes, or mixed with liquid to make a drink. The draught or liquid version was termed 'Royal Chocolate' and was consumed by nobility and high-ranking individuals.

Other people, Roblez observed, added cornflour or almonds – which was considered an inferior chocolate as it didn't keep as well – while some communities in Peru chose to add achiote to the cacao paste (a Mexican spice and colouring agent, often used in chorizo). This was considered to make an excellent diuretic. Roblez also observed that drinking chocolate at night kept people awake, which is why it was so useful to soldiers and guards. He also recommended cacao butter as a treatment for burns, tumours and even smallpox, as he believed it soothed and withdrew heat from scolds, spots or rashes. Much of this certainly testifies to what we know about chocolate today: its high levels of caffeine act as a stimulant, while it also functions as an effective laxative.

Nicasius le Febure is another of the expert contributors that Stubbe included in his book. Febure was the apothecary to the French court and was later appointed professor of chemistry to Charles II. He was also on very good terms with the king's physician, Dr Quartermaine, who recommended taking the butter of cacao (cocoa butter), melting it and then rubbing it around the anus to cure haemorrhoids. Quartermaine swore by the treatment, which not only cured the piles but also ensured they never reappeared. Le Febure maintained, like Stubbe, that chocolate should be recommended as a treatment for 'melancholy', or what we would consider to be depression today.[29]

But it was Antonio Colmenero de Ledesma who first introduced the pharmaceutical properties of chocolate to Europeans, with his *Curioso tratado de la naturaleza y calidad del chocolate (Curious treaise on the nature and quality of chocolate)* in 1631. As a Spanish physician, Don Antonio was fascinated with the characteristics of cacao, stating:

> it preserves Health, and makes such as drink it often, Fat, and Corpulent, faire and Amiable, it vehemently Incites to *Venus*, and causeth Conception in women, hastens and facilitates their Delivery: It is an excellent help to Digestion, it cures Consumptions, and the Cough of the Lungs, the New Disease, or Plague of the Guts, and other Fluxes, the Green Sickness, Jaundise, and all manner of Inflamations,

Opilations, and Obstructions. It quite takes away the
Morphew, Cleanseth the Teeth, and sweetneth the Breath,
Provokes Urine, Cures the Stone, and strangury, Expells
Poison, and preserves from all infectious Diseases.

Antonio even contributed what must be one of the earliest authentic
medicinal recipes for chocolate to be published, and he went into great
detail about the importance of the process of each step in its preparation.
This is his rather lengthy, but what he considered essential strategy for
making the perfect cup of chocolate, taken from his second book of
1644, *Chocolata Inda: Opusculum de qualitate et natura Chocolatae
(Chocolate, Or, An Indian Drinke)*.

Antonio Colmenero de Ledesma's ultimate recipe for chocolate
To every 100 *Cacaos*, you must put two cods of the Chiles, long
red Pepper, of which I have spoken before, and are called in the
Indian Tongue, *Chilparlagua*; and instead of those of the *Indies*,
you may take those of *Spaine* which are broadest, & least hot.
One handfull of Annis-seed *Orejuelas*, which are otherwise
called *Pinacaxlidos*: and two of the flowers, called *Mechasuchil*,
if the Belly be bound. But in stead of this, in *Spaine*, we put in
six Roses of *Alexandria* beat to Powder: One Cod of *Campeche*,
or Logwood: Two Drams of Cinamon; Almons, and Hasle-Nuts,
of each one Dozen: Of white Sugar, halfe a pound: of *Achiote*
enough to give it the colour. And if you cannot have those things,
which come from the *Indies*, you may make it with the rest.

The way of compounding
The *Cacao*, and the other Ingredients must be beaten in a Morter of
Stone, or ground upon a broad stone, which the *Indians* call *Metate*,
and is onely made for that use: But the first thing that is to be done,
is to dry the Ingredients, all except the *Achiote*; with care that they
may be beaten to powder, keeping them still in stirring, that they be
not burnt, or become black; and if they be over-dried, they will be
bitter, and lose their vertue. The Cinamon, and the long red Pepper
are to be first beaten, with the Annis-seed; and then beate the *Cacao*,
which you must beate by a little and little, till it be all powdred; and

sometimes turne it round in the beating, that it may mixe the better: And every one of these Ingredients, must be beaten by it selfe; and then put all the Ingredients into the Vessell, where the *Cacao* is; which you must stirre together with a spoone; and then take out that Paste, and put it into the Morter, under which you must lay a little fire, after the *Confection* is made. But you must be very carefull, not to put more fire, than will warme it, that the unctuous part doe not dry away. And you must also take care, to put in the *Achiote* in the beating; that it may the better take the colour. You must Searse all the Ingredients, but onely the *Cacao*; and if you take the shell from the *Cacao*, it is the better; and when you shall find it to be well beaten, & incorporated (which you shall know by the shortness of it) then with a spoone take up some of the Paste, which will be almost liquid; and so either make it into Tablets; or put it into Boxes; and when it is cold it will be hard. To make the Tablets you must put a spoonfull of the Paste upon a piece of paper, the *Indians* put it upon the leaf of a *Planten-tree*; where, being put into the shade, it growes hard; and then bowing the paper, the Tablet falls off, by reason of the fatnesse of the paste. But if you put it into any thing of earth, or wood, it sticks fast, and will not come off, but with scraping, or breaking. In the *Indies* they take it two severall waies: the one, being the common way, is to take it hot, with *Atolle*, which was the Drinke of Ancient *Indians* (the *Indians* call *Atolle* pappe, made of the flower of *Maiz*, and so they mingle it with the *Chocolate*, and that the *Atolle* may be more wholesome, they take off the Husks of the *Maiz*, which is windy, and melancholy; and so there remaines onely the best and most substantiall part.) Now, to returne to the matter, I say, that the other Moderne drinke, which the Spaniards use so much, is of two sorts. The one is, that the *Chocolate*, being dissolved with cold water, & the scumme taken off, and put into another Vessell, the remainder is put upon the fire, with Sugar; and when it is warme, then powre it upon the Scumme you tooke off before, and so drinke it. The other is to warme the water; and then, when you have put it into a pot, or dish, as much *Chocolate* as you thinke fit, put in a little of the warme water, and then grinde it well with the molinet; and when it is well ground, put the rest of the warme water to it; and so drinke it with Sugar.

Besides these former wayes, there is one other way; which is, put the *Chocolate* into a pipkin, with a little water; and let it boyle well, till it be dissolved; and then put in sufficient water and Sugar, according to the quantity of the *Chocolate*; and then boyle it againe, untill there comes an oyly scumme upon it; and then drinke it. But if you put too much fire, it will runne over, and spoyle. But, in my opinion, this last way is not so wholsome, though it pleaseth the pallate better; because, when the Oily is divided from the earthy part, which remaines at the bottome, it causeth Melancholy; and the oily part loosens the stomacke, and takes away the appetite: There is another way to drink *Chocolate*, which is cold; and it takes its name from the principall Ingredient, and is called *Cacao*; which they use at feasts, to refresh themselves; and it is made after this manner. The *Chocolate* being dissolved in water with the *Molinet*, take off the scumme or crassy part, which riseth in greater quantity, when the *Cacao* is older, and more putrified. The scumme is laid aside by it selfe in a little dish; and then put sugar into that part, from whence you tooke the scumme; and powre it from on high into the scumme; and so drink it cold. And this drink is so cold, that it agreeth not with all mens stomacks; for by experience we find the hurt it doth, by causing paines in the stomacke, and especially to Women. I could deliver the reason of it; but I avoid it, because I will not be tedious, some use it, &c.

There is another way to drinke it cold, which is called *Cacao Penoli*; and it is done, by adding to the same *Chocolate* (having made the *Confection*, as is before set downe) so much *Maiz*, dryed, and well ground, and taken from the Huske, and then well mingled in the Morter, with the *Chocolate*, it falls all into flowre, or dust; & so these things being mingled, as is said before, there riseth the Scum; and so you take and drink it, as before.

There is another way, which is a shorter and quicker way of making it, for men of businesse, who cannot stay long about it; and it is more wholsome; and it is that, which I use. That is, first to set some water to warm; and while it warms, you throw a Tablet, or some *Chocolate*, scraped, and mingled with sugar, into a little Cup; and when the water is hot, you powre the water to the *Chocolate*, and then dissolve it with the Molinet; and then without taking off the scum, drink it as is before directed.[30]

Edward Montagu, the 1st Earl of Sandwich, was the English Ambassador to Spain in the 1660s and he also wrote prolifically on the subject of chocolate. Dr Kate Loveman found a range of chocolate recipes in the Earl of Sandwich's journal, written after he became enamoured of the drink, while ambassador extraordinary to Spain in the 1660s. He was particularly interested in its commercial potential.

The 1st Earl's recipe for iced chocolate

Prepare ye Chocolatti … and Then Putt ye vessel that hath ye Chocolatti in it into a Jarraffa (carafe) of snow stirred together with some salt, & shaike ye snow together sometyme & it will putt ye Chocolatti into tender Curdled Ice & soe eate it with spoons, and eat also Naples Biskett alonge with it. This way is much used for pleasure in ye heate of summer, but is held unwholesome & one is oblidged for better security to Drinke Hott Chocolatti in ¼ of an houre after.[31]

The Earl of Sandwich also revealed that King Charles II paid a staggering £200 for a prized formula for spiced and perfumed chocolate 'cakes'. The recipe consisted of three pounds of cacao nuts mixed with Jamican pepper oil, aniseed, cinnamon and cardamom oil and Guinea pepper. These would make blocks of solid chocolate that could be stored. Then cacao nuts, sugar, vanilla, sugar perfumed with musk, ambergris and civet were added to these tablets to enhance the taste further.[32]

The seventeenth century's respected doctor and medical writer, Edward Strother, wrote about apothecaries in Amsterdam who made chocolates from the oil and kernels of pine nuts to help stimulate breast milk and semen.[33] He also extolled the use of chocolate to stimulate semen in his 1718 work *Criticon Febrium, or A Critical Essay on Fevers*. John Leake, meanwhile, proposed a rather unappetising sounding mix of shell lime water, milk or a dram of almond soap dissolved in half a pint of 'thin' chocolate, to be taken twice a day to relieve gall or kidney stones.[34]

It wasn't just early treaties and recipes that became popular exponents of chocolate. In 1660 Henry Hall wrote the following verse, *The Vertues of Chocolate East-India drink,* which lists its merits as virtually a cure for all, even fertility.

BY this pleasing drink health is preserved, sicknesse diverted, It cures Consumptions and Cough of the Lungs; it expells poyson, cleanseth the teeth, and sweetneth the Breath; provoketh Urine; cureth the stone and strangury, maketh Fatt and Corpulent, faire and aimeable, it cureth the running of the Reins, with sundry other desperate Diseases; It causeth Conception according to these Verses,

> Nor need the Women longer grieve,
> Who spend their oyle yet not Conceive,
> For 'tis a Help Immediate,
> If such but Lick of Chocolate.[35]

Someone who needed little help in the bedroom department, judging by the salacious accounts included in his diary, was Samuel Pepys. In 1661 he wrote about drinking a draft of chocolate, which he used as a stomach settler, following the coronation of King Charles II:

'Waked in the morning with my head in a sad taking through the last night's drink, which I am very sorry for; so rose and went out with Mr. Creed to drink our morning draft, which he did give me in chocolate to settle my stomach.'[36]

By the following century, chocolate continued to be researched, written about and showcased for its medicinal benefits. The physician and polymath John Arbuthnot's book *An Essay Concerning the Nature of Ailments* (J. Tonson, London, 1731), describes it thus:

Chocolate is certainly much the best of those three exotick Liquors, its Oil seems to be both rich, alimentary, and anodyne; for an Oil as soft as that of sweet Almonds can be extracted from the Nut, and the Indians made Bread of it. This Oil combin'd with its own Salt and Sugar, makes it saponaceous and detergent, by which Quality it often helps Digestion and excites Appetite, when it is mix'd with Vanillios or Spices; it acquires likewise the good and bad Qualities of aromatick Oils, which are proper in some Cases and Constitutions, and very improper in others.[37]

In De Chelus's *The Natural History of Chocolate* (1724) he suggests four ways it could be applied as a medicine. One of these is as a purging device: purging being a very popular treatment from medieval times, right up to the early twentieth-century, to rid the body of all manner of toxins. Tinctures were marketed and sold for centuries, concocted from a variety of herbs and plant life to cleanse the body. De Chelus also advises on mixing chocolate with grains of jalop, a strong medicine derived from the roots of a Mexican vine, affirming: 'I have had great experience of this, it is a good purge without griping [receiving sharp pains in the bowl].' De Chelus scorned people with antiquated ideas who disregarded such practices – particularly seeking out those who continued to prefer using the likes of powdered millipedes, vipers and earthworms as treatments. I would say that was pretty forward-thinking talk back in the early 1700s.[38]

Such theories on the restorative powers of chocolate continued into the nineteenth century, when Auguste Debay claimed that a balm principally made from cacao, sugar and alcohol could be used to successfully reduce syphilis. In France, chocolate was historically used as the foundation for many medicinal recipes, far more than in Britain. It was sometimes combined with iron or magnesium as a tonic or with a particular moss to aid respiratory infections. When added to quinine it was thought to alleviate the symptoms of dyspepsia, or indigestion. As a purgative, jalap – the root of the Mexican climbing plant – and chocolate were often combined, a practice also endorsed by De Chelus. But the most popular mix of cod-liver oil and chocolate was the one strongly advocated by The *Societe de Medecine de la Seine-Inférieure*, which widely published its merits as a way of disguising the unpleasant taste of the oil.[39]

As the twentieth century advanced there was no evidence of chocolate's reputation for healing and soothing diminishing. In 1929 a confectioner trading in Mayfair, London, revealed that he had some 2,000 men listed on his books as regular customers who purchased chocolate for medicinal purposes. Many were former war veterans and they regularly purchased chocolate drops or chocolate pastilles. They ate these as a way of curbing their cravings for alcohol and cigarettes.[40] The pastille shape, it seems, was often one used for other medicinal purposes, as Dr Coderre's Worm Pastilles suggest. These were marketed as: 'the nicest common-sense Worm Remedy in use. They positively eradicate worms without causing any injuries or after effects. This remedy is in the form of a VERY SMALL CHOCOLATE

PASILLE, being considered the best and simplest shape to administer to children; being small, it is easy to give, pleasant to the eye and palatable to the taste'.[41]

***

After the Second World War, chocolate was popularly received as a remedy to relieve stress. Advertisements like those promoted by Fry's chocolate showed a series of five expressions on a young boy's face alter, from desperation to sheer joy, after receiving a chocolate bar.[42]

Changes in Biomedical science and new approaches to research meant that random trials began to take place, conducted in a way that would assess the genuine merits of chocolate. Cocoa butter was viewed as a useful lubricant for the skin rashes, chapped lips and sore nipples. One wild claim also suggested it might prevent tooth decay by coating the teeth and inhibiting plaque.

All those early understandings of chocolate being used as an effective laxative also continued into the twentieth century, with a variety of tonics and drinks growing into a more legitimate 'science of chocolate'.

Cherán, a small town in Mexico, still practices the ancient art of healing alongside modern medicine. In cases of long and difficult labours, local midwives would often give the mothers hot chocolate made with water and sugar before massaging the abdomen to help stimulate delivery.[43]

Not all societies, however, are proponents of chocolate's curative properties. In parts of Jamaica cocoa and chocolate are believed to rot your bones, a theory which probably stems from chocolate's oxalic acid content, which when combined with calcium forms calcium oxalate, which can lead to a reduction of calcium in the body. During the 1970s Jamaicans strongly advocated the need to minimise the chocolate intake of local children, to one piece a day.

One of the quirkiest therapies I encountered during the research into this book was to be found in a picturesque village in Germany, where a sort of sanctuary called the 'Chocolate Cure' was established in the early part of the twentieth century, with the objective of helping people who found it hard to gain weight. The patients ate and drank chocolate every day while they admired the scenery and increased the girth of their arms, necks, shoulders and so on. It's probably too nice to appear in a dark history such as this, but at the same time there seems something disquieting to me about having to find ways to gain weight.[44]

A chocolate cake I would also like to recommend for helping with this particular dilemma is a favourite of mine and my son, making it a challenging one to share graciously in our house. The following chocolate fudge cake recipe is an early American version from 1917.

Chocolate Fudge Cake
Cream two tablespoons butter, 3 egg yolks, 1¾ cups granulated sugar. Add ¼ lb ground bitter chocolate, ¾ cup milk, ½ cup chopped nuts, 1¼ cups of flour, 2 teaspoons vanilla, ½ cup raisins, 1½ teaspoons baking powder (or bicarbonate of soda). Finally add 3 whites of eggs beaten. Bake and cut into squares.

For the Chocolate Fudge Frosting
Boil until thick – ¼ lb ground chocolate, ¾ tablespoon milk, 1 cup sugar. Add 4 tablespoons cream, add enough powdered sugar (icing sugar), until proper consistency. Add chopped nuts (walnuts or pecans) and 2 tablespoons vanilla.[45]

Adventurers and chocolate

The photographer Frank Hurley, who, together with other expeditions to Antarctica, was a member of Shackleton's tragic *Endurance* adventure of 1914, wrote about gambling being a popular pastime during these expeditions, with chocolate and candles always serving as the main currency.[46]

Chocolate is a sustaining food which frequently appears in journals relating to great expeditions, adventures and dangerous journeys. Captain Robert Falcon Scott recorded celebrating with a stick of chocolate on New Year's Eve and on his birthday a cake was presented to him covered with 'various devices in chocolate'. Chocolate is also mentioned as an essential provision throughout Scott's diary entries retrieved after the expedition party's fateful 1912 journey to the South Pole.[47]

Back in 2017 an extraordinary find of a fruit cake still in its tin, wrapped in paper was discovered in an abandoned hut in Antarctica. Made by Huntley and Palmer, the cake was considered to be 'almost edible' and dated back to Scott's Terra Nova expedition.[48] Perhaps Scott's birthday cake had been a similar fruit variety? This would have made sense considering their longevity. The existing cake was simply decorated all over with chocolate, to make it a bit more special for the occasion.

The following recipe for chocolate fruit cake hails from Fannie Farmer Merritt, a red-headed spinster who dominated American culinary society at the turn of the twentieth century. Trained at the auspicious Boston Cooking School, she went on to teach there, before opening her own training centre in 1902. Fannie was creative and passionate about food at a time when many were exacting and pedantic. She also lived with a painful disability, which makes her endeavours even more remarkable. I have included her recipe here alongside thoughts of Scott's potential chocolate-embellished fruit cake.

In addition, I have included Fannie Farmer's recipe for White Mountain Cream frosting, which covers the final cake.

Chocolate Fruit Cake
1/3 cup butter
1 cup sugar
¼ cup breakfast cocoa
Yolks 3 eggs
½ cup cold water
1½ cups bread flour
3 teaspoons baking powder (bicarbonate of soda for UK readers)
1 teaspoon cinnamon
¼ teaspoon salt
1/3 cup candied cherries
1/3 cup raisins
1½ tablespoons brandy
1/3 cup walnuts, chopped
Whites 3 eggs
1 teaspoon vanilla

Cover fruit with brandy and let stand several hours. Mix ingredients in order given and bake in deep cake pan for 50 minutes. Cover with 'White Mountain Cream' and as soon as frosting is set, spread as thinly as possible with melted chocolate.[49]

White Mountain Cream frosting
1 cup sugar
1/3 cup boiling water
White 1 egg
1 teaspoon vanilla or ½ tablespoon lemon juice.

Put sugar and water in saucepan and stir to prevent sugar from adhering to saucepan; heat gradually to boiling point and boil without stirring until syrup will thread when dropped from tip of spoon or tines of silver fork. Pour syrup gradually on beaten white of egg, beating mixture constantly and continue beating until of right consistency to spread; then add flavouring and pour over cake, spreading evenly with back of spoon. If not beaten long enough, frosting will run, if beaten too long it will not be smooth. Frosting beaten too long may be improved by adding a few drops of lemon juice or boiling water.[50]

During his 1910 safari, sponsored by the Smithsonian Institute, former US president Theodore Roosevelt regularly gave his accompanying African gun bearers chocolates in colourful wrappers, which they found fascinating. The journey was sadly as much about big game-hunting as it was about exploration.[51]

Early American presidents have a bit of a history of adventure. The Corps of Discovery Expedition of 1803 to 1806, led by Meriwether Lewis and William Clark, was commissioned by the then President Thomas Jefferson, with a view to establishing a firm American presence in newly acquired territories west of the Mississippi river, while studying the flora and fauna and initiating trade talks with native American tribes. On 6 September 1806 Lewis and Clark exchanged goods from a trading boat including beaver for hats and leather for linen shirts. Several weeks later the Mandan corn they had acquired was purchased for chocolate, sugar, whiskey and biscuits (the scone type variety), which 'our party were in want'.[52]

Lewis and Clark were accompanied by a team of other men (and one woman), who were instrumental in meeting the challenges of the expedition. Journals kept by the members of this team revealed: 'Capt. Clark felt unwell and had some chocolate made, which Mr. McClellan [a former scout with the US Army] had presented to us, after which he found great relief.'[53]

In 1803 the United States purchased Louisiana from the French, a state which is known for its culturally eclectic cuisine. Doberge Cake, invented by a pastry chef from Louisiana, is an adaptation of the Hungarian Dobos cake, a layered sponge cake with chocolate and buttercream. The original Dobos cake used as inspiration for the Louisiana version is as follows:

Dobos Cake

The foundation cake is made like a sponge cake, the recipe for which is:

7 eggs
½ lb sugar
½ lb flour
1 teaspoonful of vanilla

Beat the eggs and the sugar together till they are very light; then fold in the flour carefully, not stirring. Add the vanilla.

On flat sheets of paper, draw nine circles, each 8in in diameter. Butter the paper and place it on large baking pans. In the centre of each circle with a pastry tube, place 1/9 of the cake batter. Spread this out carefully to the circumference of the circles; and put the circles of cake into the oven to bake.

Make a chocolate butter cream filling of the following ingredients:
½ lb of sweet butter
½ lb of sugar
4 egg whites
2oz dark chocolate

Cook the sugar to a syrup and spin it slowly into the beaten whites. Add the melted chocolate and let it stand until cold. Then slowly incorporate into it the butter which has been beaten to a soft cream. Mix this with boiled custard in the proportion of 1/3 custard to 2/3 chocolate mixture.

Set the layers of cake together with the chocolate butter cream. Cover the top with a caramel brittle, made of brown sugar and water, cooked until it forms a glaze. Run the glaze into a buttered pan the same size as the cake. Take a knife and score it into any number of pieces you desire. Lay these pieces on top of the cake, so that the top will look as if it were marked. Cover the sides of the cake with the chocolate butter cream and use it in a tube to decorate the top, dividing the top into sectors and making a fancy border. Cover the sides of the cake with riced chocolate.[54]

The experienced explorer Charles Francis Hall, who once lived with Inuit communities in the Arctic, became the commander of the controversial *Polaris* expedition to the North Pole of 1871-73.

Despite his credentials, he was not a leader of men, neither was he respected by all the crew, many of whom very quickly split as supporters and non-supporters of Hall. To add to this rather challenging situation, the German researcher and physician Emil Bessels, who was rumoured to have been a rival for the affections of a woman mutually involved with both Hall and Bessels, was also part of the scientific staff and the expedition physician.

Hall mysteriously fell ill after drinking a cup of coffee. He was quick to accuse certain members of the crew of attempting to murder him and died several days later, suffering from vomiting and hallucinations.

Following Hall's death, *Polaris* got into difficulties with moving ice and some of the crew abandoned ship, while those remaining drifted before crashing and being rescued by a whaler. The remaining deserters were also eventually rescued.

Steward John Herron was one of the party left adrift on the ice raft. His journals reveal the harrowing story of their plight:

October 15 – Gale from the southwest; ship made fast to floe; bergs pressed inland nipped the ship until we thought she was going down; threw provisions overboard, and nineteen souls got on the floe to receive them and haul them up on the ice. A large berg came sailing down, struck the floe, shivered it to pieces and freed the ship. She was out of sight in five minutes. We were afloat of different pieces of ice. We had two boats. Our men were picked up, myself among them and landed on the main floe, which we found to be cracked in many places. Saved very little provisions.

His account goes on to say:

> Thursday Nov, 28 – Thanksgiving today; we have had a feast – four-pint cans of mock turtle soup, six-pint cans of green corn, made into scouch. Afternoon, three ounces of bread and the last of our chocolate – our days' feast, All well.[55]

George Tyson, Assistant Navigator, was also in Herron's stranded party and his journals reveal that initial provisions listed on 23 October included around 20lb of chocolate mixed with sugar, which mice were living in. They drank the chocolate along with coffee, made haphazardly in flat tin pans on the fire.[56] We also know from Herron's journals that this had run out just one month later following their big Thanksgiving Day feast.

And what of Charles Hall? Well, following an investigation it was concluded that he died from apoplexy, until his biographer, Chauncey Loomis, had the body recovered from the Arctic and exhumed in the 1960s. A new autopsy revealed Hall's body was riddled with arsenic.

***

It wasn't only land-based explorers who turned to chocolate for added mettle. Aviation pioneer Amelia Earhart was sustained by tomato juice and a few squares of chocolate during her 1932 solo transatlantic flight. She also swigged cocoa from a thermos.[57]

During her first team transatlantic flight from Newfoundland to Southampton, England, in 1928 with pilot Wilmer Stultz and co-pilot Louis Gordon they were stalled for thirteen days waiting for the right weather conditions. Amelia was the first woman to cross the Atlantic Ocean by plane, but travelling with Stultz proved to be stressful, as alcohol dependency consumed his days and threatened to hamper the whole expedition. When they finally departed Newfoundland, their supplies consisted of scrambled egg, sandwiches, coffee, oranges, chocolate and malted milk tablets.[58]

Earhart's famous disappearance during a leg of her round-the-world flight in 1937 has become legendary and sparked the largest sea search in history undertaken by the US Navy.

Earhart's final transmission, sent from her plane, *Electra*, from the Central Pacific Ocean was strained and anxious: 'We are on a line of position 157 [degrees] – 337 [degrees]. Will repeat this message on 6,210 kilocycles. Wait, listening on 6,210 kilocycles. We are running north and south.' Repeated requests for Amelia to reply after this never came. Neither the plane, the bodies of Amelia or her navigator, Fred Noonan were ever found.

Earhart won numerous awards throughout her career, including the National Geographic's Special Gold Medal. One French newspaper article audaciously deliberated on this, acknowledging her accomplishments, but questioning 'can she bake a cake?' Earhart's response during her speech when accepting 'Outstanding American Woman of the Year' in 1932, was, 'So I accept these awards on behalf of the cake bakers and all of those other women who can do some things quite as important, if not more important than flying, as well as in the name of women flying today.'[59]

Here is a recipe for chocolate cake from the same year that Amelia made her speech. Perhaps she could have had a go at baking it, in between changing the face of international aviation:

Chocolate Cake
Mixture for boiling:
½ cup milk
½ cup sugar
3 squares chocolate – cook till chocolate is melted, then boil and cool
½ cup butter
1 cup sugar
3 eggs
½ cup milk
2 cups flour
¾ teaspoon bicarbonate soda
1 teaspoon cream of tartar

Cream the butter and add sugar gradually. Cream together until light and fluffy. Add eggs, 1 at a time. Beat well. Sift flour, bicarbonate of soda and cream of tartar together. Add alternately with milk to mixture. Add boiled mixture. Beat all together. Bake in greased layer or loaf pans.[60]

Mint cake may have been the sweet treat shared in celebratory fashion on reaching the summit of Everest in 1953 for Sir Edmund Hilary and Tenzing Norgay, but it was chocolate that they left as an offering to the gods, at the very start of their journey.[61]

Former fashion editor, socialite and mountaineer Sandy Pittman is one of the survivors of the 1996 Mount Everest disaster. A total of eight people died attempting to reach the summit on 10-11 May that year, due in part to severe storms, delays with fixing ropes and lack of oxygen.

Pittman's original widespread and expensive campaign to become the first American woman to climb the 'Seven Summits' was thwarted when she was beaten to the summit of Everest in 1994 by an Alaskan female mountaineer. Pittman pursued her goal to come second and repeated her assault on Everest in the fateful year of 1996. She revealed to NBC news prior to her ascent that she had packed:

> Two IBM laptops, a video camera, three 35mm cameras, one kodak digital camera, two tape recorders, a CD-ROM player, a printer [together with enough] solar panels and batteries to power the whole project ... Since we'll be on Everest on Easter, I brought four wrapped chocolate eggs. An Easter egg hunt at 18,000 feet? We'll see![62]

Jon Krakauer's book tracing the events during the disaster suggests Pittman did not always garner respect from her fellow climbers and was criticised for her lack of climbing skills, etiquette and audaciousness, although other members of her team praised Pittman's enthusiasm and positive nature. I'm not sure whether they got to eat the Easter eggs or not.

Below is a recipe for chocolate eggs from the 1950s:

> 2 cups confectioner's sugar (finely ground granulated sugar)
> 1 egg white
> Water
> 2 teaspoons vanilla extract
> Melted chocolate
>
> Sift the sugar into a bowl. Beat the egg white with an equal amount of cold water and add to the sugar. Add the vanilla

extract and stir until the mixture is a creamy mass (mixture should be so stiff that it can scarcely be stirred).

Mould with hands into a large Easter egg. Roll in melted chocolate and set aside to harden.[63]

Superstition, custom and magic

From the crazy to the almost logical, superstition and chocolate have a fundamental connection, perhaps born out of chocolate's ancient origins, in times when pagan rituals and irrational beliefs were what held communities together. The intense customs and practices around its very preparation must have seemed strange and exotic to Europeans. For example, in eighteenth-century Italy it was forbidden for any young person to drink chocolate in the morning, as it was thought to both weaken their teeth and constitutions.[64] Mayan and Aztec cultures regarded cacao as divine and it was used in numerous rituals. It is this association with mysticism and ancient magic that has continued to perpetuate the enigma of chocolate throughout the ages. Even today in parts of South America, it is a tradition to read chocolate as opposed to tea leaves at the bottom of a cup. The cup is turned upside down after the contents are drunk and the patterns are read to outline your fortunes ahead.

Sadly, Spanish Conquistadors burnt many of the Aztec hieroglyphs, drawn on cloths or skins, which documented their administrative records, believing them to be connected with witchcraft. The Codex Mendoza was created not long after the Spanish conquest of Mexico in 1541. It was crafted by scholars who were possibly commissioned by Antonio de Mendoza, the viceroy of the New Spain, to provide a history of the Aztecs in the manner that information would traditionally have been recorded. Largely consisting of tribute rolls, it has remained in the care of the Bodleian Library in Oxford since the mid-1600s. It cites the importance of cacao, facts about harvesting, and its value as a currency. For example, one turkey hen was worth in the region of 100 cacao beans, while one tomato was equal to one bean.

The Codex also informs us that the cacao was ground, soaked and filtered. Water was added and the result was a reddish brown and bitter liquid to which vanilla beans, wild honey or chillies were mixed. Various vessels were used for drinking cacao: gourd, stone or pottery cups, and there were also special ceremonial goblets, some with stirring sticks.[65]

***

Written in Madrid in 1636, Antonio de Leon Pinelo's *Question moral. Si el chocolate quebranta el ayuno eclesiastico* (The Moral Question of Whether Chocolate Breaks the Ecclesiastical Fast) explores the notion of individuals responding differently to chocolate depending on their constitution, based on physical type and individual character.

According to Pinelo, hot-headed or sanguine men and women with ruddy complexions were often more cheerful and friendly, as well as being taller in stature. He recommended that they might benefit from a lighter chocolate drink without any corn-based additives, adding a dash of aniseed, chili and sugar. In order to relieve their fiery tempers a cold chocolate drink was also deemed necessary. Those with phlegmatic characters Pinelo describes as typically overweight and pallid with thinning hair. He considered phlegmatic people slow to get angry, sluggish, sleepy and lazy, who would benefit from hot baths and even hotter chocolate, flavoured with cinnamon, chilli and aniseed. Pinelo also urges caution with this recommendation, stipulating the possibility for hot and spiced chocolate to encourage lustful thoughts. On reflection, he concludes that phlegmatic personalities are so slow and cold by nature that it would be harder for them to become stimulated in this way, determining after all that hot chocolate would be the most appropriate.

As for melancholy men and women – well, according to Pinelo they led difficult and sad lives, devoid of pleasure. Being as they are, bad-tempered, prone to violence and ugly with dry skin and coarse hair, they find themselves largely unpopular. Melancholy people, he concludes, are therefore better off drinking warmish chocolate with *atole* (hot corn) and a little aniseed, without chili. They also require sweet smelling ingredients, all of which will naturally help control their flatulence and haemorrhoids. It is important to remember that Renaissance Europe was still a superstitious and largely non-scientific society, and Pinelo's theories were typical of the time.

There was a general belief in the Greek philosophy pertaining to the body's four humours – black bile, yellow bile, phlegm and blood – and it was imperative to align the humours to establish overall harmony. Black bile represented the spleen, phlegm the brain, yellow was bile and the gall bladder and blood were the heart. Equally, by mixing cold and hot foods, temperature and flavour, a person could maintain a balanced disposition and sustain good health and wellbeing.

The following recipe for a cold chocolate dish was published in the *Essex Newsman* on Saturday, 6 July 1935. Pinelo would have had access to neither bananas nor refined cocoa powder at the time of writing, but if he did, I'm certain he would have recommended this type of dish for hot-headed or sanguine men and women:

Chocolate Banana Glory

Take as many bananas as are required and mash them to a cream. Make chocolate icing by mixing cocoa and water to a smooth paste and cooking for a few minutes. Add to mixture four times as much icing sugar as cocoa and a little vanilla essence. Warm until the icing coats the spoon. Mix with your chocolate icing sufficient fresh cream, add both to the bananas, pile in custard glasses and decorate with ginger.

***

Chan Kom in Mexico is an old Mayan village, a community which was documented in the 1930s by Robert Redfield. Redfield's observations emphasised the importance of how chocolate remained integral to Mexican communities well into the twentieth century.

The Mexican Day of the Dead festival, which takes place at the end of October/beginning of November, is a time when all the souls of the dead return to earth for their annual visit, and food, particularly chocolate, plays a significant role in this. In Redfield's accounts of Chan Kom at midnight on the 30 October, a table was adorned with flowers, *jicaras* (small cups) of chocolate, bread and lighted candles. This served to welcome the dead on their arrival. Similarly, a single cup of chocolate, one piece of bread and one lighted candle were positioned in the doorway, for the benefit of any souls who no longer had living family to remember them. Another table of bread and chocolate was set up and the living ate this for breakfast the following day.

Tablets of chocolate were also consumed prior to baptisms in a ritual involving the chosen godparents, and during the process of arranging marriages between two young people in the community, with the parents of the boy visiting the house of the chosen girl. Three visits were made in total and on each occasion gifts of rum, chocolate, cigarettes and bread were made.

Mexican *rezos* (prayers) were performed regularly on each of the following occasions: seven days after a death, seven weeks after a death, seven months after a death and then again after one year had past. During these ceremonies prayers were said and chocolate was always served.[66] The remains of cacao residue has also been discovered at a variety of archaeological Mayan sites, where chocolate drinks were offered to the deceased.

The Treatise of Hernando Ruiz de Alarcón heralds from early colonial Mexico and provides a wealth of information relating to Aztec culture and religion. Alarcón was a priest who wrote an in-depth account of the religious practices of the native Indians of central Mexico. His text includes incantations and rituals with the following designed to manage anger issues, which is lengthy, but interesting:

> At first maize kernels must be sourced from early corn ears; which apparently, due to their youth, point in the opposite direction to the rest of the ear. This has the contrary effect, a reversal of all those things typically associated with the growth of crops – essence, sustenance, vitality. Instead, they are regarded with acrimony. The following words (translated from the original Aztec) are then spoken over the kernels:
>
> 1. Come here, illustrious and esteemed man, one god, you who are to placate the heart inflamed (with anger), you who are to banish from him the green anger.
> 2. I am to banish the yellow wrath and to put it to flight, for I am the priest, the Prince of spells, who I am to give the medicinal possessed one, heart-changer (for conjured one) to him to drink.
> 3. I will make it come out; I will pursue it. I am the priest; I am the nahualli-lord. I will cause it [the wrath] to drink the priest. Pahecat, Yollohcuepcatzin (or Yolcuepcatzin).

The maize is then ground down and mixed with chocolate before being drunk by the person seeking to purge their anger.[67]

You might not typically associate the celebration of a holiday, with a ritual sacrifice. But for the Aztecs, it was fairly standard, as Hernando documented:

> Most of the Indians' sacrifices are made after midnight or at dawn, and thus on the holidays of their evocations of saints, before daybreak they have already eaten. And this is the way they cut off the heads of the chickens before the fire, which is the God Xiuteuctli. This they call in their language *tlaquechcotonaliztli*. This sacrifice is made in the head man's house.
>
> Having prepared these fowls according to their way and having made tamales, after having readied pulque, *poquietes* and roses with chocolate, they divide it into two parts, one of which they offer to the fire and they pour out some of the pulque before the fire; and the other half they carry to offer at the church, putting it in *xicaras* before the altar. And in a standing *xicara* they pour out a little of the pulque and they put it in the middle of the altar and after it has been there a while they remove it and give it to the *teopan tlacas* to eat. And the same thing is done with the part offered to the fire, which is for the head man.[68]

The Aztec sauce called 'mole' derives from the ancient Aztec language, Nahuatl, with the word *molli*, meaning mix or concoction. It is a sauce characteristic of the Oaxaca and Puebla regions of Mexico. Mole sauces are dense combinations of blended chilies and spices. They have different colours depending on the types of chilies used: some examples include mole *colorado*, which is a deep reddish brown, *amarilo*, which is yellow, *coloradito*, an orangery red and mole *negro,* which is black and contains chocolate. The heritage of this sauce is ancient and there are numerous myths attached to it. The duchess of Mexican cuisine, Diana Kennedy, provides one of the best and most authentic recipes for mole *negro* in her book *The Art of*

Mexican Cooking. But this simplified recipe, to be served with pork, chicken or turkey, published in the *Los Angeles Times Prize Cook Book* is the one I have included here:

> **Mole with Pork, Chicken or Turkey**
> One pound dried dark chilies (*Chili Pasilla*), one-half pound blanched almonds, four slices dried bread, one tablespoon of unsweetened chocolate, the following Mexican herbs: two tablespoons ajunjoli, two tablespoons conimo, one tablespoon oregano, one can of tomato sauce, one teaspoon cinnamon, four large cloves of garlic, one onion, one teaspoon chili powder, one teaspoon salt.
> Cut three pounds lean pork or a hen in a piece and cook until nearly done, have one quart of liquid when at that stage. Remove stems and seeds from chili peppers, cover with water and cook twenty minutes, when cool enough to handle remove skins. Cook in hot fat. Brown almonds, herbs and bread separately in hot fat, also garlic and onion which have been cut fine. Grind all but the meat in a food grinder, making a paste. Mix all ingredients together, add cinnamon, chocolate, chili powder and salt, mix in tomato sauce, pour over meat and cook slowly one hour. The herbs may be bought at any Mexican store. Should be eaten with tortillas.[69]

***

Chocolate in the world of magic is most associated with the heart chakra, linking it to love. Its properties are believed to encourage prosperity and positive energy. It is a fire element with a ruling planet of Mars.[70] Around the world, Valentine's Day remains an important custom, a celebration of passion and love, which has become synonymous with chocolate. In Japan and Korea female industrial employees present men with special chocolates, or *giri-choco* and on 14 March (white day) those men who received chocolates return the compliment to the women by gifting them white chocolate or marshmallows.

In Korea, the 14 April marks 'Black Day', designed for any men unlucky enough not to receive a Valentine's gift, who are encouraged to meet up together and eat a meal called *jajangnyun*, which is black noodles in black sauce. This provides them with the opportunity to mourn their single status.[71]

I haven't included many white chocolate recipes in this book, simply because to me, it isn't really chocolate, as it contains no cocoa solids. It is merely cocoa butter and sugar: a sort of cheat's chocolate. But I won't deny it does taste particularly delicious when mixed with fruit, so here is a recipe for a very indulgent white chocolate and blueberry combination.

White Chocolate Chip Blueberry Brunch Cake

3 eggs
½ cup milk
1 cup softened butter
1 tablespoon baking powder (bicarbonate of soda)
1 cup sugar
1 teaspoon vanilla
2 cups flour
1 tablespoon lemon juice
1 cup blueberries
1 cup white chocolate chips

Preheat the oven for 350°F (180°C). In a large bowl beat together the eggs, milk, butter, baking powder, sugar and vanilla until well blended. Add the flour and lemon juice and mix until thoroughly blended.

Gently fold in the blueberries and the white chocolate chips.

Pour the batter into a greased 9-in x 9-in pan. Bake for 45-50 minutes, or until a knife inserted into the centre comes out clean.[72]

***

Chocolate and religion have somehow become entwined over the centuries. From the tradition of gifting chocolate at Christmas, starting in the Victorian period, to giving children chocolate eggs at Easter. This tradition stems from the ancient custom of receiving hard-boiled eggs dyed red to symbolize the blood of Christ, with the egg itself representing new life. Incidentally, breaking the shell of an egg after it has been hard-boiled prevents witches from using them for malevolent purposes.

We've all read those stories about the face of Christ appearing in a slice of burnt toast, or the Virgin Mary in a cheese sandwich, but the holy mother has also been witnessed in a pool of hardened chocolate. On 18 August 2006, kitchen worker Cruz Jacinto of Fountain Valley, California, spotted a lump of melted chocolate during her shift as a cleaner, but it wasn't just any lump of chocolate. The melted drippings had formed the image of the Virgin Mary under a large vat of chocolate, located at Bodega Chocolates, a store I understand has since closed, with Jacinto recalling: 'When I came in, the first thing I do is look at the clock, but this time I didn't look at the clock. My eyes went directly to the chocolate. I thought, "Am I the only one who can see this?" I picked it up and I felt emotion just come over me. For it was a sign.'[73]

The famed chocolate maker Bodega, launched in 1996 by Spanish sisters Martucci Angiano and Jene Paz, along with their cousin, Pat Brotman, started the business as a homage to their grandmother, Maria, and a family heritage of chocolate making that was dying out. The secret to Bodega's success was always to use quality ingredients, a philosophy which earned the company the highest reputation and the most elite of markets, from goody bags at the Oscars, Golden Globes and Emmy's to a presence in all MGM hotels and the prestigious title of Best Chocolate Maker's awarded by *National Geographic*.

Bodega truffles were based on the traditional recipes from their grandmother, the bestsellers being dulce de leche, bittersweet, caramello, mint, hazelnut, mocha and cabernet wine, along with their trademark chocolate covered pretzels and truffle cookies.[74] Sadly, it would seem, Cruz Jacinto's chocolate effigy of the Virgin Mary did little to miraculously improve business for Bodega, who went into administration in 2010.

Mint Chocolate Truffles
Makes 3 dozen
1b, semi-sweet chocolate
1¼ cups heavy cream
3 tablespoons crème de menthe liqueur
½ cup unsweetened cocoa

Chop the chocolate into small pieces, place in the top of a double boiler.

In a saucepan, heat the cream to a boil.

Right: 1. Montezuma.

Below: 2. Fresh liquid chocolate ground from the cocoa nibs. (© *Emma Kay*)

3. A cake of chocolate formed from the liquid chocolate. (© *Emma Kay*)

Above: 4. Cocoa plantation slaves waiting for their Sunday rations, taken from Henry Nevinson's *A Modern Slavery*, Harper & Brothers, London and New York, 1906.

Left: 5. Madeleine Smith in the dock, 1857.

Above left: 6. Madeleine Marguerite d'Aubray, Marquise de Brinvilliers, 1676, after her imprisonment, portrait by Charles Le Brun.

Above right: 7. Madame Du Barry, 1781, by Elisabeth Louise Vigae Le Brun, Philadelphia Museum of Art.

Right: 8. Selection of confection from Pietro Romanengo, Genoa, established in 1780. (© *Emma Kay*)

VUE DE GÊNES

Above left: 9. Bohemian Balls. (© *Emma Kay*)

Above right: 10. Chocolate pot and cup from the early 1800s. (© *Emma Kay*)

Above left: 11. Liquid chocolate mixed with spices in a copper pot. (© *Emma Kay*)

Above right: 12. Advert for Fry's Chocolate Cocoa. (*Wellcome Collection Creative Commons Attribution (CC BY 4.0)*)

Right: 13. Amy Johnson –
Scan from Foreword by
E. Royston Pike *Our
Generation*, London
Waverley Book Company,
1938.

Below: 14. Buying
drinks from a cocoa
vendor, 1829. (*Wellcome
Collection Creative
Commons Attribution
(CC BY 4.0)*)

15. Sorting cocoa beans in Trinidad, Bain News Service, Publisher. Trinidad – Sorting Cocoa Beans. [No Date Recorded on Caption Card]. (*Library of Congress*)

Left: 16. William Hogarth's illustration of Tom Kings Coffee House, 1736.

Below: 17. Original Cocoa rooms token from the 1800s. (© *Emma Kay*)

18. Tony's ethical chocolate bars. (© *Emma Kay*)

19. Dutch chocolate sprinkles. (© *Emma Kay*)

20. Chocolate balls, traditionally used for Jamaican chocolate tea. (© *Emma Kay*)

21. Cockington Chocolates, Devon. (© *Emma Kay*)

Pour hot cream over chocolate in a double boiler and continue to heat, stirring until chocolate is melted and mixed with cream.

Add crème de menthe.

Pour the mixture onto a baking sheet. Refrigerate for about one hour until mixture hardens.

Shape chocolate into individual balls, about 1 in diameter.

Place balls in refrigerator until just before serving.

Before serving, sift cocoa over balls, rolling the balls to fully cover each piece.[75]

***

History is peppered with tales of witches and their use of chocolate in spells, black masses and supernatural charms. Catherine Monvoisin, or 'La Voisin', was an all-round fortune teller, sorcerer and poisoner, who dabbled in life-threatening late-term abortions on the side, for the right price. A real charmer! She was also implicated in the much wider atrocities of Versaille's infamous 'Affair of the Poisons', which included elaborate plots to poison Louis XIV and other members of the French royal court. La Voisin became Sorceress to Madame de Montespan, the mistress of King Louis XIV. She was on hand to ensure that nothing jeopardised Montespan's relationship with the king, providing anything from Satanic worship to aphrodisiacs. Anne of Austria (who was in fact Spanish), was the mother of King Louis XIV.

We glean from the memoirs of Montespan that the queen mother had her own Spanish chocolate maker at Versailles, called The Señora Molina, mentioned previously in this chapter, who mostly looked after the needs of Maria Theresa of Spain, the king's young wife. Molina had her own separate kitchen and was best known for her clove-scented chocolate.[76] It is possible that Molina may even have prepared chocolate for La Voisin to lace with her various concoctions, including Spanish fly (a pretty green beetle, known to increase sex drive) and menstrual blood, to maintain the king's devotion to Madame de Montespan. Montespan was accused, but never tried, for any part in the 'Affair of the Poisons', unlike La Voisin who was publicly executed in 1680.

Denying any relationship with La Voisin, Montespan refers to her, along with another accusée, in her memoirs as, 'two obscure women'. A dramatization of some of these events appeared in the television series *Versailles* in 2018.

***

One other poisoner and manipulator of the Dark Arts worth including is Leonarda Cianciulli, an Italian serial killer who, being a child conceived from rape, believed herself to be cursed.

Better known as the 'Soap-Maker of Correggio', she attempted suicide on a couple of occasions from a young age, before marrying, settling and taking up the trade of soap making in the 1930s. Of the seventeen pregnancies she carried, thirteen died of various causes. Cianciulli regularly consulted with fortune tellers and travelling gypsies, all of whom predicted the loss of children, prison and madness. She took all of these portents to heart, living her life by these same predictions. In order to protect her eldest son from dying, she turned to human sacrifice as a means of preventing his death. Cianciulli's first victim was Faustina Setti, who visited her neighbour with some frequency to receive palm readings and assistance with finding a husband. It was during one of these visits that Leonarda Cianciulli drugged Faustina with wine, before killing her with an axe, cutting her body ritualistically into nine pieces and draining her blood into a basin. She described the next part of her ceremonial culling in an official statement:

> I threw the pieces into a pot, added seven kilos of caustic soda, which I had bought to make soap and stirred the whole mixture until the pieces dissolved in a thick, dark mush that I poured into several buckets and emptied in a nearby septic tank. As for the blood in the basin, I waited until it had coagulated, dried it in the oven, ground it and mixed it with flour, sugar, chocolate, milk and eggs, as well as a bit of margarine, kneading all of the ingredients together. I made lots of crunchy tea cakes and served them to the ladies who came to visit, though Giuseppe (her eldest son) and I also ate them.[77]

Cianciulli was eventually caught and tried for murder in the 1940s and sentenced to a prison sentence and also three years in a criminal asylum. She died of a brain haemorrhage when she was seventy-seven.

This horrendous crime of murder and cannibalism, which evolved from a bizarre combination of supernatural interpretation and deranged psychosis, has chocolate central to its outcomes, in the form of cakes. It is a crime reminiscent of all those ancient Mexican practices around ritualistic sacrifice and the merging of blood and chocolate; even the formation of a solid mass, reinforcing ancient beliefs in the ethereal and superstitious properties of cacao.

As the topic is rather sour, I have included a recipe for sour cream chocolate cakes, which was published around the same time as Leonarda Cianciulli's trial.

Sour Cream Chocolate Cakes
½ cup butter
1 cup sugar
2 egg yolks
¾ cup sour cream
3 squares chocolate
1¼ cups self-raising flour
1 teaspoon baking powder
1 teaspoon bicarbonate soda
½ cup pecans

Cream butter, add sugar gradually and beat well.

Add well-beaten egg yolks, beat briskly. Stir in melted chocolate, sour cream and sifted dry ingredients.

Fold in chopped pecans and turn in well-greased cup cake pans. Bake about 20 minutes in a moderate oven, 350°F/180°C. These cakes are so rich that they need no frosting.[78]

Chapter 3

Money, Markets and Merchandise: Chocolate at its Sickly Sweetest

From the seedier side of street chocolate sellers and individual makers to the strange, Machiavellian world of the Georgian chocolate houses and the families that once ruled the confectionery world: the twisted journey that chocolate made to mass production and mass consumerism was, at the same time, both tragic and impressive.

Street sellers, pedlars and independent makers

Chocolate selling was, like any other street trade, competitive, relentless and hard work. From the early chocolate beverage sellers to the solid chocolate vendors, there have been characters, criminals and clowns among them all.

French rogue, Louis Dominique Bourguigon, better known as Cartouche, masqueraded as many characters, but was essentially a highwayman and criminal. Cartouche became notorious around the streets of Paris during the 1700s and desperate attempts were made to capture him. He wore a reversible coat, blue one side, red on the other, which confused the authorities who frequently ended up chasing a criminal in blue, only to turn a corner and face a man in a red coat. On one occasion, hearing a commotion in the residence of a known local lemonade seller, police discovered a small man (Cartouche was a mere 4ft 5in tall), tearing around the room, half drunk and crazed, firing pistols indiscriminately into a crowd of men and women. On being arrested, the man declared himself to be a chocolate seller and one who had simply had too much to drink. No further charges were brought against Cartouche and he was allowed to go free. He was recaptured not long after this, in 1720, and imprisoned, before attempting to escape, and was finally sentenced to death by being broken on the wheel.[1]

Fighting against the increasing issues relating to adulteration and patent recipes during the nineteenth century, a chocolate vendor in Paris was famously known for inscribing the covers of all his chocolate with the warning 'Imitation of this chocolate will be punished with death'.[2]

Jeanne Phillipe Wagner was a German chocolate seller living in London during the 1800s. He had been disappointed at not being recognised by the board of the International Exhibition for his work as a chocolatier. The exhibition took place in May, and in August Wagner paid a man named S. J. Meany five pounds on the pretext that he would receive a medal for his services, thinking him to be a commissioner for the International Exhibition.

When it materialised that no medal was on the way, Wagner took Meany to court for fraud. However, the court rejected the case based on the evidence that Meany never actually stated that he was a commissioner, but rather implied it, leading Wagner to simply assume that he was.[3]

Here is a recipe for German chocolate sauce, which, interestingly, suggests scrimping on the chocolate and using dry flour as a substitute.

German Chocolate Sauce

A piece of butter, and four yolks of egg, are to be thoroughly mixed together in the pan, and instead of flour, a quarter of a pound of chocolate is to be used; pour in wine and a little water and add sugar to the taste; then boil the whole together into a thick sauce. For the sake of economy, we may use less chocolate, and supply its place by dry burnt flour.[4]

It wasn't until the 1880s that evidence presented in the census records suggests a boom in independent chocolate makers and chocolate manufacturing. By the 1890s these occupations decreased significantly, only to increase again by 1901, with more specific job titles appearing. These included chocolate canerers, chocolate coverers, refiners, dippers, finishers and even chocolate van drivers, distributing it all over the country and suggesting a move away from the more independent chocolate makers to the large factories and mass production.

By 1911 there are nearly 10,000 names listed with an association to chocolate manufacturing in some form, compared to the 250 or so of the previous decade, demonstrating a staggering shift in the British chocolate economy. As late as the 1940s children of at least fourteen years of age could still be found selling chocolate on the streets, while those children lucky enough to get an education would have been in a better position to eat the stuff rather than have to sell it.

Charles Duff's *Ireland and the Irish* provides an account of a life spent on and off in Ireland. His schooldays in the early 1900s in Dublin are recounted with fear, his only solace being Sunday afternoon recreational time spent in Phoenix Park. He befriended a chocolate seller who was able to help him practise his German and Italian languages. This chocolate seller was described as 'a sturdily built, clean-shaven native of Trieste, a young man with longish fair hair who used an engaging patter to sell his chocolates,' and he was particularly memorable on account of the fact that he would give away bars of chocolate to any of the schoolboys who were short of cash. He would also take at least half an hour out of the busiest day of the week to chat and introduced some of the boys to the local cinema, where his colleague let them watch films for free.[5]

Some chocolatiers clearly aspired to middle-class ambitions. In 1919 Charles John Atkinson, a chocolate vendor, announced his intention to stand as an independent 'working man's' candidate for Spen Valley at the General Election.[6] This was reported in a couple of newspapers at the time and presented quite an amusing little story for journalists. Atkinson applied for his nomination papers, but sadly received no nominations.[7] A similar situation arose in Paris in 1863, when a Monsieur Devinck, a chocolate-maker, also ran for election. Whether he was popular with the people or not is difficult to determine, with one newspaper declaring 'M.Thiers [another candidate] has stamped his name upon history, M.Devinck only on chocolate.'[8]

The FA Cup Final, which took place in London on 24 April 1920, between Aston Villa and Huddersfield, was the first since the end of the First World War. The chocolate hawkers who positioned themselves outside Stamford Bridge were said to have had 'a great time'.[9] Some sports ground chocolate vendors, it seems, liked having a bit too much of a good time. Like chocolate seller Edward Topps who stole £1, 7s and 10d in 1914 during a match at Sheffield Wednesday football ground. The amount of cash he returned failed to meet the actual sales of chocolate that day, which he was selling on behalf of a Mr Jonas Quastel. He immediately absconded and was eventually tracked down in the army, serving in Dublin.[10]

Stories appearing in the media at the time suggest there was a significant correlation between chocolate sellers working in football stadiums during the first half of the twentieth century and young men taking trials for some of the bigger football clubs – and often becoming successful. It seems to have been a natural springboard for ambitious players.

Cocoa sellers in London would sometimes be in possession of little bells which were used to grab the attention of thirsty passers-by. In Henry Mayhew's *London Labour and the London Poor* (volume 1, 1861), these hot drinks were kept in large cans and sold alongside bread and butter, currant cake, ham sandwiches and boiled eggs. They charged 1d a mug or ½ d for half a mug and another ½ d for the sandwich, etc. The cocoa would have been purchased by the pound from a local grocer, for which they'd pay about 6d a lb, compared to the coffee which cost 1s a lb and tea 3s a lb. So it would have been much cheaper for traders to purchase cocoa during this particular period, with tea and coffee costing about eight times as much. Coin-operated vending machines selling hot drinks, which evolved during the earlier half of the twentieth century, would have eventually led to the demise of the hot chocolate peddler. Incidentally, it was Ludwig Stollwerck, of the famous German Stollwerck chocolate family, who contributed significantly towards the development of the first automated vending machines in nineteenth-century Europe.

Despite the advent of mass consumerism, men and women continued to sell chocolate on the streets well into the twentieth century. On Thursday, 1 March 1934, an SOS was broadcast in an attempt to track down John William Bond, who sold chocolate to commuters outside Victoria Station in London. It seems that no one had been able to contact Mr Bond to inform him of his father's serious illness.[11] There were also tenacious opportunity-seekers like Cecil Twort, who, in 1948, was charged with obstructing a footpath in Aylesbury and littering the area. Twort had set up shop in the street one day, selling Crunchie bars (originally created by J. S. Fry & Sons in 1929) out of large boxes. A queue of people formed on the pavement causing an obstruction. Some members of the public came forward to challenge Twort about his illegal practices, which is when he got angry, shouted abusive language and threw empty boxes around. He failed to appear in court, sending a letter instead. He was fined 20s.[12]

Undoubtedly the biggest chain of chocolate vendors trading in the nineteenth century, and possibly any century, must have been the Temperance Cocoa Rooms, which emerged out of an increasingly lawless society which had become dependent on alcohol.

In the parish of St Luke, London, in 1846 Mary Murray was drinking with Martin Jennings in one of the many local gin shops. Jennings accused her of stealing a shilling from his pocket and, when Mary denied it, he struck her violently in the face. She continued to deny the theft before he struck her again. In an attempt to get away from Jennings, Mary staggered to the door, but was followed and struck again. A member of the public raised the alarm and Jennings escaped, leaving Mary to die on the ground.[13] In 1771 a Captain Pierce anchored at Bristol and lured a nine-year-old girl on board his ship, plied her with alcohol to get her drunk before raping her. He was discovered and later executed.[14] And in Thames Street, Nottingham, 1894, Catherine Freeman was remanded in custody for being drunk, dropping her baby and giving the child a concussion of the brain.[15]

By the nineteenth century, alcohol, and, in particular, moonshine gin, had become a significant social issue in Britain. Many families struggled to survive, and with both men and women too drunk to secure work, domestic violence increased and children were being neglected.

Quakers, many of whom abstained from alcohol, sought an alternative to the public houses and gin palaces with their new Temperance Movement, jointly formed with the Salvation Army, Catholic groups and the League of the Cross, fighting back against the evils of drink. Various campaigns were launched to persuade people away from alcohol, but very little changed until the emergence of the cocoa rooms.

These 'cocoa rooms' were the successors of the old coffee and chocolate houses. Brass tokens were issued to entice people out of the public houses (often situated next door). They could be obtained at a cost of thirteen tokens for a shilling. These tokens were sold as an alternative to the paper tickets issued to those in need of soup kitchen hand-outs by parish officials. It was thought these tickets had a stigma attached to them, whereas the tokens didn't. This is because it wasn't possible for others to determine whether you were paying with a coin or a token.

Although many of these houses were run in conjunction with the church, they were also owned by individual businesses which had a commercial interest. They were initially opened under the British

Workmen's Public House Company, but Lockhart's Cocoa Rooms, owned by the former Liverpudlian metal broker turned social reformer and avid Presbyterian, Robert Lockhart, soon ran the monopoly, with outlets that originated in the Liverpool and Newcastle regions expanding into London and other major cities across the UK. There were some eighty-five general cocoa rooms in Liverpool alone listed in Kelly's directory of 1894. Lockhart, speaking at a meeting of the National Association for the Promotion of Social Science in 1874, explained that the first cocoa room opened in 1873 in Liverpool, with a further twelve emerging the year after. These establishments opened at 5.00 am to catch men and women employed in manual labour on their way to work. These same workers were then encouraged to bring their dinner with them on their return home and stop again for another drink of cocoa.[16]

Lockhart died of bronchitis in 1880, at the comparatively young age of fifty-eight. It would appear that the legacy of cocoa rooms became a little tainted over the following decade, with newspapers often reporting on the gambling that took place in these establishments after hours.[17] Other competitors during this century offered similar services, like John Pearce's 'Pearce and Plenty' dining rooms and 'The People's Refreshment House Ltd', a company which acquired over 233 licensed premises, transforming them into non-alcoholic houses of refreshment.[18]

How ironic to think that a drink considered so sinful and provocative some 200 years before was now seen as the saviour of a depraved and broken society. Even more ironic when you consider that colonial Trinidad in the 1830s was planning to establish a similar 'chocolate shop', where only chocolate and coffee would be available. This was welcomed on an island where the increasingly detrimental effects of alcohol abuse were beginning to encourage behaviour which, according to the *Falmouth Express and Colonial Journal* of 14 April 1838, 'brutalized' society. In general, the labouring classes of the island would start their day drinking raw spirits in the local grog-shops, the effects of which would lead to ill-tempers and sluggish productivity. There were offers of free newspapers, among other incentives, to be granted to the first person prepared to open one of these chocolate shops. To think that Trinidad, with its 200-year history of cacao production, was encouraging locals to replace alcohol with the very product that was also enslaving them, seems paradoxical somehow.

Curiously, in the UK it's also worth mentioning that chocolate houses, certainly those in operation from the mid- to late-1800s, were denied licenses for music and dancing, while taverns were granted a range of entertainment licenses. Whether this has anything to do with music and dance being thought of as provocative and therefore unsuitable for the principals of teetotalism is unclear, but it's an interesting outlook for the time.

Numerous cookery books were published by the Temperance movement during the nineteenth century, unsurprisingly many included a wealth of chocolate recipes. Here are two recipes from Mary G. Smith's *Temperance Cook Book.*

Chocolate Blancmange

Half a box of gelatine, soaked till dissolved, in as much water as will cover it, four sticks of grated chocolate, one quart of sweet milk, one cupful of sugar; boil milk, sugar and chocolate five minutes more, stirring constantly; flavour with vanilla and put into moulds to cool and eat with cream.

Chocolate Pudding

Three fourths cup of chocolate, one quart of milk, which has not been skimmed, let it boil, then set it to cool; beat until very light and thick, add the yolks of four eggs, with one cup of sugar; flavour delicately with vanilla; put it in a baking dish and bake slowly. To make meringue: Beat up the whites till they stand alone, add four tablespoonfuls powdered sugar, flavour with vanilla or lemon, then the pudding is again cooled; put the meringue over the top and brown slightly. This quantity is enough for six persons.[19]

Chocolate manufacturers

There was a time when major independent manufacturers of chocolate were mostly businesses established by families and which continued to trade over successive generations. Many floundered during the First and Second World Wars due to restrictions on cocoa and an inability to source the required ingredients. Others thrived in times of conflict in environments where cheap labour could be exploited and contraband could be accessible with the right connections.

It would be impossible to document every major chocolate manufacturer in this part of the book, but I have tried to include as many bleak and murky historical elements as possible about some of the world's biggest confectionery competitors. The chocolate industry as a whole is continually justifying issues related to sustainability and ethically questionable practices, but they are frequently implicated in all manner of other controversies, from employee accidents to sullied profiles. Companies such as Meiji, a large-scale Japanese corporation initially established in 1917, specialising in a range of low-cost, high-quality chocolate, who, in 2011, came under intense scrutiny for the high levels of radioactive caesium found in their baby formula: or the American Mast brothers, whose artisan chocolate has faced years of allegations regarding the use of third-party chocolate, melted down and mixed with other ingredients, before being retailed as their own unique invention.

One of the inventors of the Toblerone, Theodor Tobler, was known as an ardent follower of the famous Folies Bergères, a risqué burlesque dance troupe in Paris. The iconic Matterhorn-style peak, was purported to resemble one of the Folies' popular routines, with straplines such as 'lose yourself in the Toblerone triangle'. They also launched their 'Ballerina Assortment' in the 1950s, so perhaps there is some truth in the rumours.[20]

Toblerone Rocky Road

Makes sixteen squares, using a 23cm² cake tin lined with
   greaseproof paper.
Prep: 15 minutes.
Chill: 4 hours minimum.
150g unsalted butter
3 tablespoons runny honey
200g Toblerone dark chocolate, plus extra for decorating
50g raisins
200g Oreo cookies, roughly chopped
100g mini marshmallows
150g mini Toblerone milk chocolate chunks

Melt the butter, honey and dark chocolate in a large saucepan over a gentle heat. Remove from the heat and stir in the raisins, cookies and half of the marshmallows until completely coated in the chocolate. Stir in half of the marshmallows until completely coated in the chocolate. Stir in half of the mini chocolate chunks and pour into the prepared tin. Flatten with the back of a spoon and sprinkle over the remaining chopped dark chocolate, marshmallows and mini milk chocolate chunks.

Cover with clingfilm and chill in the fridge for at least 4 hours until set or keep in the fridge until ready to serve. Cut into sixteen squares and store in an airtight container for four to five days in the fridge.[21]

By 1900 Huntley and Palmer, the British firm of biscuit makers, were selling some 400 varieties of biscuits, many of which would have contained chocolate. Despite senior partner George Palmer being an active campaigner against slavery, it would have been very hard for any of the large-scale manufacturers of the Georgian and Victorian age to have avoided commercial involvement in the slave trade. In fact, the reality is that some of today's chocolate-making practices are still shrouded under a dubious cloak of forced labour, human trafficking and wretched conditions. Still today, stories break involving one of the big chocolate players linked to child slavery, poverty or complications with damaging environmental issues: too many, in fact, to mention here.

Huntley and Palmer launched a special chocolate range between 1930 and 1939, which included a selection of wafers: the chocolate finger wafer, the chocolate Ascot filled wafer and the summer wafer.

I discovered this rather unique chocolate wafer roll recipe, which mostly seems to contain whipped cream, while having the audacity to suggest being served with more whipped cream.

Chocolate Wafer Roll
30 wide chocolate wafers
1-pint whipping cream
Maraschino cherries

Whip cream stiff, and spread a layer on a wafer. Cover with another wafer and cover this with another layer of whipped cream. Repeat until all the wafers are used, but be careful to keep the roll straight. Cover all sides of the roll with the rest of the cream and decorate with the Maraschino cherries.

Place in the ice box for several hours. To cut, place the roll
on its side and make diagonal slices. Served with more
whipped cream, if desired.[22]

I had no idea that Cuba was once a centre of cacao production, with over
sixty plantations listed there in the nineteenth century. Most of these
were destroyed during the Wars of Independence, but the American
giant Hershey bought up old sugar mills during the First World War to
mill sugar for chocolate production. This is perhaps as good a place as
any to start.

Hershey, USA

Starting his trade in the caramel business, Milton Hershey faced bankruptcy
several times before investing in new machinery in the 1890s, machinery
which he used to start manufacturing chocolate bars. Today, the standard
Hershey Bar, with its distinctive reddish-brown wrapper and bold white
font, remains one of the most iconic brands of confection in the United
States, if not the World. But if it hadn't been for a business commitment
obliging him to leave three days earlier than planned, following a vacation
with his wife in France, the world would never have known of his talents.
This is because Milton Hershey and his wife had booked their original
return passage via the ill-fated *Titanic* in 1912.

Nonetheless, one tragedy Milton Hershey was unable to dodge in
earlier life was that of the untimely death of his sister, Serena, who, at
the age of four, contracted scarlet fever, the effects of which she endured
for several months, before finally succumbing to the infection in 1867.
The impact on the Hershey family was understandably devastating, with
his mother rejecting his father, and the eventual decline of the family
business. The grief of this event stayed with Milton for the rest of his
life and was perhaps one of the driving forces behind his ambitions.[23]
Incidentally, If you ever wondered why its characteristic flavour might
remind you a little of vomit – as I discovered as a child in New York,
tasting my first ever Hershey Bar – it is because, allegedly, the milk
Hershey uses goes through a process called lipolysis, which breaks
down the milk's fatty acids, producing butyric acid, the chemical also
found in sick.[24]

I appreciate the need to include some dietary recipes in the book and this one was originally a cake recipe taken from the back of a Hershey's box of cocoa. The author of the recipe made some adjustments to ensure it was gluten free and came up with the final result:

Gluten-free chocolate cake
2 cups GF flour, minus 2 tablespoons
1 teaspoon xanthan gum
1 cup sugar
3 tablespoons cocoa powder
2 teaspoons bicarbonate of soda
1 cup sparkling water
1 cup GF mayonnaise
1 teaspoon vanilla

Keep testing the cake as it bakes. Gluten-free recipes often require longer in the oven and the heat adjusted accordingly.[25]

Ferrero, Italy

Pietro Ferrero founded his confectionery business in 1942 at a time when ingredients were scarce and the Italian economy was fragile. Hazelnuts, however, were abundant in the region and by 1946 the hazelnut cream, *pasta gianduja*, based on an existing hazelnut paste from the Napoleonic era, was born. Its low price and moreish consistency made it an instant success.[26]

As chocolate became more accessible after the war, Ferrero began experimenting and diversifying with products that merged chocolate and hazelnut together, until he died suddenly of a heart attack at the age of fifty, followed just a few years later by his brother, Giovanni, who helped run the business.[27]

By the consumerist boom of the 1960s, Pietro's son, Michele Ferrero, had developed the famed household brand of hazelnut chocolate spread, Nutella. Twenty years later and Michele launched Ferrero Rocher, individually golden-wrapped hazelnut chocolate rock, or rocher, allegedly named after a grotto in Lourdes. Pietro eventually passed the business down to his sons, Giovanni junior and Pietro junior, the latter of whom died of a heart attack aged forty-eight during a cycling trip in South Africa 2011.[28]

Giovanni now retains the title of Executive Chairman of the Ferrero group, which includes Nutella, Ferrero Rocher, Kinder and Tic Tac.

Hazelnut Paste for Chocolates

Grind 1lb (2 cups) of roasted, blanched hazelnuts. Put through grinder three of four times until the nuts are finely mashed.

Cook 1lb (2 cups) granulated sugar and 1 cup water to 240°C on a thermometer.

Remove from the stove and add the ground hazelnuts and ½ cup caramel flavour made as follows:

Put 1 cup of granulated sugar in a saucepan over the fire and stir until it melts and browns and burns just a little. Add slowly 2 cups of water and let boil until the caramel is all dissolved. Beat until thick and creamed and turn out on a marble dusted with powdered sugar.

When cold mould into balls and coat with sweet chocolate.[29]

Cadbury, UK

Trinidad was once the location of most of Cadbury's plantations. But by the early 1900s they were importing around fifty-five per cent of their cocoa from the Portuguese colony of São Tomé in Central Africa. The firm claimed to use workers who could be free to leave their jobs whenever they chose, but in 1901 William Cadbury received an offer to purchase a nearby estate for £3,555, which included land, vehicles, cattle and 200 black labourers. The offer of workers for sale along with cattle concerned him and from that day Cadbury began a long and protracted campaign for Portuguese labour reforms.[30]

Around this time the journalist Henry Nevinson's investigations in the same region were revealing widespread examples of slavery, which would later lead to significant new legislation. Nonetheless, despite the evidence, Cadbury failed to boycott their trading activity in São Tomé for another eight years. Following the ongoing investigations and campaigns for change, the company, along with Fry's, Rowntree's and German manufacturer Stollwerck, did finally cease production.

This would be the start of a long, ongoing debate about commercial chocolate manufacturers and their relationship with unethical practices, not just on cacao plantations but also on sugar plantations as the two are mutually dependant for the commercial chocolate economy. It should be said that the Quaker ethics of Rowntree, Fry and Cadbury were built on strong values and their work ethics reflected a holistic approach to wealth, one which benefitted the community, society and their own workers.

Other companies such as Nestlé, not that much younger in its origins, is a controversial company frequently criticised for flouting human rights laws, engaging in modern-day child slavery and trafficking, and the destruction of forest habitats, despite their broad public zero-tolerance approach.

Ironically, in 1918 Egbert Cadbury became managing director of the British Cocoa and Chocolate Company, which was formed out of a merger between J. S. Fry & Sons and Cadbury Brothers Ltd. Despite the vehement Quaker commitment to pacifism, Egbert, who served in the First World War, shot down two Zeppelins, killing both sets of crews.

The following recipe comes from *Cadbury's Practical Recipes*. The company published several editions of this book throughout the mid-twentieth century.

Chocolate Soufflé
3 eggs
½ gill water (about 2fl oz)
2oz caster sugar
½ oz gelatine
1 dessertspoon. Bournville chocolate
1½ gills cream or evaporated milk (about 7fl oz)
vanilla essence
To prepare the soufflé dish

Cut a strip of paper long enough to go round the dish and sufficiently deep to reach from the bottom to about 2in above the top of the dish. Place around the outside so that if fits exactly. Pin or tie firmly into position.

Method: Put the sieved cocoa, egg yolks and sugar into a bowl and heat over a pan of hot water until thick and creamy. Whip the cream or evaporated milk and add this with the vanilla essence to the thickened mixture. Dissolve the gelatine in the hot water. Stir into the other ingredients. Allow to cool and then fold in the stiffly beaten egg whites. Pour into the prepared dish and stand in a cool place until firm.

Carefully remove the paper from side of the soufflé and decorate.[31]

C. J. Van Houten & Zoon, Holland

It is thanks to the Dutch that we have chocolate in solid form today. In 1828 Casparus van Houten senior invented a way to press the fat out of the cacao bean and reduced the cocoa butter to almost half, creating a 'cake' that could then be ground down into cocoa powder – the basis for all types of chocolate. His clever hydraulic press made drinking chocolate easier to make, in addition to enabling chocolate powder to be mixed with sugar and then remixed again with cocoa butter, producing a solid bar. Once the patent expired it opened the doors to all chocolate makers to produce solid chocolate in this way and British company J. S. Fry was one of the first to take advantage.[32]

Casparus had a son, Coenraad, who took his father's invention a step further by treating cocoa powder with alkalines – a process known as 'Dutching' – making a radically smoother product. To add even more confusion, Coenraad had a son, also called Casparus, who joined the Van Houten company, bringing a flair for marketing and taking the company into new commercial directions. In 1897 Casparus junior started building himself a giant 99-room villa in Weesp, in North Holland, on the back of his dynastic fortune. Work was finally completed in 1901, the year he died.[33] There is also a frequently quoted urban myth about Van Houten's, which suggests they once paid a condemned man to shout out their company name at the moment just prior to his hanging. Personally, I'm not sure whether that's favourable publicity or not, but it makes for a good story.

Advent Dutch Chocolate Cookies (This is a recipe to be stored and eaten at a later date)

1 cup molasses
2 cups brown sugar
1 cup grated chocolate
1 cup butter
1 teaspoon baking soda/bicarbonate of soda
Flour

Mix the ingredients to make a stiff batter, using just flour enough to roll. Cut out with a cookie cutter about 1½ in in diameter. Bake the cookies in a hot oven on greased paper.

Then when baked and cooled, put in a stone crock in a cool place and keep for a month or six weeks before eating. (The early Dutch baked them at Thanksgiving time for Christmas use). The result is a soft, chewy cookie with a caramel effect.[34]

Charbonnel et Walker, France

In 1875 Charbonnel et Walker opened their premises in New Bond Street, London. Former confectioners at Maison Boissier in Paris, Virginie (Eugenie) Charbonnel and Mary Anne (Minnie) Walker were allegedly persuaded by Edward VII, the then Prince of Wales, to relocate and establish their own business across the channel.

In 1891 a twenty-three-year-old clerk, Alexander Albert, shot himself on the premises of their chocolate shop having been rejected by the manageress of the store. She had taken pity on him and nursed through an illness, but, unfortunately, Alexander's behaviour towards the manageress became obsessional. He followed her, behaved aggressively when drunk and threatened suicide if she didn't marry him.[35]

Charbonnel et Walker was also a famous tea shop, with one visitor writing about her experiences in 1888, describing the hot chocolate as 'the best I have ever tasted in this country,' and remarking on the genuine pheasant and hare skins stuffed with chocolates.[36] We would undoubtedly consider this macabre today, but in the 1800s it was *de riguer*. The relationship between the two women declined over the years, climaxing in a significant libel case over the use of the store's name elsewhere.

Charbonnel et Walker were renowned for their bon-bons. So, what better recipe to include here than one from Queen Victoria's chef himself, Charles Francatelli, from 1867.

> ### Chocolate bon-bons
> To half a pound of course-sifted sugar add two ounces of the finest French chocolate, dissolved in a wineglass-ful of water in a separate boiler or stewpan and after mixing this with the sugar in its boiler, stir on the fire until it arrives at almost simmering heat; and lay out the drops of the size of a sixpenny-piece.[37]

Terry's, UK

Robert Berry opened a shop in York in the 1760s selling lozenges, candied peel and other sweets. William Bayldon joined the business not long after, establishing Robert Berry & Co. confectionery. Meanwhile, Joseph Terry, an apothecary's assistant, opened his own chemist, before meeting and marrying the sister-in-law of Robert Berry. Joseph soon took over from William Baylden and the business premises moved to St Helen's Square. On the death of Robert Berry, his son, George, went into partnership with Joseph, creating the jauntily named Terry and Berry, a partnership that ceased after just three years, leading to expansion and the distribution of Joseph Terry and Sons products in at least seventy-five towns across the country.

Following Joseph Terry's death, Joseph junior took over the reins, creating a new factory and extending the shop premises to include a ballroom and restaurant. Joseph was knighted several times for his success in expanding the new commercial chocolate market. On his death in 1898, his sons, Thomas and Frank, took over the business.

The first of the Terry family tragedies occurred in 1910 when a biking accident led to blood poisoning and death by sepsis for poor Thomas Terry.[38] A third brother, Noel, who had a career in banking, was drafted into the family business. Noel dodged an early death in the First World War One when a silver cigarette case was thought to have deflected a bullet, shattering his leg instead of killing him. Noel was the brain-child behind the conception of the chocolate orange and Terry's iconic 'All Gold' selection in the 1930s. He married Kathleen Leetham, whose father killed himself at their family home by blowing his brains out with a rifle. He was just sixty-two years of age. Evidence suggests he had suffered from insomnia and depression for some time.[39] Noel and Kathleen Terry's son, Kenneth, died during a training exercise in the Second World War when his aircraft mysteriously crashed into the sea over Germany in 1944. Less than one year earlier, Kenneth had taken forty-eight-hours' leave to marry Ivy Denyer.[40] Ivy submitted a written memorial to the *West Sussex County Times*:

> Deep in our hearts you are living yet,
> We loved you too dearly to ever forget,
> Although the place where you lie
> We cannot see,
> You will live forever in our memory.[41]

As one of Terry's most acclaimed creations was the chocolate orange, I have included a recipe here from *The Home Confectioner* for what the author has christened Chocolate Orange Pralines. As there are no nuts involved, I have boldly decided to rechristen them as Chocolate Orange Fondants, which was a variation of the standard method for preparing chocolate drops.

Fondant
2lb granulated sugar
1 cup water
¼ teaspoon cream of tartar

Place the above ingredients in a pan and stir until melted. Cover and cook for 2-3 minutes until the sugar starts to boil, turns thick and forms a soft ball when dropped into cold water.

Pour the mixture onto a stone or marble slab or into a tray sprinkled with cold water. The mixture should be about ½ in thick. Let it cool for just a minute and then start to work the fondant until it becomes a hard-white lump.

Spread a damp cloth over the top and leave for half an hour. Knead it again, cover and store until required. It will keep for around 2-3 weeks.

Chocolate Orange Fondants (pralines)

Take as much fondant as required and have icing sugar to hand. Mix the fondant with some icing sugar to make small balls or oblongs, while adding the juice of one orange as you work the mixture.

Place the individual drops onto baking paper and let them rest, until they are dry enough to handle.

Dip each one in chocolate, either by hand or using a small fork. Place on baking paper and leave them in a cool place to set.[42]

Elite Chocolate, Israel

The Strauss Group's Elite chocolate started life as Laima Chocolate, in Riga, Latvia, where there was a significant Jewish diaspora. Confectioner Eliyahu Fromenchenko was forced to join this community having fled Russia, where many Jews were being excluded from economic life towards the end of the nineteenth century.

When the Nazis came to power Fromenchenko was once again forced to move on and he sold Laima in 1933. This time he emigrated to British-controlled Palestine with his business partner, Yaakov Arens. He bought property in Ramat Gan, Tel Aviv, where production of the new 'Elite' chocolate line began in 1934. Fromenchenko took to the streets to promote his wares which included chocolate-covered waffle cookies and chocolates encased in sesame seeds.

Today, Elite Chocolate and Confectionery is now a major brand in Israel, controlled by the international food and beverage company, Strauss Group.[43] Elite are particularly well-known for their praline chocolates, so I thought it fitting to add a recipe for slightly more authentic pralines here:

Chocolate Pralines

½ lb (2 cups) almonds
10oz lump-sugar
Coating chocolate

Blanch and shred the almonds, then slightly brown them in the oven.

Rinse a saucepan out with cold water, put the sugar into it and melt it slowly; then boil it until it is a golden-brown colour. Pour it onto an oiled or buttered slab or plate and leave it until cold.

Pound the sugar, then pound the almonds. Mix them together until they can be formed into small shapes. Melt the chocolate in a double boiler; dip each praline into it and place on waxed paper to dry.[44]

Mars, USA

Jaqueline Badge Mars collided with a minivan in Northern Virginia and killed one of the passengers in 2013. Her father, Forrest Mars, Sr., pioneered the Mars chocolate empire when he opened the factory in Slough, England, in the 1930s. He followed in the footsteps of his father, Frank, who founded the Mars factory and developed the unique and highly profitable Milky Way bar in the 1930s, with successful businesses in Minneapolis and Chicago. Frank died suddenly of a heart condition at the age of fifty. Unlike other major chocolate manufacturers, Mars never made their own chocolate. Instead, they bought it wholesale from Hershey's.

During the Spanish Civil War soldiers ate little chocolate pellets coated with a hard candy shell to prevent them from melting; this gave Forrest the inspiration for M&M's. Hershey, who already supplied all the chocolate for the military, had the capacity to supply Mars with their own chocolate and sugar to manufacture M&M's during the Second World War.

There are two theories attached to the M& M name. Firstly, it represented the surnames of the two company heads, Forrest Mars and Bruce Murrie. The second is that it formed an alliance, following the strained relationship between Forrest Mars and his late father, Frank Mars.[45]

The basis for many of the Mars confectionery products is nougat, a process involving the mixing of hot sugar syrup with fluffy egg whites until it stiffens. The recipe I have included here for chocolate nougat is a commercial one, so you may want to consider scaling it down if you're just planning on making a few bars.

Good Commercial Chocolate Nougat
4lb (1.8kg) sugar
3lb (1.3 kg) glucose
1-quart (2 pints) water
8 egg whites
85-113g of bitter chocolate

Cook the sugar, glucose and water to 260°F. While cooking beat the egg whites firm. When the sugar has reached 260°F set off and stir with a paddle until it looks creamy, add the bitter chocolate then add the beaten egg whites, stir well and pour in a box lined with wafers or onto a slab with wafers, cover, weigh down and set for 2 to 3 hours, when it will be ready to cut into bars.[46]

Fry's, UK

Fry's was a Bristol-based company that operated from 1728 until 2011. On 11 September 1935, Swiss born Jacob Gloor, chief confectioner for J. S. Fry & Sons Ltd, sent Rowntree and Co. Ltd a letter requesting £5,000 in exchange for information relating to the recipe and method of manufacturing Fry's famed Crunchie bar brand. The letter was accompanied by a tin of Crunchie bar samples. On receiving the letter, staff at Rowntree rejected the offer, but did not reply. Two further letters were received from Gloor (who used a false name), before Rowntree's contacted senior staff at Fry's, informing them of the proposed scheme.[47] Gloor was charged with corruption and fined £50. He was just a month away from receiving his retirement package of £4 a week, equivalent to just over £200 in today's currency. It transpired that he needed the £5,000 (equivalent to about a quarter of a million) because he had invested unwisely and lost a great deal of money.[48] Ironically, it was Jacob Gloor who had solely developed the

Crunchie recipe for Fry's and created the unique process of forming, shaping and cutting the bar.

Despite Fry's creating the first solid chocolate bar and becoming the official chocolate-makers to Queen Victoria, they were unable to make it a commercial success. One of the alleged reasons for this is that they scrimped on quality and used powdered milk instead of fresh milk, which was less palatable, in their bars,

One of the most iconic chocolate bars of the twentieth-century was Fry's Turkish Delight, launched as early as 1914. There will even be some of you reading this who will recall the unforgettable slogan 'Full of Eastern Promise' which accompanied the iconic television campaign from the 1960s to the 1980s.

Turkish Delight
1oz sheet gelatine
½ teaspoon cream of tartar
1lb granulated sugar
1 cup water
Juice and rind of one orange
Juice of one lemon
Soak the gelatine in ½ cup water for several hours.

Boil the sugar in ½ cup water; when boiling add gelatine and boil for 20 minutes. Remove from the fire, add flavouring, strain and pour into pans rinsed with cold water. When stiff, cut into squares. Coat with sweet chocolate, before rolling in sugar.[49]

Australian chocolate

The Cadbury brand identity war with Australian chocolate manufacturer Darrell Lea has been raging for years. The antipodean company's controversial use of purple packaging continues to ruffle the directors at Cadbury Schweppes, who consider the colour to traditionally connect with Cadbury's chocolate. Having recently lost the long-running dispute, Cadbury continue to appeal, with their marketing experts reinforcing that 'consumers may mistakenly link

Cadbury with Darrell Lea, and vice versa, having become connected in consumers' minds through the common use of purple.'[50] Subsequent attempts at trademarking the colour purple have also been defeated in international courts, but Cadbury continue with their fight. Incidentally, Cadbury's acquired MacRobertson's, once the largest manufacturer of chocolate in Australia, who were the original creators of Freddo Frog. Darrell Lea are now a completely palm oil free brand, recognising the importance of ethically sourced ingredients in the modern world. Mondelez on the other hand, who supply palm oil for Cadbury's chocolate, are the world's worst offenders, threatening the extinction of orangutans every year.

In 1914 chocolatier Ernest Hillier opened his business, providing locally made chocolate. Prior to this, all chocolate in Australia had to be imported from the US and Europe. Because of the distance and climatic conditions and transport restrictions, the chocolate always arrived in poor condition.

Rabbits were introduced to the Australasian continent in the eighteenth century by European settlers, but they have steadily become an unwanted pest, creating economic and environmental damage and importing myxomatosis. The Easter bunny, therefore, isn't quite as welcome in Australia as it is elsewhere. During Easter, Haigh's Chocolates promote their range of chocolate Bilbies, an endangered marsupial that is rather more endearing down-under than a bunny.

The Haigh's website contains a selection of glorious chocolate recipes, including this ridiculously indulgent one:

Celebration Chocolate Mousse Cake
3 extra large eggs, lightly beaten
1¼ cups (310ml) buttermilk
1¼ cups warm water
½ cup (125ml) rice bran oil
2 teaspoons vanilla extract
2½ cups (300g) self-raising flour
2½ cups (300g) raw caster sugar
1¼ cups (150g) cocoa powder
2 teaspoons bicarbonate soda
1¼ teaspoons salt

Chocolate & orange buttercream mousse
2 x 200g Haigh's dessert blocks, chopped
300ml thickened cream
1½ tablespoons (30ml) golden syrup
1 teaspoon orange zest
2 tablespoons Grand Marnier or Cointreau (optional)
340g unsalted butter, slightly softened

Method
Preheat the oven to 180°C (160°C fan-assisted). Lightly grease three 20 cm round cake tins and line the bases with baking paper.

Using an electric stand mixer, combine eggs, buttermilk, warm water, oil and vanilla, slowly beating until well combined. Add flour, sugar, cocoa, bicarbonate soda and salt, mixing slowly until mixture is smooth and well combined.

Using a set of scales, evenly divide batter among the three prepared cake tins.

Bake cakes in preheated oven for 35 minutes or until a skewer comes out of the centre of each cake clean. Remove from oven and allow to cool for 10 minutes, before turning onto a wire rack to cool completely. Using a bread knife remove the domed tops from each cake, creating three even layers.

For the buttercream mousse, place chocolate, cream, syrup, zest and liqueur together in a medium saucepan over a very low heat, stirring constantly until chocolate has melted, making sure mixture does not become too hot. Remove from heat and allow to cool to room temperature.

Once chocolate mixture has cooled, place in mixing bowl of an electric stand mixer with a balloon whisk attachment. Beat mixture on a medium-high speed, adding butter a little at a time until mixture becomes pale, smooth, glossy and mousse like.

To ice cake, place each cake layer on a baking tray, making sure the top layer is cut side down. Place butter cream in a disposable piping bag, snipping the end. Pipe little icing kisses by pushing down as you squeeze the icing and then lift up to create a point. Repeat this process until all the cake layers are covered in icing kisses. Place baking trays in refrigerator for 30 minutes, to allow buttercream mousse to set.

To serve

200g mixed fresh berries (e.g. strawberries, raspberries, blackberries, blueberries)

1 punnet fresh edible flowers (e.g. violas, snap dragons, pansy)

Place the bottom layer of the cake in the centre of a cake stand or serving plate. Place a few berries around the outside. Carefully place the middle layer on top and again place some berries around the outside. Finally place the top layer carefully on top, making sure it is centred. Carefully scatter berries and edible flowers over the top. The cake is best refrigerated until serving, making it easier to slice, as the mousse remains set.[51]

Guittard, USA

Etienne 'Eddy' Guittard emigrated to the US from France in the 1860s to become a gold prospector. He also brought French chocolate with him to trade in bulk in San Francisco. While the prospecting was not very prosperous, he was persuaded by the stores where he sold his wares to try his hand at manufacturing chocolate, a trade in which he was already trained. Etienne returned to France, saved enough money to buy the required equipment and opened a store of his own in San Francisco.[52]

His son, Horace, took over the business in 1906 when it was destroyed by the infamous San Francisco earthquake. To his testament, Horace rebuilt the business and moved the premises, although forty years later the store was forced to move once again to accommodate a new road scheme – the Embarcadero Freeway.[53]

Today, the company is owned and managed by the fourth generation of Guittards and is the oldest continuously family-run chocolate making business in the United States.

This recipe was contributed by Miss Anna Gerichten, a resident of San Francisco, as part of a compilation of old Californian dishes.

Chocolate Macaroni

Three tablespoons ground chocolate, three ounces macaroni, one glass milk, three tablespoons sugar, four eggs, a pinch of salt, one teaspoonful vanilla, juice of half a lemon.

Dissolve the chocolate in a little hot water. Boil the macaroni in the milk until very soft. Beat the eggs light and add the sugar, salt and flavouring. Mix well, add chocolate and macaroni. Bake in a buttered mould. Serve very cold with whipped cream.[54]

Rowntree's/Nestlé, UK/Switzerland

The Nestlé narrative is a complicated one. It was originally born from two Swiss entrepreneurs in the 1860s who cornered the market in milk-based baby products and condensed milk, before adding chocolate into the mix – or rather powered milk to chocolate, a decade later. What followed was a list of mergers, partnerships and expansions, worthy of its own book.

In the 1980s they acquired Rowntree Mackintosh, which had once operated as one of the largest chocolate and confectionery manufacturers in the world, with well-known brands including Quality Street and Kit-Kat.

Nestlé has a string of human rights abuses against it, including flouting child labour laws on their cocoa farms. As the largest food company in the world with thousands of brands, Nestlé has dealt with numerous scandals over the years, including contaminated baby milk, cookie dough and noodles. They have also been accused of chocolate price fixing, forced labour and deforestation. One wonders what Henry Isaac Rowntree, with his mild manner and Quaker principles, would make of all this today.

The following recipe is taken from *Rowntree's Little Cookbook of 'Elect' Recipes*. Rowntree created a cocoa powder called Elect, launched in 1887, which proved to be very successful right up until the two World Wars.

Chocolate Rock Cakes
½ lb flour (one breakfast cup)
3oz sugar (three level-tablespoons)
3 oz margarine (three level-tablespoons), or clarified dripping
One good teaspoonful baking powder/bicarbonate of soda
One dessertspoonful Rowntree's Elect Cocoa
One egg, fresh or dried
Milk

Mix flour and cocoa. Rub in the margarine. Add sugar and baking powder. Beat the egg, pour in, make into a stiff mixture with about one tablespoon of milk.

Place in little rough heaps on a greased tin and bake in a fairly quick oven for 15 minutes.

Makes about fifteen small cakes.[55]

Menier, France

The French Menier dynasty was once one of the largest producers of chocolate, with factories in France and London and a distribution centre in New York. Their distinctive marketing image, created by Firmin Buisset in 1892, of a little girl scrawling the words 'Menier Chocolate' on a wall or glass, using a piece of chocolate, became iconic and immediately recognisable around the world. The company fell into decline between the two World Wars, with Antoine Gilles Menier becoming the last member of the family to run the business until the mid-1960s.

Henri Menier, CEO between 1853 and 1913, was a bit of an eccentric and an adventurer. In 1895 he purchased the Canadian-owned Anticosti Island, discovered by Jacques Cartier in 1534 and occasionally referred to as the 'Cemetery of the Gulf' due to the high number of shipwrecks that occurred off its coasts. Henri constructed a village on the island, which he christened Port-Menier, and ran a fish and shell-fish canning business from there. He also introduced various species of game, including deer, reindeer, moose, otters, beavers, mink, elk, frogs and rabbits, for the sport of hunting. The indigenous animals were black bears and foxes. A chateau – 'Villa Menier' – was also built on the island, but was sadly demolished in the 1950s.

Following his death, ownership of the island moved to Henri's brother, Gaston, before being sold to a large paper corporation. For forty years the Meniers used the island every summer, hosting numerous guests who stayed in the purpose-built cabins or in pavilions situated at the mouth of rivers. Each one was designed to accommodate six people.[56]

This hunting and fishing paradise is quirky in itself, but Anticosti was once inhabited by just two families established at either end of the 100-mile-long island to provide aid to castaways.[57] Prior to this it was associated with piracy and cannibalism and fell into the hands of many different colonial powers.

Perhaps its most interesting resident was the renowned sea rover Louis-Olivier Gamache, a man known for his dark supernatural powers, with a reputation so terrifying that no one disturbed him on the island until he died in 1854. It is more likely that Gamache was merely a knowledgeable man, perhaps a practitioner of white magic who had crafted his reputation for the purposes of seeking isolation. It has been documented that Gamache returned from a hunting trip one winter to find his wife and children had frozen to death in his absence. This tragedy made him even more reclusive, until he eventually died one morning, allegedly while taking a slug of navy rum at breakfast.[58] Gamache Bay, one of the safer harbours on the island, is named after him and he has become immortalised as the 'Robinson Crusoe' of French Canada. Today, there are around 200 residents living in the Port-Menier district of the island, which has also recently applied for World Heritage status.

Although Menier was acquired some years ago by Nestlé, it continues to retail a small range of products and its website includes a wealth of delicious chocolate recipes, including this one for curried lamb stew with bitter chocolate:

Curried Lamb Stew with Bitter Chocolate
Serves 4-6
Ingredients:
1 large onion, peeled, roughly chopped and puréed
2 tsp mustard seeds
2 tbsp root ginger
10 curry leaves
8 cloves
½ tsp cardamom, ground

1 tsp Kashmiri chilli
2 green chillies, roughly chopped
600g lamb shoulder, diced
4 medium potatoes, peeled and diced
800g tinned tomatoes 1 litre chicken stock
½ tsp turmeric
2 cinnamon sticks
100g vegetable oil
30g Menier dark chocolate
1 tsp ground coriander
4 garlic cloves, crushed
1 tsp salt
Generous pinch pepper

Pour the oil into a large, thick bottomed saucepan and place on a medium heat. Once the oil is hot, put in the cloves, mustard seeds, curry leaves and cinnamon sticks and cook for approximately 1 minute. Remove from the heat, take out the spices with a slotted spoon and set aside, then place the saucepan back over the heat. Once hot, add the diced lamb. Fry for approximately 5 minutes, stirring frequently to ensure all sides of the lamb are browning. Once the lamb has browned, remove from the saucepan and set aside, retaining the hot flavoured oil in the saucepan. Place the saucepan back on the heat and add the garlic, puréed onion, ginger and green chilli. Fry over a low heat, stirring frequently, until the onions start browning. Add the ground spices – cardamom, Kashmiri chilli, turmeric, coriander – and cook for about 10 minutes over a low heat, stirring frequently. Add the lamb and the fried spices from earlier – cloves, mustard seeds, curry leaves and cinnamon sticks – and stir, ensuring that all is mixed well. Add the tinned tomatoes, chicken stock, salt and pepper and bring to the boil. Cover with a tight-fitting lid, lower the heat and simmer for about an hour.

Add the potatoes, stir and bring to the boil. Cover again, lower the heat and cook gently for a further hour, or until the lamb and potatoes are tender. Once cooked, remove from the heat and gently stir in the dark chocolate, making sure you don't break up the lamb and potatoes. Taste and adjust the seasoning accordingly.

To serve: Spoon the curry into pre warmed bowls and top with a dollop of natural yoghurt and a handful of coriander leaves. This recipe is great served with steamed coconut rice.[59]

Godvia, Belgium/Turkey

Founded in Brussels in the 1920s by Joseph Draps, Godiva was to become a brand that focused on producing premium chocolate with sophisticated and elegant packaging. Draps named his company after the medieval noblewoman Godgifu, (meaning gift of God) who is most associated with riding through the streets naked, with only her hair covering her modesty. Godgifu, or Godiva, is believed to have done this in protest against the harsh taxes imposed by her husband, Leofric. Although Godiva herself is well documented and recorded in the Doomsday Book, there is no direct evidence to support this particular legend.

Today, Godiva has hundreds of retail stores throughout the world, but why exactly Daps decided to name his company after her is debatable. She was certainly courageous and challenging, to take on her husband in the way she did, if there is any truth to the legend. And Draps was indeed tenacious in building a company that represented style, exclusivity and quality.[60] This reputation has been sustained over the years, despite Godiva being one of the major companies to consistently be linked with flouting child labour laws. It should also be emphasised that Godiva do not actually make their own chocolate, the Belgian chocolatiers Callebaut are their main suppliers.

Neuhaus, Belgium

Understood to be the inventors of praline, Jean Neuhaus and his wife, Louise, have additionally always been credited with the creation of the ballotin box in 1915. Before this decorative little cardboard container became available, chocolates were generally sold in paper cones. Charbonnel et Walker were certainly selling their chocolates in similar boxes, like the boite blanche, at least six years prior to this supposed invention, so perhaps other manufacturers were also using similar packaging. Maybe this is one fact that should be re-considered in the overall archives of the chocolate narrative.

Tony's Chocolonely, Netherlands

The last manufacturer to add to this section is a misfit in the world of confection, in that Tony's go beyond the chocolate pale, striving for slave-free chocolate. Teun van de Keuken is a Dutch journalist with a reputation for investigating the issues surrounding fair trade. One of his documentaries led to the formation of Tony's Chocolonely, a chocolate manufactured in a completely slave-free way. Van de Keuken was so appalled by the extent to which the major manufacturers of chocolate abused their business practices in Ghana and the Ivory Coast that he staged a one-man protest in a police station by purchasing and consuming as many chocolate bars as he could, before requesting to be arrested as a criminal who had participated in the illicit trade of child labour. While his case proved futile in the courts, his protest made an impact worldwide. Tony's mission is to make slave-free chocolate the standard way to manufacture. They work directly with farmers, who are also paid a premium, receive training and education. Tony's are one of the few chocolate brands that know exactly where their beans come from. Their chocolate bars are also visually divided into a pattern, opposed to uniform squares. This symbolises how the money from cocoa production is unevenly divided. It's a little glimmer in a sector which sadly remains very dark indeed.

Chocolate Houses

The first chocolate house to open in Paris was in 1675, some twenty years after the first in England, in Queens Alley, Bishopsgate Street, London, and, ironically, run by a Frenchman. Along with royalty and noblemen, it was the fops, or 'beaux', who frequented the theatres, chocolate houses and pleasure gardens of eighteenth-century London. They cut the latest fashions with their wigs, fancy coats and powdered faces, all vying for the title of marquis.

London in particular was a city of dandies. Recreation and spending money on going out was the new fashion in the Georgian age. The pleasure gardens like Vauxhall and Ranelagh in Chelsea offered covered and lit walkways, band stands, performers, fireworks, and food and drink, which included the sale of chocolate, while the smaller tea gardens of Marylebone attracted the likes of politicians and musicians. As women were allowed access to these venues, they rapidly became popular alternatives to the coffee houses. These gardens were also fuelled with an erotic ambience, a place where a modest entrance fee gave way to the possibility of a romantic frisson. The lifestyle of these privileged members of society is succinctly put in Macky's, *Journey Through England*, 1714:

> We rise by nine and those that frequent great men's levees find entertainment at them till eleven. About twelve the beaux monde assembles in several coffee or chocolate houses. We are carry'd up to these places in chairs or sedans. If it is fine weather we take a turn in the park till two, when we go to dinner. The general way is to make a party at the coffee-house to go to dine at the tavern, where we sit till six, when we go to the play, except you are invited to the table of some great man. After the play the best company generally go to Tom's and Will's coffee-houses, near adjoining, where there is playing picket and the best of conversation till midnight.[61]

Tea, coffee, chocolate and sometimes sherbet were all served in the coffee-houses, drawn from large wooden barrels. Each coffee and chocolate house took on its own identity depending on the clientele. There were Whig and Tory houses, houses that attracted writers and performers, houses that had particularly less than salubrious reputations. There was usually an admission fee of 1 penny, with a hot beverage costing tuppence. If you were a regular you had your seat reserved. They opened around 9.00 am, often closing at around 2.00 am the following morning.

Numerous fights and brawls took place inside and directly outside of these venues. In 1717 there was a quarrel that escalated out of control outside the Royal Chocolate House in St. James's Street, London. Three of the men involved were mortally wounded and a fourth (a Colonel Cunningham) was only spared by the quick-thinking actions of his footman who dashed in front of his master and physically removed him from the scene.[62] At the Guildhall Coffee House, Cheapside, a murder took place in the early hours of Saturday, 15 August 1846, in which the kitchen maid, Susan Tolliday, had her throat cut by the cook, John V. Smith. His execution took place on 21 August that same year.[63] When asked why he did it, Smith replied, 'I was drove to do it. She had been calling me all the rogues she could think of, all the morning. I have a wife and four children as was I afraid I should lose my place at night from what she had said.'[64]

***

One of the most disreputable of these houses was King's, a venue based in London's Covent Garden, owned and run by the intriguingly highly educated Tom King and his fierce wife, Moll, a one-time street nut vendor who inherited the premises on his death. The house was a front for prostitution and worse, with Moll frequently up before the courts for running a disorderly business. 'Here you might see Ladies of Pleasure, who apparelled like Persons of Quality, not at all inferior to them in dress, attended by Fellows habited like Footmen, who were their Bullies (Pimps), and wore their disguise, the more easily to deceive the unwary Youths who were so unhappy as to Cast their Eyes upon these deceitful Water-Wag-Tails'.[65]

A book, *Covent Garden in Mourning*, was published paying satirical homage to Moll King's life in 1747. Indeed, so notorious was this madam and felon that she was even immortalised on canvas by the painter Hogarth. Moll King is also frequently linked to the main character of Daniel Defoe's *Moll Flanders*, published in 1722. A verse was published as part of a compilation of British poets by Thomas Parks in 1818, which is damning in its accusations of Moll. Her character is painted bleakly as a wild, fearsome woman who was infamous in Covent Garden. It also insinuates that she died of syphilis, a hugely painful and debilitating sexually transmitted disease that was rife in eighteenth-century society. A different account of her in 1854 recalls a woman who was 'very witty', with King's described as a venue where 'persons of every description' frequented. Moll would happily serve 'chimney-sweepers, gardeners and the market-people, in common with lords of the highest rank.'[66]

The story of King's Coffee House exemplifies the disreputable and salacious activity of some of these venues, but is also an insight into the way in which women of Georgian society were viewed and judged. Customers drank chocolate, but chocolate houses were also places where people came together, shared gossip and witticism, political debate or to do business. They also plotted and planned the most underhand of schemes.

***

Patrick Daly's Chocolate House, established in Dublin around the 1750s, was one of the most notorious clubs in Ireland, best known for its gambling and allegedly where half the landed estates in Ireland changed hands. Numerous patrons were documented being thrown out of windows, while duels with swords and pistols were commonplace.[67]

White's chocolate house was opened in 1693 by Francis White at a house on the site of what was known as Boodle's Club. Francis then moved it in 1697 to 69/70 St James Street. He died in 1711 and his widow took over, before passing it onto John Arthur in 1725. It was entirely destroyed by fire in 1733. This scene was captured by Hogarth in the *Rake's Progress* (Plate 6) which shows a group of men so engrossed in their own activities that they fail to notice the fire. It also highlights the diverse nature of the clientele, including a highwayman, noblemen and money-lenders. Following the fire, the club/chocolate house was moved to Gaunt's coffee house, on the west side of the street, before moving again in 1736.[68] It became a private gambling house, its principal members including the Duke of Devonshire, and Earls of Cholmondeley, Chesterfield and Rockingham amongst others and was dubbed 'the most fashionable hell in London'.

Other notorious chocolate houses included The Smyrna in Pall Mall, Mrs Rochford's and Robin's which apparently attracted 'Ambassadors, foreign consuls and strangers in general'. Other notable meeting places included the British Coffee House on Cockspur Street, the chocolate house on Blackheath and The Spread Eagle. The literary men and characters of the day frequented John's, Child's and Baston's or Button's in Covent Garden.[69] Truby's, apparently, was mostly patronised by the clergy, and Sir Issac Newton and Hans Sloane would drink at The Grecian in Devereaux Court, while Samuel Johnson supped at The Turk's Head in the Strand.

Charles II briefly banned chocolate houses in 1675, with his 'Proclamation for the Suppression of Coffee Houses,' in an attempt to flush out the radical politics they encouraged.[70] His bill failed spectacularly, undoubtedly due to the popularity of the drink and its associated leisure pursuits by London's elite. After all, these were the places where the downfall of kings was plotted.

Many chocolate houses in London became synonymous with the area of St James's. This association dates back to the reign of William III, and as a consequence of a fire in January 1697-8 which ravaged the Palace of Whitehall, thus reinstating the royal court to St James's. There were only two chocolate houses – White's and Ozinda's – based in St James's Street and Pall Mall before the fire. Then came the Cocoa Tree, in 1698, the Smyrna, in 1702, the Thatched House Tavern, 1704 or 1705, and the St James's Coffee House (1705), all catering to the new elite residents of the neighbourhood, attracted by the Court of St James's.[71]

During its long career the Cocoa Tree occupied three different houses in Pall Mall and then moved to No 64 St James's Street. It finally ceased to exist in 1932, following a diverse career as a club and a victualler's. The only West End club, in fact, together with White's, whose heritage traced back to the original chocolate houses of the 1600s.

John Tallis published a series of beautifully drawn street views of London in the mid-1800s. One such illustration shows the Cocoa Tree in 1839, described as having:

> three main storeys and a garret, with a continuous iron balcony railing at first-floor level and a band course at the level of second-floor sills. The bottom storey was irregular, having a modest square-headed front entrance door between a wide square-headed passage entrance on the north, leading to Blue Ball Yard, and a three-light sash window on the south. Three round-headed windows, the central one emphasized by being placed in a shallow round headed recess, gave light to the second storey. This central motif was repeated on a smaller scale in the third storey, where it was flanked on either side by a single square-headed window. The result was to over-emphasize the centre, and give a slight touch of pretentiousness to an otherwise modest front.[72]

The Cocoa Tree appears to have been frequently patronised by the satirist Jonathan Swift, best-known today for his novel *Gulliver's Travels*, and it was a favoured Tory rendezvous. During the eighteenth century it became a club for members only. In his Journal of 1762, the revered historian and writer Edward Gibbon recorded:

[I] dined at the Cocoa-tree with Holt … We went thence to the play … and when it was over, returned to the Cocoa-tree. That respectable body, of which I have the honour to be a member, affords every evening a sight truly English. Twenty or thirty, perhaps, of the first men in the Kingdom, in point of fashion and fortune, supping at little tables covered with a napkin, in the middle of a Coffee-room, upon a bit of cold meat, or a Sandwich, and drinking a glass of punch. At present, we are full of Privy Counsellors and Lords of the Bedchamber; who, having jumped into the Ministry, make a very singular medley of their old principles and language, with their modern ones.[73]

During the nineteenth century the Cocoa Tree was less about politics and hot beverages and more about heavy drinking, entertaining the likes of The Prince of Wales, Sheridan and Byron. Its final incarnation was as a Gunsmith's, which was severely damaged by fire in 1926, leading to its closure in 1932. It is said that when builders drilled down into the foundations, a tunnel was revealed leading to a tavern in Piccadilly. Undoubtedly, this would have provided traitors with a means of escape when the chocolate house was raided.[74]

George II's wife, Queen Caroline, was dropped next to the steps of Ozinda's Chocolate House while being carried in a sedan chair. The action of the chair dropping broke her opera glasses, but the queen remained unharmed.[75] Ozinda's was located on the north side of St James's Palace. The owner, a Mr Osenda, returned to his native France in 1724, putting the chocolate house and all its contents up for sale, including snuffs, liquors, wines and cinnamon water. Like the Cocoa Tree and Whites, Ozinda's was a popular Tory hangout.

The man sometimes referenced as the founder of the city of Richmond in Virginia, William Byrd, wrote about Ozinda's in his diaries, as a place where the drinking of chocolate, betting and reading newspapers were the main activities of the clientele.[76] William Byrd's diaries in fact reveal much more about the man and his insatiable sexual appetite, including countless sexual advances towards his servants and slaves and numerous encounters with prostitutes during his visits to

London. He wrote several diaries in code, from 1709 to 1741, which remarkably survived. His writings are riddled with revealing insights into sexuality and misogynist outbursts in the Southern states. He was preoccupied with control and entitlement and relentlessly assaulted his female staff, from kissing and groping to intercourse, often in earshot of his wife. He also wrote about his friends and male companions and their ongoing attempts at forcing themselves on young girls and women in all aspects of society.[77]

Chocolate makers

King Charles II enjoyed his chocolate and drank it regularly on the advice of his doctor, Dr Quartermaine, who swore by its abilities to alleviate constipation. The king would drink a cup in the morning, then retire for half an hour, during which time it 'never fail'd to give him a stool as soon as he was up.'[78]

But it was King William III and Queen Mary who were responsible for legitimising a royal chocolate-maker in the 1690s and built a special chocolate kitchen at Hampton Court Palace, a trend which was sustained by the royal household and guaranteed the importance of chocolate generally in society. William and Mary were both also, somewhat contradictorily, responsible for agreeing to raise additional duties on tea, coffee and chocolate in 1695.

By the time of George I, Thomas Tosier, the king's personal chocolate-maker, not only had his own kitchen, but his own rooms too, where he slept, in order to be on-hand with the king's morning and evening chocolate. His wife, Grace Tosier (Tozier), was a chocolate house keeper in Blackheath, London, a building also known as the Assembly Rooms. Grace was highly esteemed and respected. Her second marriage was to a brewer thirty years her junior.[79] She was a bit of a celebrity around town, hosting respectable balls and dinners at her chocolate house, and always to be found wearing flowers and exaggerated hats.

Such was Grace's success in the community that the artist Bartholomew Dandridge painted her portrait in 1729. The print became a collectible and has immortalised her legacy. Like all chocolate houses of the seventeenth and eighteenth centuries, however, Grace's venue attracted controversial groups and gangs, including the Anti-Gallicans, a society dedicated to maintaining ongoing hostilities towards France – from its people, to its culture and goods.[80]

Although Thomas Tosier had long since departed, the last person to see King George II alive was his chocolate maker, who as custom dictated, watched while the king drank his cocoa in the morning, during his 'levee' (the ritual of getting dressed in front of a select few) before he opened the window declaring a walk was in order. Having left the room, the chocolate maker then heard a sigh and a thud and ran to the king's aid, only to find him lying on the floor with an injured head, from which he never recovered.[81] Royal household accounts during the reign of George II in 1750 list a monthly expenditure detailing the lowest amount spent on tea, coffee and chocolate in December at £16 and 15 shillings, while the highest consumption was during August and September – a staggering £24 and 9 shillings (over £2,000 today).[82] Incidentally, Queen Caroline, the wife of George II, had her own chocolate maker, Mr Teed, who resided at St James's Palace. The chocolate maker of her predecessor, Queen Anne, must have been super busy, adding to her ongoing health issues by allegedly providing her with some ninety pint-pots of chocolate a month.[83]

One of the most spontaneous crimes against a chocolate maker was that of Thomas Rawlins who was murdered by Foster Snow, the proprietor of The Feathers Alehouse in Holborn, London, in 1725. Rawlins was stabbed in the chest. According to the notes from the trial Rawlins was described as a man who owed Snow quite a bit of money and was prone to bad behaviour when drunk. The two exchanged words when Rawlins entered the inn requesting his rabbits to be cooked for his supper. Rawlins' wife arrived and she and Snow also exchanged heated words, before he struck her across the face. As the couple got up to leave, Snow followed, grabbed a knife from a nearby dresser and stabbed Rawlins to death. He was found guilty and sentenced to death on 7 October 1725.[84]

It seems that other chocolate makers of the eighteenth century were prone to criminal wrongdoings. Daniel Cable, an 'eminent chocolate maker', was tried for perjury in 1748, while Hosea Youell, whose only work had been as an assistant to a chocolate maker, was tried for the robbery and murder of Captain Joseph Johns in October 1747. Hosea was caught while Johns lay dying from his stab wounds over a period of several days in rooms nearby. He was brought to Johns' bedside, where the captain identified him, just before he died, declaring, 'You barbarous villain, you are the rascal that stabbed me.' Hosea denied the charge, but was subsequently arrested.[85]

Sometimes it was the chocolate makers themselves who were on the receiving end of atrocities. During the siege of San Sebastián, which was ruled by France before Wellington's troops captured it in 1813, the city was besieged by tired, drunk and riotous British and Portuguese troops following the city's takeover. Numerous statements were gathered about the brutal and hideous acts of the soldiers themselves who looted, pillaged and burned the city, killing and raping as they went. One such statement listed the deaths and rapes of specific people residing in the city, including a priest, the wife of a silversmith, a chocolate maker, whose shop was also ransacked, and a second chocolate maker, who was married to a prominent servant, known simply as the 'Good Girl', who would almost certainly have been violated.[86] After the event the remaining townsfolk met and sent word to Wellington that they needed financial help and support following the atrocities committed by his own men. Wellington denied the citizens anything and refused to acknowledge the accusations. Today, the Spanish city continues to remember this period in history and the people who suffered, with an annual memorial service.

Jewish communities who were driven into Portugal during the Spanish inquisition established themselves as great authorities on chocolate making, having learnt their craft in the 1500s from some of the very first recipes. They then took this knowledge into the Basque region, including San Sebastián, and Bayonne in present-day France. Robert Linxe, the founder of the acclaimed La Maison du Chocolat, Paris, now a major international chain of chocolate boutiques, learnt how to make chocolate in Bayonne and this is the native recipe that he was taught:

Robert Linxe's Bayonne Chocolate

Take 1l of heavy cream and bring it to a boil. Pour it slowly over 3lb 12oz of semi-bitter chocolate until the chocolate melts. Whisk it like mayonnaise until thickened. Add 3½ oz of softened, high-quality butter.

Remove pits from Itxassou cherries (a variety from the village of Itxassou in France), and put the cherries through a food mill until a fine pulp is produced. Heat the pulp, add a little alcohol (brandy or local fruit alcohol), and reduce the liquid. Incorporate in the chocolate mixture. Chill it. Then cut it in pieces and dip in melted *couverture* (covering chocolate). This is a bit difficult, but you can always shape it into balls and roll them in cocoa powder as truffles.[87]

Linxe, apparently, sometimes mixed the chocolate filling with citrus juices from Spain, before forming it into little flat rectangles and dipping in chocolate. He called this creation *Arneguy*, which is also a village in south-west France.

Historically, Jewish tradesmen and women have had to experience persecution and prejudice throughout the world. One look at the British newspapers of the 1800s demonstrates the level of underlying animosity towards the significant community of Jewish bakers active in London at that time.

Babka, or *kranz* as it's called in Israel, is a traditional sweet braided bread of Eastern Europe, which is stuffed and rolled with a variety of fillings, chocolate being one of the most popular. The recipe I have included here is a combination of the dough and topping from online lifestyle magazine *delish.com*, with the chocolate filling provided by Shannon Sarna's *Modern Jewish Baker.*

Ingredients for the *babka* dough
1/3 cup (80ml) milk, lukewarm
1 (0.25oz) packet instant yeast
1/3 cup (70g) granulated sugar, divided
1 2/3 cup (212g) all-purpose flour, divided
2 large eggs, divided
1 tsp (6g) kosher salt
6 tbsp (84g) butter, softened

For the filling
6oz dark chocolate, cut into pieces
¾ cup unsalted butter, at room temperature
½ cup sugar
1/3 cup cocoa powder
¼ teaspoon cinnamon
Pinch fine sea salt

Instructions for filling

In a microwave-safe bowl, heat chocolate in 30-second intervals until completely melted, stirring vigorously in between with a small spatula.

Allow to cool for 2 minutes.

Beat butter and sugar until smooth. Add cocoa powder, melted dark chocolate, cinnam on and salt. Use to spread inside *babka*.[88]

For the *streusel* topping

3 tbsp (21g) powdered sugar
3 tbsp (21g) all-purpose flour
1 tbsp (14g) butter
1/2 tsp ground cinnamon
Pinch kosher salt

For the egg wash

Reserved egg white
1 tsp granulated sugar
Pinch kosher salt

Method

Make the dough: To the bowl of a stand mixer fitted with the hook attachment, add lukewarm milk, yeast, ⅔ cup flour, and 4 teaspoons sugar. Using a spatula, mix until well combined, then cover with and let sit for at least 30 minutes, up to 2 hours.

Once the dough has formed some air pockets, add in 1 whole egg and 1 egg yolk (reserving the egg white for the egg wash), remaining 1 cup flour, remaining ¼ cup sugar, and salt. Mix on low speed until well combined, then gradually increase to medium-high speed. Continue mixing, scraping down bowl every 2 to 3 minutes, until dough becomes elastic and pulls away from the sides of the bowl, 6 to 8 minutes.

With the mixer running, add in butter gradually, 1 tablespoon at a time, letting each tablespoon fully incorporate into the dough before adding the next, 5 minutes. Continue mixing on medium-high speed until the dough is glossy and passes the windowpane test, 3 to 5 minutes more. Cover bowl and refrigerate for at least 2 hours, up to overnight.

30 minutes before you're ready to assemble the *babka*, make chocolate filling: In a microwave-safe bowl, melt together butter, cream, and 1 cup chocolate chips in 20-second increments until smooth, stirring between each heating to prevent burning. Stir in zest, if using, and salt. Let cool before using.

Make streusel: In a small bowl, whisk together sugar, flour, cinnamon, and salt. Using your fingertips, work in butter until evenly distributed and tiny clumps of streusel form. Refrigerate until ready for use.

Make egg wash: In a small bowl, whisk together reserved egg white with sugar and salt.

Transfer chilled dough out onto a floured surface and roll out into a thin 16-in square. Brush dough with melted butter. Using an offset spatula, spread chocolate filling into an even layer across the dough, then sprinkle remaining ¾ cup chocolate chips on top. Tightly roll dough into a rope, then fold the rope in half and braid the two segments around each other with three twists.

Line an 8½ in x 4½ in loaf pan with parchment. Place braided dough into loaf pan, tucking in the ends of the rope underneath. Gently press dough into an even layer. Brush more egg wash over the entire loaf, then sprinkle on streusel and press lightly to adhere to loaf. Cover and let proof until dough rises almost to the lip of the pan, about 1 hour to 1 hour 30 minutes. Preheat oven to 375°C for 15 minutes before you're ready to bake.

Bake until deeply golden on top and the centre of the loaf registers between 190°C and 205°C, 45-50 minutes.

Lift loaf out by the ends of the parchment and transfer onto a cooling rack. Let cool completely before slicing.[89]

Chapter 4

An Audience with Chocolate

For decades chocolate has featured in films with an edgier or ironic theme: *Charlie and the Chocolate Factory*, *Chocolat*, *Bread and Chocolate*, *The Chocolate War*. It has also been the focus of theatrical plays like Phillippe Blasband's *The Chocolate Eaters* which explores the repercussions of chocolate addiction.

Representation of Chocolate in the arts is simultaneously adverse and seductive. Songs, literature and poetry are full of cocoa-inspired references. Songs like *La Femme Chocolat* by Olivia Ruiz, the Bee Gees' *Chocolate Symphony* and Kylie Minogue's *Chocolate* all have bittersweet undertones running through their lyrics. Similarly, poetry and prose writers of famous literary works have dwelt on the changing significance of chocolate. Poisoners who chose chocolate as their method have also been the inspiration for works of fiction, like the American author John Dickson Carr's *The Black Spectacles*, based on the Christina Edmunds case, and in Mary Ann Evans' (George Eliot) gothic novella, *The Lifted Veil*, the unsavoury character of Bertha is said to reflect the chocolate poisoner Madeleine Smith (both of whom you can read about in chapter one).

The Lindt chocolate company made wrappers for their milk chocolate in the 1960s using illustrations from Walt Disney's animated film of *Snow White* and we all know how surreal that story turned out.[1] Chocolate in visual art is often symbolic of its combined charm, wantonness and sinister connotations.

Slave narratives are also integral to understanding the darker side of chocolate. The rot that lies beneath the shiny sweet capitalist pleasures is reflected historically through music, dance and ceremony. The blues and folk music are rooted in the pain of displacement, injustice, immorality and the survival of the soul, and evolved from plantation elegies.

Historical literary chocolate

Satirists of the seventeenth century seized upon the notion of writing about the introduction of chocolate into society. In *The Way of the World* (1700), English playwright William Congreve sets the first scene of his satirical drama in a chocolate house in which the dialogue revolves around gambling, cheating and deception, highlighting at once the idleness and low morals of the main characters.

Robert Gould aligns sexuality, lust and laziness with chocolate in his 1693 Restoration poem *Corruption of the Times:*

> Our *Laziness* their *Labour* does debauch
> Who'd think at ten a clock it shou'd be said
> That the great Lady's soaking in her bed?
> When to repair the *sensible decay*
> That twelve hours *hearty Sleep* has took away,
> Dish after Dish for *Chocolate* she calls;
> (She must be rais'd that often falls).
> That strong back Liquor *hoops'em* in the *Chine*,
> No other *Nectar* they allow *Divine*;
> *Vain Sex*! at once both *Foolish* and *Unjust*,
> To think they need *Provocatives* to *Lust*:
> Were all their Lives to be *one Nuptial Night*,
> Their *Stock* would never be *exhausted* quite;[2]

Similarly, Matthew Prior's 1704 poem *Hans Carvel* describes the protagonist's wife as someone who is frivolous, whose pleasures only extend to 'music, company and play'. She doesn't wake until 10.00 am, at which time she drinks chocolate before retiring back to bed for another two hours. The rest of her day is spent frolicking with her lover and staying out as late as possible to ensure she enjoys all the entertaining delights of London's eighteenth-century nightlife. Chocolate is placed at the heart of her superficial day, reminding us of just how much this drink was once associated with hedonism and loose morals.[3]

Alexander Pope's satirical poem *The Rape of the Lock* also mocks contemporary society of the eighteenth century, comparing mythical gods to actual characters and events of the time. He compares the preparation of chocolate with the punishment of Ixion, expelled from Olympus for attempting to seduce Hera, the Queen of the Gods.

> Or, as Ixion fix'd, the wretch shall feel
> The giddy motion of the whirling Mill,
> In fumes of burning Chocolate shall glow,
> And tremble at the sea that froths below![4]

We are reminded once again of the sexual connotations that have historically aligned themselves to chocolate since its earliest introduction into society in Carlo Goldoni's *La bottega del caffè* (*The Coffee House*, 1750). Chocolate as a beverage becomes a dialogue of innuendo between two salacious characters – Eugenio, a gambling addict, and Lisaura, a dancer:

LISAURA: "Your most humble servant."

EUGENIO: "Has it been long Signora, since you got up?"

LISAURA: "I got up just this moment."

EUGENIO: "Have you had your coffee?"

LISAURA: "Not yet. It's still early."

EUGENIO: "May I see to it that you are served?"

LISAURA: "Much obliged, but don't trouble yourself."

EUGENIO: "It's no trouble at all. Boys, bring the lady coffee, chocolate, all that she wants, I am paying."

LISAURA: "Thank you, thank you, but I make my coffee and chocolate at home."

EUGENIO: "You must have good chocolate."

LISAURA: "It is quite perfect."

EUGENIO: "You make it yourself?"

LISAURA: "My servant is quite talented."

EUGENIO: "Would you like *me* to give your chocolate a little whip?"

LISAURA: "Ah, you shouldn't worry about it."

EUGENIO: "I will come and drink it with you, if you let me."

LISAURA: "It is not for you, Sir."

EUGENIO: "I should be pleased to accept anything at all. Come now, open the door and we'll spend a little while together."

LISAURA: "Forgive me, but I don't open the door that easily."

EUGENIO: "Well, tell me, do you want me to come through the back door?"

LISAURA: "People who come to my house have nothing to hide."

EUGENIO: "Come now, open the door, let's not make a scene."[5]

The references to back doors and whipped chocolate are enough to read between the lines of this saucy exchange, at a time when the consumption of chocolate was considered licentious.

In the eighteenth century, with the exception of a few culinary recipes, chocolate was still largely identified as a drink. It was a period of war, progress and science, with the industrial revolution on the horizon. It is also recognised as a time of mixed morals and discord among the classes. Hannah Glasses' recipe for Sham Chocolate sits very nicely within this social framework.

Sham Chocolate
Take a pint of milk, boil it over a slow fire, with some whole cinnamon and sweeten it with Lisbon sugar; beat up the yolks of three eggs, throw all together into a chocolate pot and mill it one way, or it will turn. Serve it up in chocolate cups.[6]

William Makepeace Thackeray makes numerous references to chocolate houses in his writings. In his anecdotal work, *The Four Georges*, which, as the title might suggests, is a colourful journey through the reigns of George I through to George IV, Thackeray notes: 'Fancy the beaux thronging to the chocolate houses tapping their snuff boxes as they issue thence their periwigs appearing over the red curtains.' And, 'tis a rule with the English to go once a day at least to houses of this sort, where they talk of business and news, read the papers and often look at one another without opening their lips. The chocolate-house in St. James's Street, where I go every morning to pass away the time, is always so full that a man can scarce turnabout in it.'[7]

By the late 1600s any self-respecting coffee-house would have included the sale of chocolate to cater to the changing tastes and fashions of the wealthier consumers of the day.

Richard Briggs, an eighteenth-century cook, who also worked at the Temple Coffee-House, which was a known location for men of the law to congregate, wrote *The English Art of Cookery* in 1788. It contains a recipe for chocolate puffs, baked on writing paper (not sure how that would have worked out):

Chocolate Puffs

Take half a pound of double refined sugar, beat and sift it fine, scrape into it one ounce of chocolate very fine and mix them together; beat up the white of an egg to a very high froth, then put in your chocolate and sugar and beat it till it is as stiff as a paste; then strew sugar on some writing paper, drop them on about the size of a sixpence and bake them in a very slow oven, when they are done take them off the paper and put them in plates.[8]

The prolific Victorian novelist L.T. Meade wrote at some length about her school day 'cocoa parties' in her many books written for young people. These parties saw fellow schoolgirls coming together to meet and chat. Meade, who was brought up in Ireland, described one scene : 'The cocoa-table was drawn up in front of the fire and on a quaintly shaped tray stood the bright little cocoa pot and the oddly devised cups and saucers.'[9] She informs us that five or six girls would regularly attend these parties, organised by one of the school mistresses in her quarters, where they would lounge about, chat and laugh around copious cups of cocoa.

It would appear that nineteenth-century female students had a reputation for illicit late-night snacking. The antics of attendants of the all-female Vassar College in New York allegedly popularised chocolate fudge, which was introduced to fellow students by Emelyn Battersby Hartridge, who acquired her recipe including cream, sugar, butter and chocolate from a friend in Baltimore. This craze for chocolate fudge-making spread widely across other US women's colleges such as Smith and Wellesley, who added their own twists of brown sugar and marshmallow respectively.[10] Below is an early US published recipe for Vassar College Fudge from 1899 (contributed by S. G. Bronson).

Vassar College Fudge

2 cups sugar, 1 cup milk, 5 teaspoonfuls Baker's Breakfast Cocoa; boil, stirring constantly until it hardens, in water; pour into buttered pans; in about 5 minutes cut in caramel squares.[11]

The Baker's chocolate listed in this recipe is most likely referring to The Baker Chocolate Company, Dorset, Massachusetts, the oldest manufacturers of chocolate in the United States, established in the 1770s but now owned by Kraft Heinz Foods. One of Bakers' founding chocolatiers, John Hannon, famously disappeared on a trip to, reputedly, purchase cacao beans from the West Indies, never to be seen again.[12]

Charlotte Brontë's novel *Villette* contains several references to chocolate. A tale of love, cross-cultural issues, separation and a protagonist, Lucy Snowe, whose journey to self-discovery and independence is both tragic and passionate. She shares simple meals of chocolate and rolls, hot chocolate and new-laid eggs, and chocolate as a refreshment with the man she falls in love with, Paul Emanuel. These are served in jest by Lucy herself acting as hostess. The references to chocolate could be considered symbolic of their underlying passion, a luxury which they share intimately on so many occasions. Ironically, it is even hinted towards the end of the book that Emanuel dies *en route* to the West Indies, the very place where so much cocoa was traded.

Slavery is imagined in a great deal of literature during the nineteenth century, the one that most resonates with me being Charlotte Brontë's *Jane Eyre*. When reading the book it's hard not to analyse the situation of Mr Rochester's 'madwoman in the attic', his wealthy Creole heiress, abandoned and locked away. Who was she exactly, what is her story? And did her behaviour justify such extreme treatment? Jean Rhys went some way to explore these questions in her 1966 novel *Wide Sargasso Sea*. Some writers, like Samuel Taylor Coleridge, were also public anti-slavery advocates. His 'Ode to the Slave-Trade' formed part of a series of lectures delivered in Bristol in 1795, damning man's obsession with social greed. He cited rum, cotton, log-wood, cocoa, coffee, pimento, ginger, indigo, mahogany and conserves as completely unnecessary luxuries.[13] Coleridge, however, was disdainful of the Emancipation Act of 1833 at a time when social evolution in the higher echelons of society was considered vulgar.

Charles Dickens' references to drinking chocolate in *A Tale of Two Cities* implies its outdated association with the French aristocracy. By the Victorian period, drinking chocolate as a beverage, opposed to eating it in solid bars, was no longer considered fashionable.

'Monseigneur was about to take his chocolate. Monseigneur could swallow a great many things with ease, and was by some few sullen minds supposed to be rather rapidly swallowing France; but, his morning's chocolate could not so much as get into the throat of Monseigneur, without the aid of four strong men besides the cook.'[14]

Here is a recipe for chocolate pudding, published the same year as Dickens' *A Tale of Two Cities,* showing how far in culinary terms chocolate had moved on from its origins as a beverage by this time.

Chocolate Pudding

Scrape down very fine two ounces of prepared chocolate, and add to it a tea-spoonful of nutmeg and cinnamon mixed. Put it into a saucepan and pour over it a quart of rich milk, stirring it well; cover it and let it come to a boil. Then stir up the chocolate and press out all the lumps; repeat this until it is quite smooth. Then stir in by degrees while it boils a quarter of a pound of sifted sugar and set it to cool. Beat eight eggs very well and pour through a strainer to the chocolate stir well and bake. This pudding should be eaten cold.[15]

One of the most famous Latin American writers of the twentieth century, Gabriel García Márquez, perhaps as a consequence of his heritage, refers to chocolate throughout many of his works. In *One Hundred Years of Solitude* he suggests that chocolate possesses the unique ability to levitate a priest, such are its magical powers. While James Joyce's *Ulysses* illustrates the shift in the accessibility of chocolate, then available in solid bars for wide consumption: 'The navvy, staggering forward, cleaves the crowd and lurches towards the tram siding on the farther side under the railway bridge bloom appears, flushed, panting, cramming bread and chocolate into a sidepocket.'[16]

***

By the mid-twentieth century, chocolate was being used in all manner of preparations, from pies, puddings and cakes to biscuits, confection and treats galore. When India gained its independence in 1947 many female writers came forward with their stories, like *Prison and Chocolate Cake*, published in 1954 by Nayantara Sahgal.

In this book of memoirs, written through the eyes of a young girl growing up in Allahabad with her parents and her uncle, Jawaharlal Nehru, who would become the first prime minister of India, Nayantara talks about how the family only had bread and butter for tea. So she is surprised one day when they are all served up a delicious 'rich, dark cake, chocolate through and through, with chocolate swirls on top'.[17] Little does she know that the cake represents a literal sweetener prior to the police descending to take away their father. One of many prison visits the family would encounter, for the good of the freedom movement.

This is an Indian recipe for *khoya* chocolate twists. *Khoya*, or *khoa*, is widely used across the Indian Subcontinent and is a type of curd, made simply by heating and thickening full-fat milk over several hours.

Khoya Chocolate Twists
250g khoya
2 tbsp cocoa powder
1 tbsp chocolate powder
1½ tbsp sugar (ground)
3½ tbsp walnuts (chopped)

In a dry hot karahi or a saucepan fry the khoya lightly till cooked.

When slightly cool add chocolate and cocoa powder and sugar and knead. Make thin rolls.

Spread chopped walnuts in a plate. Take each roll and roll in walnuts so that the walnuts stick to the roll.

Take two rolls and twist them together. Press both ends.

10 rolls will give 5 twisters.

You may decorate these with silver foil.[18]

Children's literature

There is a folk tale from the Netherlands called *The Chocolate House*. This is a story that was sent to a collector of folktales in the 1890s by a woman from Utrecht. It is essentially a Hansel and Gretel type scenario where two children get lost in the woods and stumble across a house entirely made of chocolate. Not believing their luck, they begin devouring the house, until a shrill voice cries out: 'Who's nibbling on my house? Surely tis a little mouse.'

An old lady appears and feeds the children at a table made of chocolate. They eat and drink from cups and plates of sugar, until they soon discover that their fate is to work for the witch forever, or they will both be turned into animals. The little girl manages to trick the old lady one day into leaning over the well in the garden, just a bit too far, before pushing her in. The children are reunited with their family in the woods, find the witch's treasure and live happily ever after. It's interesting that this version replaces the house with chocolate – a more contemporary seducer than gingerbread.[19]

The Dutch have a penchant for buttered bread covered in chocolate sprinkles. It is a real breakfast treat. The sprinkles even have a name, *Hagelslag*, meaning hailstorm. The falling sprinkles sound like falling hail. This is a custom which harks back to medieval times, when Dutch folk sprinkled anise seeds onto rusk bread, particularly on the arrival of a new baby. The fashion grew and the sprinkles became more elaborate. By the 1800s they were called *muisjes* (little mice) and came in a variety of colours. Even the shapes of these decorative hundreds and thousands alternated, with a smooth sugar coating prepared for a girl and a rough prickly coating for boys.[20] With the arrival of chocolate and its adoption as the favoured European start to the day – chocolate and bread in France, Italy and England, churros in Spain, and so on – it wasn't long before the Dutch were indulging in chocolate sprinkles on their bread.

***

Easily the most memorable of references to chocolate in fantasy literature is with the Harry Potter books. Chocolate frogs make a regular appearance, not least with introducing Professor Dumbledore to the readers, as well as to Harry, in *The Philosopher's Stone*. While a block of chocolate helps Harry recover following his encounter with a Dementor in the *Prisoner of Azkaban*. On the official site for Harry Potter and Fantastic Beasts, J. K. Rowling cryptically wrote, perhaps in reference to mental health generally:

> The mood-enhancing properties of chocolate are well known in both the Muggle and wizard worlds. Chocolate is the perfect antidote for anyone who has been overcome in the presence of Dementors, which suck hope and happiness out of their surroundings.
> Chocolate can only be a short-term remedy, however. Finding ways to fight off Dementors – or depression – are essential if one is to become permanently happier. Excessive chocolate consumption cannot benefit either Muggle or wizard.[21]

Enid Blyton's work is full of culinary references, although the phase 'lashings of ginger beer' never actually appeared in any of her books. In *Five Get into Trouble,* new boy Richard, temporarily joins the gang, and in a bid to impress brings 'a magnificent chocolate cake he saw in a first-class cake-shop' to one of their picnics. The book contains all the usual Blyton investigative plot antics, from mistaken identities, kidnapping, a lonely old house, imprisonment and escape, and the bad guys locked up by supper time.[22] Blyton was obsessed with strong morals and it has been quoted by some that she found children intrusive and irritating, which is why she preferred to engage with them through her writing.

The Chocolate Touch is a modern-day twist on the morals presented in the Greek legend of Midas, whose greed spawns his ability to turn all he touches into gold. Patrick Skene Catling's novel replaces gold with chocolate, which ultimately leads to youngster John Midas learning some scary lessons in self-control, excess and selfishness when his mother turns to chocolate as he kisses her on the cheek. The book is essentially a coming-of-age narrative, exploring many of the challenges that young children experience when advancing into their teenage years.

There are of course numerous other children's books that focus on the valuable lessons to be learnt from devouring too much chocolate.

The most obvious being *Charlie and the Chocolate Factory*, the film of which I have chosen to concentrate on later in this chapter. Then there's Robert Kimmel Smith's *Chocolate Fever* in which a young boy experiences the physical consequences of over-indulgence. Similarly with *Chocolatina* by Erik Craft, a book which finds the tiny heroine, Tina, take the phrase 'you are what you eat' to a whole new disturbing level. Then there's probably the scariest of them all, Chris Callaghan's *Chocopocalypse*. Yes, that's right, an impending disaster across the world that threatens the very existence of chocolate forever.

Film

For years the scene in Roald Dahl's classic *Matilda*, adapted for the screen in 1996, when Bruce Bogtrotter is forced to eat an entire chocolate cake in front of his classmates, haunted my dreams (still does a little, if truth be told). To see a child humiliated and tortured in such a degrading way, despite the humorous undertones is quite distressing and dark.

Here is a recipe for a chocolate cake worthy of recreating this scene (without the sinister elements), taken from an edition of *Life Magazine* in 1939.

> ### Double Mocha Chocolate Cake
> 2 cups sifted self-raising flour
> ¾ teaspoon salt
> 1 teaspoon bicarbonate of soda
> 4 squares unsweetened chocolate
> ½ cup butter
> ½ cup coffee syrup
> 2 cups sugar
> ¾ cup sour milk or buttermilk
> 2 teaspoons vanilla
> 2 eggs, unbeaten

To make coffee syrup: bring 1 1/3 cups of water and 3 tablespoons sugar to a boil; add ¾ cup ground coffee. Remove from the heat, cover and let stand for 5 minutes. Strain well.

Sift flour, add salt and bicarbonate of soda and sift well.

Combine chocolate, butter and ½ cup coffee syrup in top of a double boiler; place over boiling water and cook until chocolate has melted, stirring constantly. Cool and add sugar. Add flour and milk alternately in two parts, stirring until blended. Add vanilla and eggs and beat 2 minutes. Bake in two greased 9-in layer pans in moderate oven (350°F) for 30-35 minutes. Spread coffee butter frosting made with remaining coffee syrup (see below), between layers and on top and sides of cake. Decorate with a border of chopped pecans.

Coffee Butter Frosting
2/3 cup butter
5 cups sifted icing sugar
5 tablespoons coffee syrup

Cream butter. Add part of sugar gradually, blending after each addition. Add remaining sugar, alternately with coffee syrup, until of right consistency to spread.[23]

***

Como agua para Chocolate (Like Water for Chocolate) is a successful Mexican film from 1992, based on the 1989 novel of the same name by Laura Esquivel, with a Mexican female cook at the heart of a complex love story which ends in the tragic, unexpected and untimely death of both the main protagonists. Cooking represents the vessel through which love and hate are expressed, but it is also indicative of a lifetime of servitude for the central character, Tita. Numerous recipes from a cookbook are central to the plot, including this one for making chocolate tablets, which Tita prepares during the moment she suspects she is pregnant with her lover's child.

The first step is to toast the chocolate beans. It's good to use a metal pan rather than an earthenware griddle since the pores of the griddle soak up the oil the beans give off. It's very important to pay attention to this sort of detail, since the goodness of the chocolate depends on three things: that the chocolate beans used are good and without defect, that you mix several different types of beans to make the chocolate, and finally the amount of toasting.

It's advisable to toast the cocoa beans just until the moment they begin to give off oil. If they are removed from the heat before then, they will make a discoloured and disagreeable-looking chocolate, which will be indigestible. On the other hand, if they are left on the heat too long, most of the beans will be burned, which will make the chocolate bitter and acrid.

When the cocoa beans are toasted, as described above, they are cleaned using a hair sieve to separate the hull from the bean. Beneath the *metate* (grindstone) on which the chocolate is to be ground place a flat pan containing a hot fire; once the stone is warm, begin grinding the chocolate. Mix the chocolate with the sugar, pounding it with a mallet and grinding the two together. Then divide the mixture into chunks. The chunks are shaped by hand into tablets, long or round, according to your preference and set out to air. The dividing points can be marked with the tip of a knife if you wish.[24]

***

Chocolate has frequently been the catalyst in the darker side of many books and films dealing with human nature over the years. *Merci Pour le Chocolat* is a French film released in 2000 and based on the novel *The Chocolate Cobweb* written by Charlotte Armstrong in 1948. This is a suspenseful, family-based drama where one of the characters is suspected of poisoning a chocolate drink regularly prepared each evening.

The Chocolate War is a brutal American coming of age film of the 1980s, based on Robert Cormier's 1974 novel of the same name. Set in a Catholic boys' school with a plot around selling chocolates for fundraising, this is essentially a book about male power struggles, bullying, manipulation and psychological warfare. It contains violence, fear and skewed moralities.

Here is an American recipe for chocolate caramels with nuts from the early twentieth century. You probably wouldn't be able to sell these at school today, due to nut allergy protocol, but I'm sure all nut lovers will enjoy indulging in this simple recipe.

Chocolate Caramels with Nuts

Take one cup granulated sugar, two cups brown sugar, one cup milk, butter the size of an egg, two squares of bitter chocolate, one teaspoon of vanilla.

Boil until it hardens when dropped in cold water.

Remove from fire. Add one cup chopped nuts and turn into a buttered tin to cool.[25]

Romantics Anonymous or *Les Émotifs anonymes* is a French/Belgian film from 2010 with the central plot revolving around a small, old-fashioned failing chocolate manufacturer. It was adapted into a musical for the stage in 2017. Containing themes relating to social anxiety, recovery and rehabilitation it's probably rather more upbeat than the other black comedy set in a chocolate factory, *Consuming Passions*. Based on a play originally written by a team of writers including Monty Python legends Michael Palin and Terry Jones, the story involves the horrific consequences of three factory workers dying in a vat of chocolate and chopped into raspberry creams, which are destined for the open market retailing as new brand called *Passionelles*. The new brand becomes an instant success, leading, in Sweeney Todd fashion, to the issue of the factory owners having to come up with inventive ways of replicating the ingredients.

***

The most famous chocolate factory of all to be immortalised on the screen provides even broader themes of peculiarity, with Roald Dahl's character Charlie Bucket, whose family circumstances involve sharing a room with both grandparents in one bed, in a town overshadowed by the successes of a secretive, eccentric, genius chocolatier. *Charlie and The Chocolate Factory* has become a universally recognised classic novel and film, known and loved by millions, adapted frequently and critiqued by many. Inspired by Dahl's school days, during which Cadbury invited children in South Derbyshire to taste test new ranges, *Charlie and The Chocolate Factory* includes outrageously over-the-top characters, led by maverick confectioner Willy Wonka whose creations include the jaw-dropping spectacle of the river of chocolate, complete with edible surrounding foliage, and a description of a palace of chocolate made for an Indian prince. This contained hundreds of rooms 'made of either dark or light chocolate! The bricks were chocolate and the cement holding them together was chocolate and the windows were chocolate and all the walls and ceilings were made of chocolate, so were the carpets and the pictures, and the furniture and the beds; and when they turned on the taps in the bathroom, hot chocolate came pouring out.'

The blond, blue-eyed boy whom many of us associate with eleven-year-old Charlie Bucket was originally meant to be black, but was sadly changed to a white character at the bequest of Dahl's agent who felt a black child would not appeal to readers of the book. This is in stark contrast to criticisms of the original text portraying Oompa Loompas as black African pygmies, a racist accusation that persuaded Roald Dahl to rewrite the characters as hippy dwarves.[26]

Sophie Dahl is Roald Dahl's granddaughter, a model-turned-cook and recipe writer. This is her recipe for 'Uncle's Chocolate Soufflés with Brandied Cherries':

Uncle's Chocolate Soufflés with Brandied Cherries
3½ oz/100g really good-quality dark chocolate, chopped, chopped
4 egg whites
¼ cup/50g superfine sugar
2 egg yolks

For the brandied cherries
A handful of pitted cherries
1 tablespoon brandy
1 tablespoon sugar
1/3 cup/80ml water

Preheat the oven to 300°F/150°C. Using a knob of butter, grease the inside of four small ramekins.

Place your chocolate in a heatproof bowl over a saucepan of boiling water. Stir the chocolate so it melts evenly. Keep over low heat. In a very clean, dry bowl, whip the egg whites (an electric mixer makes life very easy). When the egg whites are glossy and stiffening, start adding the sugar bit by bit.

Take your chocolate off the heat and whisk the egg yolks into it. Very gently add the chocolate to the egg whites. The key is to fold rather than mix or whisk because you want the whites to stay as light as a feather. Gently divide among the ramekins, smoothing the edges with your thumb, which will help them rise. Place the ramekins on a baking sheet, place in the oven (and don't you open that door for twenty minutes). Serve immediately.

Make the cherries while the soufflés bake. In a small saucepan, combine the cherries with the brandy, sugar and water. Cook over low to medium heat for about 10 minutes, or until the cherries are soft and sloppy, but still holding their basic shape. Serve alongside your soufflés.[27]

***

Joanne Harris's *Chocolat*, both book and then hugely successful box office screen adaptation, is perhaps one of the best-known mainstream films with this sweet, exotic marvel at the heart of the narrative. Young, single, attractive mother Vianne and her daughter appear from nowhere to open a chocolate shop in a small French village during the start of Lent. The book focuses on Vianne's magical powers of persuasion with the locals, predicting their favourite flavours, winning their hearts at a time of fasting and coming into conflict with the local priest, Francis Reynaud. It's a book tied up with small village superstitions, magical undertones, resistance to conformity and fading traditions, with violent undertones of domestic abuse and prejudice. Reminding us that chocolate is never simply just about pleasant sugary indulgences.

Vianne is an enchanted and enchanting woman, with abilities to create bewitching confection, a nod to the enticing, seductive and magical properties of chocolate. Harris is from Yorkshire and grew up in an environment that revolved around her grandparents' sweet shop.

With the description of the opening of Viannes' shop, the reader imagines a mouth-watering visual feast of delicacies of which Harris is clearly familiar:

In glass bells and dishes lie the chocolates, the pralines, Venus's nipples, truffles, mendicants, candied fruit, hazelnut clusters, chocolate seashells, candied rose petals, sugared violets […] And in the middle she has built a magnificent centrepiece. A gingerbread house, walls of chocolate-coated pain d'epices with the detail piped on in silver and gold icing, roof tiles of Florentines studded with crystallized fruits, strange vines of icing and chocolate growing up the walls, marzipan birds singing in chocolate trees.[28]

In 2002 Harris published her cookery book, *The French Kitchen*, which includes a recipe for Nipples of Venus, actually an Italian recipe, but Harris found it impossible to omit.

Nipples of Venus
Makes about 70

For the filling
225g dark chocolate (70 per cent cocoa)
300ml double cream

For dipping
100g dark chocolate (70 per cent cocoa)
50g white chocolate

For the filling, break the chocolate into small pieces and place in a heatproof bowl. Make a bain-marie (put the bowl over a saucepan of simmering water) and allow the chocolate to melt. Heat the cream in a small saucepan and add it to the melted chocolate, mixing until evenly blended. Leave to cool for 2 hours. Then, using an electric whisk, beat until the mixture becomes stiff and holds its shape.

Line 3 baking trays with baking parchment. Put the filling mixture into a piping bag with a 1cm plain nozzle and pipe little mounds – or nipples – onto the baking parchment. Put in the fridge to chill and set.

Melt the dark chocolate in a bain-marie.

Take each chilled nipple and dip in the melted dark chocolate. Return to the parchment paper and leave to set for an hour.

Melt the white chocolate in a bain-marie.

Take each dark-chocolate nipple and dip the tip into the white chocolate. Leave to set.

Enjoy![29]

***

Lessons in Chocolate (*lezioni di cioccolato*) is a 2007 Italian film set in the legendary chocolate landscape of Perugia. This is a bittersweet comedy, naturally, as it centres around chocolate and wouldn't be in this book if it wasn't gritty in some way. It deals with issues concerning immigration, illegal work practices, social injustice and a sense of redemption. The focus of the film is a chocolate-making class, which takes place at the world-famous Baci (chocolate kisses) factory. According to their website, Baci Perugia are made from eight simple ingredients, including the central hazelnut which is never positioned in the same place apparently. That's quite a claim to boast.

Blood and Chocolate is a collaborative multinational film of the fantasy-horror genre, with a partial backdrop of a Romanian chocolate shop. It was adapted for the screen from a 1997 book in which the writer, Annette Curtis Klause, describes the heroine, Vivian, wrestling with the conflict of relenting to her destiny as a werewolf or remaining in the human world of the chocolate shop, which her aunt owns (and who is also a werewolf).

Romanian chocolate cream cakes, or *prajitura cu ciocolata*, which simply translates as 'cake with chocolate', is typical of the Romanian layered, torte-type of cakes that are popular throughout the country and which contain anything from pears to walnuts. They are also very popular additions at festivals and special occasions. There are quite a few 'fake chocolate' recipes in Romanian culture, like the chocolate salami, a no-bake treat made from crushed biscuits and a variety of fruit, moulded into a log, refrigerated and cut into slices. These were created during the Communist era, between the 1940s and 1980s, a time when food was scarce and chocolate certainly would have been an even scarcer luxury that was occasionally imported from China.

Prajitura cu ciocolata
Makes eight

For the sponge discs
3 eggs, separated
60g (2½ oz) caster sugar
1 tsp cream of tartar
Juice and zest of 1 lemon
75g (3oz) plain flour

For the filling
150g (5oz) double cream, at room temperature.
30g (1¼ oz) icing sugar
125g (4oz) dark chocolate, melted

For the syrup
100ml (31/2 fl oz) water
100g (31/2 oz) caster sugar
50ml (2fl oz) rum or brandy

For the chocolate glaze
100g (31/2 oz) milk chocolate, melted

To assemble
200ml (7fl oz) double cream, whipped
Cocoa powder (optional)

Preheat the oven to 180°C/350°F/gas mark 4. Line a baking tray with baking paper and use a pencil to draw sixteen 8cm (3in) diameter circles onto the paper.

To make the sponge discs, whisk the egg whites until they form soft peaks, then add the sugar and cream of tartar, whisking to the consistency of stiff meringue. Add the egg yolks and lemon juice and zest, sift the flour and fold gently until well incorporated. Pipe or spoon equal quantities of the mixture into each drawn circle, if possible forming a slight dome shape. Bake for 15 minutes, or until firm and golden in colour and cool on a wire rack.

To make the filling, whisk the cream with the icing sugar until thick, then gently add the melted chocolate, combining well. Transfer to a piping bag and refrigerate to firm up.

To make the syrup, bring the water and sugar to the boil in a pan over a medium heat and stir in the rum or brandy. Leave to cool.

To assemble take half the sponge discs and dip the tops one by one into the chocolate glaze, then set aside – the chocolate doesn't even have to be around the edges. Take the unglazed discs and brush them with a little of the rum syrup, then pipe the chocolate cream filling on top. Place the glazed discs on top of the filling, then spoon over or pipe a little of the whipped cream onto each one and dust with cocoa powder, if liked. Serve on the day of making.[30]

***

In *Rosemary's Baby,* both book and film, Minnie Castevet makes a series of herbal drinks for Rosemary Woodhouse, the targeted vessel for Satan's spawn, and demonstrates her skills in pharmacopeia by making her a chocolate mousse on the night that the Woodhouses plan to conceive. Rosemary complains about the chalky taste and refuses to finish the dish, but falls unconscious moments later.

Here is a recipe for chocolate mousse from the 1960s, the time when *Rosemary's Baby* was introduced to the world.

French Chocolate Mousse
The writer advises: Made at home for one tenth of what it costs in shops, this mousse gives an idea of what a real one tastes like. Since it's about as rich as desserts come, a small pot de crème per person is as much as one can take. A good dessert when eating out of doors. Serve in sealed paper cups with wooden spoons.

Fills one glass dish or about 12 ramekins. Prepared in 30 minutes with electric beater. Chill before serving.

8oz sweet chocolate
1oz bitter chocolate
5 tbsp granulated sugar
3 tbsp liquid coffee

6 eggs separated
2 sticks sweet butter
½ cup heavy cream whipped

Stand eggs at room temperature for 20 minutes (cold eggs don't whip up nearly so well). Put chocolate, butter, coffee and sugar in top of double boiler, be sure hot water doesn't touch the top pan and melt chocolate over a low fire. It melts by itself in about 10 minutes – stir occasionally. Meanwhile whisk egg whites and cream in separate bowls. Check melted chocolate for graininess due to unmelted sugar; if grainy, cook a little longer and stir before removing from fire; mixture should be smooth. Pour it into a large mixing bowl, add egg yolks, one at a time creaming them in until smooth, and so on until the last egg. By then the mixture is shiny like satin. Stand mixing bowl in cold water if necessary until just warm. Fold in the whipped cream, then fold in the egg whites. Pour in glass dish or cups. Chill before serving.

Mousse keeps several days under refrigeration.[31]

***

In the USA today there exists the very real problem of dealing with a growing number of illegal *churro* vendors, particularly in New York City where female street vendors in particular are arrested with some frequency for operating without permits. In 2019 a picture of a woman selling *churros* being handcuffed in a Brooklyn subway station went viral. One week later another woman selling churros was arrested nearby in a similar way. Mobile food vending has become a black market for licensing. With only 2,900 permits issued each year in New York, demand significantly exceeds supply, with many permit owners leasing them out to other vendors – often poor, immigrant families who are charged over 100 times the price. There is no paperwork to go with these transactions.

A recent survey investigating female street vendors operating in New York City determined that of the fifty women surveyed, thirty-six were either from Mexico or Ecuador, with an average age of forty-six. They were also the main wage earner in the family. Seventy-two per cent of these women did not have permits.[32]

The short film, *Churros*, released to critical acclaim in 2019, tackles this contemporary social issue through the story of a young teenage Mexican boy who lives with his street vending single mother and younger sister in Brooklyn. Torn between his extraordinary abilities as a break-dancer, the lure of a better life and loyalty to his family, *Churros* provides remarkable insight into this dangerous and desperate world. Spanish *churros* (fritters), are basically elongated fried dough sticks, made of flour, water, salt and oil, similar to doughnuts and then eaten after being dipped in thick hot chocolate. Mexican *churros* are often coated in cinnamon and served alongside chocolate or sometimes *dulce de leche*. In Uruguay they also eat them stuffed with cheese. There is confusion as to the origins of the *churro*, but it is likely that they are an adaptation of the similar Chinese *youtiao*, replicated by visiting Portuguese merchants. Traditional street sellers would squeeze the batter into cans of boiling oil.

***

The Licensing Act of 1737 was introduced by British Prime Minister Walpole, who was tired of being ridiculed in satirical works for the stage. This new act forbade the performance of any plays 'for gain, hire or reward' and plays were only allowed in theatres located within the City of Westminster, limiting performances to Drury Lane and Covent Garden. Theatre managers got around this legislation by offering free plays while buying a pint of ale, or charging for other events where plays were performed during the intermission or during an art exhibition. All of this was frequently accompanied by the lure of dishes of chocolate for sale, with which you could enjoy your 'free' play.[33]

Theatres were affected for a number of years in the earlier part of the twentieth century when it was illegal to sell chocolates after 8.00 pm. Numerous venues were prosecuted for doing so. I include cinemas in the term 'theatres' as the two were somewhat intertwined by this time. The rise in talking pictures from the late 1920s led to a radical change in the way theatres operated, with live entertainment becoming more about movie watching.

Chocolate retail legislation had everything to do with shopkeepers who were regulated by The Early Closing Act losing out financially. Why should the shops suffer a loss of trade when theatres could continue selling their chocolatey wares? Equally, the theatres criticised the decision of

Parliament, with chocolate sellers parading London's streets on 26 May 1920 in protest at the 'no chocolates after 8.00 pm' restrictions.[34] A month later some 200 London music-hall chocolate sellers arrived outside the Houses of Parliament and sailed up and down the Thames on a barge and a steam tug, protesting against the chocolate legislation.[35] This was challenged further in 1921 with demands for theatrical venues to extend their retail hours to 9.30 pm.[36] Apparently, chocolate sales represented 10 per cent of all turnover in theatre refreshment departments in 1919, so it's unsurprising perhaps that so much political pressure was being placed on government at the time to loosen the restrictions on legislation.[37]

Of the sixteen general chocolate sellers listed in the 1911 census, ten were under the age of eighteen, one was nineteen, two were in their sixties and the other three aged thirty-seven, forty-one and fifty-four. It seems that it was probably more of a young person's game at this time, perhaps because children and young people were easy to exploit and cheap to employ. Three of the chocolate sellers who were also among the youngest listed are specifically identified as working in theatres, but that's not to say the others weren't also engaged in this capacity, as many vendors were moving off the streets and into the warm embrace of burgeoning retail opportunities.

Not all young cinema chocolate sellers were to be pitied though. Two youths, one of whom was only twelve years of age, selling chocolate at the Picture Palace, Millom, were charged with stealing films and selling them onto collectors.[38]

There were risks too for vulnerable young people working as chocolate sellers in the theatres and picture houses of the earlier part of the twentieth century. As the case of a fourteen-year-old girl employed in Uxbridge demonstrates, when she accused cinema operator Gilbert Wright of sexual assault. Having missed her last train, she ended up going home with Wright, telling him she was afraid of returning so late, perhaps in anticipation of a scolding from her parents. It was in Wright's bedroom where the girl accused him of the assault. She left early in the morning, agreeing to meet up again the following Saturday, and went to find a friend in Ealing to set her up in accommodation. Having failed to secure a bed, she ended up walking the streets of London all night, before being found by police. She informed the officers that she was unhappy living with her stepfather and that she had planned to commit suicide. Gilbert Wright denied knowing the girl was just fourteen and told the court that he had tried everything to get her to go home and talk things through with her family. He demonstrated an excellent character and witnesses came forward to vouch for Wright, which led to a lenient sentence of just two months.[39]

These sorts of incidents clearly weren't isolated either. Sixteen-year-old Francis Denvers Mohur was accused of housebreaking and to 'have associated with a fourteen-year-old girl chocolate seller' in London in 1916.[40] Perhaps one of the most disturbing stories of all is that of Betty Buckingham, who, in 1938, was sixteen-years-old and working as a chocolate seller at the Regent Cinema, Chelmsford. One day Betty received a letter, simply addressed to 'the chocolate girl'. The writer expressed his admiration from afar and invited her to meet with him at a place where she would not be harmed, but would be expected to watch as he horsewhipped himself. He requested she cut her hair short and included a ten shilling note along with the letter, equal to a week's salary for a chocolate seller at that time.

Frightened by the note's content, Betty took it to the police who arranged for her to meet the man, together with several disguised detectives acting as vagrants in the vicinity. Sure enough, Betty's 'admirer' appeared out of the darkness, holding a whip and announcing himself. As instructed, Betty coughed loudly, signalling to the police to jump out and apprehend the stranger who was later questioned back at the station.[41]

***

One final note to add to this section on theatrical venues is something that continues to threaten the sanity of many an audience member today – be it live or film action – the dreaded loud talker, mobile phone user or snack paper rustler. It seems that this must have been a similar issue in the early twentieth century, with Rowntree's of York developing a special box of chocolates in 1929 specifically designed for theatre-goers. There were no paper wrappings and the chocolates were packed between soft wads of soundless tissue. They could be found on sale in theatres nationwide at 2s a box.[42] That would be around £5 in today's money.

If you didn't have that sort of additional cash to flash after all the expenses of paying for your performance and getting to the venue itself, perhaps there was an option to bring your own snacks. If so, these macaroons, the recipe for which was published in the *Rowntree's Little Cook-Book of 'Elect' (Cocoa powder) Recipes* may have been ideal.

Elect Macaroons
(makes eighteen)
Two egg whites beaten stiff
One cup sugar
One cup rolled oats
¼ tsp vanilla essence
1 tbsp Elect cocoa
Pinch of salt

Mix the sugar, salt and cocoa, add to the well beaten whites of eggs. Add the rolled oats and vanilla.

Drop from a teaspoon on to a buttered tin and bake in a very slow oven for about half an hour.

These biscuits keep well if stored in a tin box.[43]

Music and art

Chocolate can now be manipulated and moulded into any shapes, from chocolate skulls to penises. *Death by chocolate,* by the American conceptual artist Stephen J. Shanabrook, depicted a dismembered human body complete with graphic entrails and was exhibited at The Museum of Old and New Art in 2011. Shanabrook worked in a chocolate factory during his early youth and has become best known for working with this particular medium in a somewhat morbid way. He has travelled around the world to take casts in chocolate of fatal wounds, including gunshots and protruding eyeballs. These were wrapped in shiny paper and placed in a gift box entitled *Chocolate Box Morgue.*

British artist Tom Martin paints hyper-realistic images of food, in particular chocolate. Martin's paintings are so life-like they almost appear to be photographs. His same-scale naked woman alongside packets of Aero and Crunchie, titled *Contemplation*, is a reflection of modern society's pressures on women fixated with image over confection, while his impossibly seductive *Chocolate Donut*, with the light glistening on the surface of the icing is designed to tempt and tantalise the viewer.

In contrast to Louis Marin Bonnet's eighteenth-century painting, *The Proposal*, it demonstrates how little the association between chocolate with love, sex and seduction has altered. In the painting, a man proposes ardently on one knee to a woman in a beautiful room, with the main focus on the table and its silver chocolatiere.

The antithesis to this must surely exist in controversial performance artist Karen Finley's live spectacle in which she covered her entire body (wearing only pants and a bandana) in chocolate and sprinkles while performing a piece called *We Keep Our Victims Ready* to audiences at the Sushi Gallery, San Diego, in 1989. Mocking women's tired old association with all things sweet, she screams 'smear chocolate all over body until you are a human shit – eat Suzy Q's chocolate-covered cherries.' Finley's work dealt with issues of misogyny, with chocolate representing the verbal and physical abuses of women. Suzy Q's is an American brand of chocolate snack cakes with a white crème filling.

The following recipe for Suzy Q's has been taken from cookpad.com and was contributed by Raven Decatur.

Suzy Q Cakes with cream filling
11/3 cups plain flour
1 cup granulated sugar
2/3 cup unsweetened cocoa powder
1 tsp bicarbonate of soda
1/2 tsp salt
1 cup milk or buttermilk
2 eggs
1 stick softened butter

Filling
1 stick softened butter
11/4 cup confectioners' sugar
11/4 cup marshmallow fluff
1 tsp vanilla extract

In a large mixing bowl, combine flour, sugar, baking soda, cocoa powder and salt. Combine well.

Next add eggs, milk and butter, dash of vanilla extract (optional)

On low, mix until well combined, turn mixer to high and whip until fluffy. About 2 minutes.

Preheat oven to 350°F. In a 9 x 13-in baking dish, spray with non-stick spray. Add cake mix and smooth evenly.

Bake for 20-25 minutes or until toothpick inserted in middle comes out clean.

Cool on wire rack.

While cake is cooling, mix filling ingredients until light and fluffy. Whip on high until smooth.

When cake is completely cooled, either cut into circles with biscuit cutter and split in half, or rectangles for individual servings. Cut in half. Spread filling between layers. Top with other half.

You can also just cut cake in half, cut each half into two layers and fill in between layers. You can also just use filling as frosting.[44]

***

Music and chocolate historically afford a powerful and evocative combination, from the working songs of the plantations to more contemporary associations. The Cocoa Panyols are a very specific and unique ethnic group who represent a blend of Venezuelan and Trinidadian people who share a mixture of racial origins including African, Spanish and Amerindian (indigenous peoples of the Americas) ancestors. This is a fading culture which over the centuries has become merged through mixed marriages amongst Trinidadian or French Creole communities.

Panyols were once a tight-knit society of their own, created by the presence of existing Spanish communities in Trinidad, who settled there following the Spanish colonization of the fourteen-hundreds, alongside slaves of African origin who were transported to Trinidad by the Spanish around the sixteenth century. These communities were then joined by large numbers of Venezuelan peasants and agricultural workers entering Trinidad to seek work in the developing cocoa industry in the nineteenth century.

The peoples of all these groups merged and lived amicably together, perhaps out of a shared bond symbolic of their struggles and displacement. They lived and worked together successfully on the cocoa plantations in the north of the island.

The Caura Valley was once recognised as the main Panyol community until the British government, which controlled Trinidad, moved all the inhabitants out during the 1940s in order to construct a dam. It was this move that largely ended up dividing the Panyol society, although many also moved together to an adjacent valley.

There are still aspects of their culture that have sustained, including Parang, a form of folk music played on the mandolin or violin, accompanied by percussion instruments like maracas. It is a form of music most associated with Christmas or waking people from their beds, as the musicians serenade from house to house.[45]

The Garland Encyclopedia of World Music suggests that the Zarabanda, a popular dance of Guatemalan and Mexican origin, may be one that evolved in Spanish colonial cacao slave plantations. Robert Stevenson elaborates on this theory by entertaining the possibility that early Mexicans danced the Zarabanda, or Sarabande while honouring the gods in their temples.[46] It is described as a provocative and libidinous dance. So perhaps it may well have been performed after indulging in cacao.

Certainly, the Cocoa-Rina-Dance is one which remains in use today on some plantations, even acting as a participatory tourist attraction on the Caribbean island of St Lucia. Workers perform barefoot on the cacao beans to polish them. This is the final act of preparation before the beans are bagged up. Singing would frequently accompany this dance. If you have an urge to listen then the Library of Congress have a cocoa-dancing song in their archives, recorded in 1942 in Trinidad.

Michael Humphrey's memoirs of growing up in the Caribbean in the 1940s, *Portrait of a Sea Urchin: A Caribbean Childhood,* talks about the bawdy nature of some of these accompanying ballads, which covered adult themes, the like of which included challenging unfaithful men.

Kalinda (Calinda) was another dance/stick fight that evolved in Trinidad and Tobago in the 1720s, created by Africans who were sold into slavery. Johnny Coomansingh talks about the regular Saturday stick-fighting contests that took place on his godmother's cocoa plantation in his memoir, *Cocoa Woman.* These would be staged in a sort of arena called a *gayelle.* The blood from the wounds was collected in a 'blood hole'. It was a ritualistic process, with African drums and chanting echoing all around the estate. He also recalls his godmother making Creole chocolate tea served with *sada roti*, a basic flat bread.[47]

Cocoa production in Trinidad and Tobago has been in the hands of the British, the French and the Spanish, and as a consequence the type of cocoa grown has become a hybrid of different variants, giving it a unique flavour. The chocolate tea (chocolate being the 'tea of the gods') of this region therefore bears little resemblance to our traditional expectations of European hot chocolate. Creole chocolate tea is a blend of chocolate with a variety of spices, creating a pungent and heavier drink. The drink is made from solid balls of ground-up cocoa beans, or sticks of cocoa, which are grated finely and boiled up with cinnamon and nutmeg in water, before adding sweetened milk or honey.

The following account of cacao production, taken from an observer known only as B.A., writing in the *Colonial Magazine and Commercial Maritime Journal* of 1844, describes their experiences of a visit to the Reconocimiento plantation in Trinidad, one of the largest in the Caribbean:

> Cacao is prepared for market in the following manner: the pod having been gathered from the tree by the hand, or by means of a hooked pole, where that mode is impracticable from the branches being too high, it is collected into large heaps on the ground and allowed to soften, or sweat as it is termed by the planters for three or four days. The pods are then opened by means of a longitudinal cut with a cacao knife, and the seeds and pulp extracted with the fingers and thrown into another heap, where the mass is allowed to sweat for two or three weeks more. At the end of this period fermentation has loosened the seeds from their pulpy bed when they are easily separated from it and taken to the drying house in baskets. The nuts are now daily spread in the sun upon a large cemented, or sometimes only carefully swept, esplanade in front of the drying house, where they are turned frequently and carefully during the day. At night they are again housed. The drying-house is furnished with large trays in which the cacao is received during the process of drying and which can be run out at ports in the

side of the building when the uncertainty of the weather may render that plan advisable. The operation of drying is continued for about three weeks more or less, according to the favourable or unfavourable state of the weather, when the nuts become sufficiently dry and are packed for sale and shipment. Coarse bags made of Oznaburgs sacking, having been prepared each large enough to contain a fanega in weight. They are filled with the produce which is now ready to be conveyed to market in Port of Spain, on mules backs or in carts, as the nature of the roads will admit, where it is usually immediately sold and shipped for Europe, as it is an article which deteriorates by keeping.

***

The Spanish enslaved Africans in Venezuela as early as the 1600s. The village of Chuao is recognised as one of the oldest and most renowned cocoa plantations in that region. Today it continues to yield some of the most expensive, high quality cacao in the world. The area remains inhabited by descendants of African slave populations and is accessible only by boat. The plantation fell into the hands of the Roman Catholic Church in the mid-seventeenth century, where it remained until the early part of the 1800s, becoming the property of the University of Central Venezuela, before it fell under the jurisdiction of the State.

Due to its remote location and its religious past the village has adopted a local integration of African and Spanish Catholic traditions and cultures. The most famous of these, now recognised by UNESCO, revolves around the Corpus Christi celebrations and the ceremony of Los Diablos Danzantes (dancing devils) held around the end of May/ beginning of June. The foundation of these festivities is rooted in the arrival of African slaves to cultivate the cocoa and closely identifies with the African drumming rhythms of the *golpes de tambor*, a combination of drum, dance and verse. Despite being organised by the women of Chuao, only the men are allowed to beat the drums, while the women sing and the two come together for the dancing. These are sexualized dances combining both African and Spanish techniques, the thumping of the feet and the swishing of skirts. Hot chocolate and rum are consumed in order to sustain participants as they continue part of the procession throughout the night.[48]

The following recipe is an old traditional recipe for *Marquesa de Chocolate*, or Chocolate Marquise, which I sourced from a Venezuelan tourist site online. It is not a recipe which can be found that readily in books and often requires translation as this one did. It seems to be a recipe which has many impersonators, from soufflés to mousse. The original version is a no-bake layered cake which originates from Venezuela and requires the acquisition of specialist *Maria* biscuits, popular in some European and Latin American countries, with a very similar consistency to English rich tea biscuits.

Marquesa de Chocolate, or Chocolate Marquise
750g Maria cookies/Rich Tea biscuits
1l milk for the pudding and milk for soaking the biscuits
Chocolate sprinkles

For the chocolate pudding
1l milk
4 egg yolks, beaten
300g dark chocolate
2 tbsp butter
125g sugar
1 tsp vanilla
2 tsp corn flour dissolved in 2 tblsp milk.

In a pot with a heavy bottom place the milk, the sugar and the vanilla. When it is warm add the previously beaten egg yolks, stir constantly. In a double boiler melt the chocolate with the butter, when it is melted, pour it onto the milk mixture and continue stirring. Dissolve the cornstarch in a little milk and add it to the previous preparation. Continue stirring until it thickens, lower the heat and reserve.

To make the chocolate marquise, take a packet of Maria cookies and presoak in milk. In a large glass oblong dish place a layer of chocolate pudding, followed by a layer of the soaked cookies. Continue layering ending with the chocolate pudding. Set in the fridge overnight.

It can be garnished with chocolate sprinkles or chocolate chips, there are also those who use sliced and toasted almonds or cookies, others dip the cookies in liquor.[49]

***

Early cocoa plantations like Chuao in Venezuela would initially have served to produce chocolate for medicinal purposes. It wasn't until the 1800s that it began to be commercially recognised as a product for eating, and this is when demand would have soared.

Chocolate would originally have been sold in apothecaries and pharmacies throughout Europe and of course in America where the celebrated drugstore culture has now become legendary.

As Britain's apothecaries evolved into pharmacies dispensing modern medicines, the same happened in the United States around the time of the Civil War era. But one addition that Britain lacked was the soda machine. No self-respecting drugstore in America would have been without a soda fountain, a trend that continued right up until the latter part of the twentieth century. Undoubtedly these served communities particularly well during the prohibition years.

Sodas quickly extended to malted drinks, ice creams and milkshakes, becoming stores in their own right, called malt shops. Malt shops were incredibly popular with teenagers and young people in 1950's America, a time immortalised in Doris Day's 1947 song, *A Chocolate Sundae on a Saturday Night*.

A chocolate sundae on a Saturday night.
What a way to make an evenin' end right.
The moo-oon was fine, the dancin' divine.
Let's head for the drug store at Maple and Vine.

Try this Chocolate Sundae Pudding recipe and feel yourself being transported back to 1950's America.

Chocolate Sundae Pudding
1 cup flour
½ tsp salt
2/3 cup sugar

2 tbsp melted butter
½ cup chopped nuts
2 tsp baking powder
2 tbsp grated chocolate
½ cup milk
1 tsp vanilla

Topping
¼ cup white sugar
3 tbsp grated chocolate
1 tsp vanilla
½ cup brown sugar
¼ tsp salt
1 cup boiling water

Sift the flour, baking powder, salt, sugar and chocolate and add milk, melted butter, vanilla and finally the nuts. Spread in a pan and make the topping.

Combine the sugar, chocolate and salt thoroughly and spread over the mixture in the pan.

Put the vanilla in the boiling water and pour all over. Do not stir.

Bake at 350°F or 180°C for 35-45 minutes.

Perhaps due to the historic popularity of the soda fountain, there has always been a much wider variety of fizzy watered-down drinks in America than Europe, all falling within the broad category of what is known as soda. This includes chocolate sodas, which were prepared with a chocolate syrup. *The American Druggist and Pharmaceutical Record* of 1894 reported that the most popular soda at that time by far was the chocolate variety.[50] This is perhaps because soda fountain chocolate syrup was always prepared in-house at the drug-store, to ensure it competed with all the other leading brands.

The addition of a high-quality chocolate was considered imperative for the true success of a chocolate soda.[51] A university study in 2010 took ninety samples of beverages from soda fountains across a 22-mile radius in Roanoke, Virginia. Almost half of the samples tested positive for faecal contamination, with some samples also containing E.coli and antibiotic-resistant microbes. In fact, many of the sample beverages fell below drinking-water regulations set by the US Environmental Protection Agency. These findings were published in the *Journal of Food Microbiology*.[52]

If that wasn't disturbing enough, the location of the research is part of a much wider and chilling piece of American history, involving an abandoned colony of families, established by Sir Walter Raleigh in 1587 in attempt to secure a settlement in that part of Virginia. Despite financial support from England, the men, women and children at Roanoke were abandoned. Supplies were delayed for several years as a consequence of the Anglo-Spanish war and by the time assistance arrived, the settlement was empty, everyone had disappeared. Aside from the fortified camp, the only other remaining evidence was one word carved into a tree – CROATOAN.[53]

Chocolate Soda

Serves 1

3 tbsp chocolate syrup

2 scoops chocolate ice cream

1 scoop vanilla ice cream

1 cup soda or sparkling water

Place the syrup in a 12-oz glass. Add the ice cream, alternating the chocolate with the vanilla. Add soda water and stir until foamy. Serve immediately.[54]

***

The Beatles 1968 song *Savoy Truffle* has an upbeat Blues/rock riff, dedicated to the band's friend, musician Eric Clapton's love of chocolate. Written by George Harrison, it lists Clapton's favourite flavours, along with a stark warning for his teeth. The varieties listed in the song came from a well-known box of chocolates, popular at the time, called Mackintosh's Good News Chocolates. Mackintosh's was established by John Mackintosh and his wife towards the end of the nineteenth century and they were best known for their toffee. The company merged with Rowntree to become Rowntree Mackintosh in the 1960s, which was later absorbed by Nestlé. The savoy truffle of the song title was alleged to have been the most prized of all the eleven flavours in the box.

Creme tangerine and Montelimart
A ginger sling with a pineapple heart
Coffee dessert, yes, you know it's *Good News*
But you'll have to have them all pulled out
After the Savoy truffle.

In 1895 a French patisserie in the Savoy region in the French Alps (named after the famous House of Savoy family) is said to have invented truffles. So, perhaps the savoy truffle is just a traditional creamy dark chocolate ganache mix in the shape of a sphere. Or is it connected to the Savoy Hotel in London? There is also a mushroom truffle, which grows in Savoy, noted for its garlic flavour and which can grow to up to 2lb in weight.[55] Or could it even be a relative of the fatless sponge cake, the Savoy cake, also from the Savoy region and popular in the 1700s? The possibilities are boundless.

Montelimar nougat is a very old French creation, named after the town in which it was conceived, although nougat itself undoubtedly has Middle Eastern origins. It was the Arnaud-Soubeyran collaboration of confectioner and manager-wife team that made Montelimar nougat a commercial success. Their life and legacy lives on at the Montelimar Museum and the town's oldest factory, where you can purchase just about any type of nougat. The Arnaud-Soubeyran website provides an old nougat recipe, which happens to be one of the few non-chocolate recipes I have included in this book. To transform it into the Good News boxed chocolate of the Beatles song, simply dip and cover the finished product in your favourite melted *couverture*.

Nougat from Arnaud-Soubeyan, Montelimar
575g whole almonds with or without skin
230g of crystal sugar
230g of lavender honey
A sheet of unleavened bread.

In a saucepan melt the honey and sugar, bring the temperature to 160°C.

Stir in almonds.

Spread the hot dough over a sheet of unleavened bread and let cool.

Store away from moisture.[56]

Another historic confectioner, Elite Chocolate, which you can read more about in Chapter Three, is remembered in the words of the Israeli author, poet and lyricist, Yehonatan Geffen, who wrote the song, *The Smell of Chocolate*:

At the edge of Ramat Gan there's a special place
Where you can stand and smell Chocolate in the air
There's a big tall house
With three chimneys and no windows
And thirty machines inside working all day and night
Seventy workers in aprons and mitts
Making chocolate of every kind.

Chorus:
Small chocolate, big chocolate (sho-ko-ko-)
Expensive chocolate, cheap chocolate
Chocolate with nuts and plain
For the rich people, and for us all
And the smell is free
so all the citizens
Stop to sniff the air (mmm...).[57]

Geffen has been criticised for his outspoken, extreme left-wing ideals and for exposing controversial military and government atrocities, making him a target for political intimidation.

The following recipe for Chocolate Cheesecake has been taken from the Elite Chocolate website:

For the Base
150g biscuits with cacao
75g butter

For the Stuffing
320g (4x80g) Elite bitter chocolate
1 package (200ml) cream
400g mild cream cheese
1 water glass condensed yoghurt
1 water glass sugar

3 eggs
1 package vanilla

For the Top
100g Elite bitter chocolate
1 package cream
1 tsp butter

To prepare the cake base, crush the biscuits until they get as small as flour. Melt the butter and pour it onto the biscuits, mixing until they feel smooth. Spread this dough in a cake mould or tray with your hands. Put the cake mould into the fridge.

For the stuffing: Put Elite bitter chocolate and cream in a pot and warm them up until they melt, stirring continuously. After the mixture gets smooth, take it off the stove until it gets cool.

In another bowl, mix the mild cream cheese, condensed yoghurt, sugar and vanilla together. Break the eggs one by one and mix for 20-30 seconds after each egg. Finally, pour the melted chocolate into this mixture and stir them well.

Take the cake base out of the fridge and pour the stuffing. Put it into the preheated oven (180°C) and cook for 50-55 minutes. When you turn off the oven, it may still feel soft; however, it will get stiffer as it gets cooler.

For the top: In a small pot, put the chocolate, cream and butter; cook them until the chocolate melts. Take it off the stove, stir occasionally until it gets cooler. After getting cool, pour the mixture (ganache) onto the cake and leave the cake in the fridge at least for 4 hours. You can put different nuts to ornate your cake.[58]

***

When I initially approached this book I hadn't imagined that it would take me on a journey discovering so many diverse chocolate based connections – murderers, pirates, adventurers and disasters – and

I certainly would never have associated chocolate with the arts to the extent that I have.

It still amazes me, even after writing this book, how very much society relies on the cacao bean. How did we become so dependant and wanton with it? Imagine what the world would be like if we hadn't usurped the ancient folklore of the Mayans and Aztecs. Did their venerable superstitions curse the burgeoning European societies of the seventeenth century, gifting us a life-long product that would yield the destruction of whole communities, with the capacity to destroy, seduce and debauch.

Yet, conversely, chocolate undoubtedly has the power to nurture, revive and restore the spirit, with a capacity for such versatility that it can be equally at home in a cup of boiling water, moulded into confectionery, baked into light and fluffy creations or grated into rich savoury casseroles.

The range of recipes that have been carefully sourced and included throughout hopefully reflect the diverse nature of chocolate. Many of them are old and may at times require adapting or a little additional research. This is an historical account after all, which demands relevant context. It is interesting to observe the extent to which recipes incorporating chocolate have evolved over the centuries: from simple drinks and medicinal remedies to the gradual realisation that it might work in rudimental baking, the experimental years and into the artistic and elaborate projects that can be seen today everywhere, in shop window displays and on reality television programmes.

The greatest example of this in recent years has to be the brand Choccywoccydoodah, specialist chocolatiers originating in Brighton and famed for their unusual and intricate chocolate creations. Founded in 1994, the company went on to provide a range of masterpieces for high profile celebrities and featured in a long-running television series. The business went into administration in 2019 as a consequence of a challenging trading environment. Whether this was related to the huge explosion in high-street and online specialist 'artisan' chocolatiers in recent years, or the changing value of cocoa generally is not clear. However, one quick online search reveals a rather saturated market.

There are of course those who stand out: the many illustrious and historic manufacturers who have stood the test of time and the new, experimental chocolate makers such as Paul A. Young, who isn't so new anymore, but who does seem to rise above the masses. Perhaps it's his natural approach, his understanding and appreciation of where each bar of chocolate comes from, together with his experimental flair.

I visited Cockington Chocolates in Devon a year or so before writing this book and was introduced to Ruby chocolate, which, to my shame I had not really much experience of. Ruby chocolate has evolved from a specific variety of Brazilian cocoa beans, whether it is actually a new variety of chocolate, or simply another marketing scam, it does seem to be growing in popularity.

There is a current trend for novelty chocolate, including hot chocolate bombs, hollow chocolate spheres filled with cocoa powder and marshmallows. The ball is simply added to a mug of hot milk, where you can observe it melting, revealing the mallowy chocolate within. While the marshmallow rises, the cocoa powder and the shell of the original chocolate ball mix with the milk, creating a decadent hot chocolate.

But what next for chocolate? Has it anywhere new to go? With increasing demand on resources and worldwide pressures to maintain ethical practices, in an industry which is anything but ethical most of the time, how will it survive? There are new burgeoning trends to mix savoury items with the contrasting sweetness of chocolate, to ensure chocolate is more plant-based and free of additives, and, as mentioned at the start of this book, a concerted effort to find alternatives to chocolate production, including genetic modification.

At the time of writing many chocolatiers have resorted to online retail during the pandemic, with reports of domestic comfort eating rising. Boom time for chocolate perhaps?

One thing is certain, society has become reliant on chocolate and ways will always be found to ensure demand is met. It continues to be the backbone for activities that require endurance, boosting performance and energy. Chocolate remains a drug as well as a food and it still has the potential to mask other more potent drugs. I'm willing to bet it remains highly prized in the military too.

When you next reach for that little bit of comfort food, that sweet Christmas gift, that tempting cake or biscuit, do try and remember the legacy of chocolate, its origins, how far it has travelled – both spiritually and in terms of environmental footprint. And consider those who have sweated and tormented over its production, and, most importantly, remember what it is capable of.

In the wake of annihilation, homicide, genocide, disaster and despair, I wanted to end this book on a positive note. Although I remain a little sceptical still of what exactly Fairtrade defines in terms of the realities of a limited economic model and principals versus practice, it remains at least one movement actively working towards improving working conditions and increased salaries for all farmers, including those on sugar and cacao plantations, in the developing world.

The Fairtrade Foundation website includes a feast of recipes to help direct consumers towards a more ethical approach to cooking. The following nutritious and Fairtrade chocolate mousse is easy to make, with principled ingredients, including a much-underused pairing of chocolate with lemon. The recipe was originally published in Anna Jones' *The Modern Cook's Year.*

Anna Jones' Fairtrade Sea Salted Chocolate and Lemon Mousse
For the mousse
200g Fairtrade dark chocolate (at least 70 per cent cocoa solids)

A good pinch of flaky sea salt

2 tbsp runny honey (Hilltop Honey do a great Fairtrade one)

The seeds from 1 vanilla pod (Ndali Vanilla do excellent Fairtrade vanilla pods)

The zest of 2 unwaxed lemons

For the quick brittle
60g sesame seeds, plus extra to finish
2 tbsp maple syrup

Method
This is a pretty maverick way of making a chocolate mousse, which was brought to my attention by a great chef friend. It's based on a technique by the French chemist Hervés. Don't worry, it's really quite easy, though you do have to follow the recipe to the tee. It uses water, not cream, and the mousse is whipped over a bowl of ice, which chills the chocolate. The result is a cleaner, less cloying mousse that is unadulterated chocolate, backed up by a little lemon, salt and vanilla.

Lemon is rarely paired with chocolate but I think it works incredibly well. If you'd prefer, orange or even lime could be added too.

Half-fill a large mixing bowl (or saucepan) with water and ice, then sit another mixing bowl inside it.

Put the chocolate, salt, honey, vanilla and lemon zest into a saucepan with 175ml of cold water. Place on a low heat and stir until it all comes together and the chocolate has just melted.

Use a spatula to scrape the mixture into the mixing bowl, set over the ice bath and whisk with a balloon whisk (an electric one will be too powerful). Keep whisking until it looks shiny but isn't yet set (like a thick chocolate sauce) – the whisk will make little ribbons of chocolate on the mousse when lifted. You will be whisking for about 3 minutes, but keep an eye on it, as the mousse will thicken really quickly, and will set in the fridge as it cools. Have a taste and check you're happy with the flavour. If the mousse tastes a little grainy, it is probably because it has been over-whisked. Don't panic, just scrape the mixture back into the original saucepan, melt and start again.

Once ready, spoon into ramekins and place in the fridge. Chill for at least 3 hours before serving.

To make the brittle, have a plate lined with greaseproof paper ready. Toast the sesame seeds in a pan on a medium heat until well browned, then add the maple syrup and take off the heat. Scoop the seed mixture onto the greaseproof paper and leave to cool completely.

Serve the mousse topped with sesame seeds and the brittle.[59]

List of Illustrations

Bibliography

Afoakwa, E.O., *Chocolate Science and Technology*, (Wiley-Blackwell, Chichester, 2011).

Aleman-Fernandez, C.E., *Corpus Christi and Saint John The Baptist: A History of Art in an African-Venezuelan Community.* (ProQuest, United States, 1990).

Allen, E.W., *The New Monthly Magazine Volume 124*, (1862).

American Home Economics Association, *Journal of Home Economics, Volume 44, Issue 7,* 1952

Arbuthnot, J, An *Essay Concerning the Nature of Ailments*, (London, 1731)

Arnot, R, *Memoirs of the Comtesse du Barry*, (Dustan Society, 1903)

Aslet, C *The Story of Greenwich*, (Harvard University Press, 1999)

Bainton, R, *The Mammoth Book of Superstition: From Rabbits' Feet to Friday the 13th,* (Hatchette UK, London, 2016).

Ball, J, *Angola's Colossal Lie: Forced Labor on a Sugar Plantation,1913-1977.* (Brill, Boston, 2015)

Barnard, C.I., *Paris War Days: Diary of an American,* (Library of Alexandria, 1914).

Bashor, W, *Marie Antoinette's Darkest Days: Prisoner No.280 in the Conciergerie*, (Rowman and Littlefield, New York and London, 2016)

Beals, R.L., *Cherán: a Sierra Tarascan village*, (U.S. Government, Washington, 1946) 167

Bellin, M, *Modern Kosher Meals*, (Bloch Publishing Company, 1934)

Berdan, F, Anawalt, F, *Codex Mendoza: Four Volume set*, (University of California Press, 1992).

Binda,V, *The Dynamics of Big Business: Structure, Strategy and Impact in Italy and Spain.* (Routledge, 2013)

Blyton, E, *Five Get Into Trouble*, (Hatchette UK, 2014).

Briggs, R *The English Art of Cookery,* (G.G.J. and J. Robinson, London 1788)

British Newspaper Archive *Aberdeen Herald and General Advertiser* (Saturday 11 July 1857).

British Newspaper Archive *Belfast Telegraph*, (Tuesday 20 October 1925).

British Newspaper Archive *Berwickshire News and General Advertiser*, (Tuesday 26 December 1871).

British Newspaper Archive *Cornish and Devon Post*, (Saturday 11 January 1908).

British Newspaper Archive *Northampton Chronicle and Echo* (Tuesday 14 November 1911).

British Newspaper Archive *Northern Whig* (Friday 08 April 1898).

British Newspaper Archive *The Bridgeport Evening Farmer* (16 September, 1913.

British Newspaper Archive *The Scotsman* (Thursday 15 July 1920).

British Newspaper Archive *Weekly's Freeman's Journal*, (Saturday 18 February 1922).

British Newspaper Archive *Western Times* (Saturday 24 May 1890).

British Newspaper Archive, *Daily Herald*, (Thursday 10 June 1920).

British Newspaper Archive, *Derby Mercury*, (Thursday 08 February 1733).

British Newspaper Archive, *Hull Daily*, (Saturday 07 December 1935).

British Newspaper Archive, *Leeds Times*, (Saturday 21 March 1846).

British Newspaper Archive, *Manchester Courier and Lancashire General Advertiser*, (Saturday 29 January 1881).

British Newspaper Archive, *Newcastle Courant*, (Saturday 14 October 1721).

British Newspaper Archive, *Nottingham Evening Post*, (Friday 09 February 1894).

British Newspaper Archive, *Pall Mall Gazette*, (Monday 15 August 1921).

British Newspaper Archive, *Yorkshire Evening Post*, (Saturday 18 July 1891).

British Newspaper Archive, *Aberdeen Evening Express* (Wednesday 10 September 1986).

British Newspaper Archive, *Bell's Weekly Messenger*, (Saturday 02 August 1862).

British Newspaper Archive, *Bucks Herald*, (Friday 27 February 1948).

British Newspaper Archive, *Daily Mirror*, (Saturday 19 February 1938).

British Newspaper Archive, *Eastbourne Gazette*, (Wednesday 29 May 1867).

British Newspaper Archive, *Evening Herald (Dublin)*, (Saturday 14 January, 2006).

British Newspaper Archive, *Falkirk Herald*, (Wednesday 27 April 1887).

British Newspaper Archive, *Globe*, (Saturday 24 April 1920).

British Newspaper Archive, *Hampshire Chronicle*, (Saturday 05 September 1846).

British Newspaper Archive, *Hastings and St. Leonards Observer*, (Saturday 20 September 1919).

British Newspaper Archive, *Lancashire Evening Post* (Thursday 27 May 1920).

British Newspaper Archive, *Leeds Mercury*, (Friday 02 March 1934).

British Newspaper Archive, *Millom Gazette*, (Friday 12 September 1913).

British Newspaper Archive, *Newcastle Daily Chronicle*, (Friday 12 December 1919).

British Newspaper Archive, *Newcastle Daily Chronicle*, (Wednesday 26 November 1919.

British Newspaper Archive, *Sheffield Evening Telegraph*, (Friday 08 May 1914).

British Newspaper Archive, *Shepton Mallet Journal*, (Friday 27 July 1923).

British Newspaper Archive, *Sussex Advertiser*, (Monday 03 November 1760).

British Newspaper Archive, *Taunton Courier and Western Advertiser,* (Saturday, 20 November 1943).

British Newspaper Archive, *The Editor's Box*, (Wednesday 06 November 1929).

British Newspaper Archive, *Truth*, (Thursday 20 December 1888).

British Newspaper Archive, *West Sussex County Times*, (Friday 01 October 1943)

British Newspaper Archive, West Sussex County Times, (Friday 27 April 1945).

British Newspaper Archive, *Western Daily Press*, (Saturday 23 November 1935).

British Newspaper Archive, *Whitby Gazette*, (Saturday 06 June 1863).

British Newspaper Archive, *Daily Mirror*, (Monday 20 May 1929).

British Newspaper Archive, *Daily Record*, (Thursday 15 October 1914).

British Newspaper Archive, *Hampshire Advertiser*, (Wednesday 20 December 1899).

British Newspaper Archive, *Illustrated Police News*, (Thursday 24 January 1918).

British Newspaper Archive, *Liverpool Echo*, (Thursday 08 June 1995).

British Newspaper Archive, *Newcastle Courant*, (Saturday 16 August 1746).

British Newspaper Archive, *Portsmouth Evening News*, (Tuesday 21 December 1926).

British Newspaper Archive, *Stamford Mercury*, (Wednesday 08 March 1721).

British Newspaper Archive, *Sunday World*, (Dublin) (Sunday 04 August 2002).

British Newspaper Archive, *Uxbridge & W. Drayton Gazette*, (Friday 29 August 1930).

British Newspaper Archive, *Pall Mall Gazette*, (Saturday 01 July 1916).

British Newspaper Archive, *Western Mail*, (Tuesday 18 February 1913).

Brown, N. I, *Recipes from Old Hundred: 200 Years of New England Cooking*, (M.Barrows and Company, U.S.A.,1939).

Burke, J, *Amelia Earhart: Flying Solo,* (Quarto Publishing Group, U.S.A, 2017).

Burnett, J, *Liquid Pleasures: A Social History of Drinks in Modern Britain*, (Routledge, 2012)

Buttar, P, *Russia's Last Gasp: The Eastern Front 1916-17*, (Bloomsbury Publishing, 2016).

Cabell, C, *Captain Kidd: The Hunt for the Truth,* (Pen & Sword Maritime, Yorkshire, 2011).

Cadbury, R, *Cocoa: All About It*, (S. Low, Marston, Ltd, 1896).

Casanova, G, *The Complete Memoirs of Casanova, the Story of My Life, (*Benediction Classics, 2013*).*

Casanova, G, *The Memoirs of Casanova*, (Musaicum Books, 2017)

Chalmers, C, *French San Francisco*, (Arcadia Publishing, 2007)

Chiller, A, *German National Cookery for English Kitchens,* (Chapman and Hall, London 1873)

Chronicling America. Historic American Newspapers. Lib of Congress. *New York Tribune* (12 January 1911)

Chronicling America. Historic American Newspapers. Lib of Congress. *New York Evening Post*, (1750).

Chrystal, P, Dickinson, J, *History of Chocolate in York*, (Remember When, Yorkshire, 2012).

Civitello, L, *Cuisine and Culture: A History of Food and People*, (John Wiley & Sons, 2008) 232.

Claire, M, *The Modern Cook Book for the Busy Woman*, (Greenberg, New York, 1932).

Clarke, C,G., *The Men of the Lewis and Clark Expedition*, (University of Nebraska Press, 2002)

Clemens, F.A. *Practical Confectionery Recipes for Household and Manufacturers*, (Pittsburgstates,1899).

Colmenero de Ledesma, A, (Translated by Capt. James Wadsworth), *Chocolate, Or, An Indian Drinke*, (John Dakins,London 1652).

Coomansingh, J, *Cocoa Woman: A Narrative About Cocoa Estate Culture in the British West Indies*, (Xlibris, 2016).

D'Anghiera's, P. W., *The Decades of the Newe Worlde or West India Conteynyng the Nauigations and Conquestes of the Spanyardes,* (Edward Sutton publishers, London, 1555).

D'Antonio, M, *Hershey: Milton S.Hershey's Extraordinary Life of Wealth, Empire and Utopian Dreams,* (Simon & Schuster, New York, 2006).

D'Arcy, B, *Chocolagrams: The Secret Language of Chocolates*, (Chocolate Boat Press, 2016)

D'imperio, Chuck, *A Taste of Upstate New York: The People and The Stories Behind 40 Food Favorites*, (Syracuse University Press, U.S.A.,2015)

Dahl, S *Very Fond of Food: A Year in Recipes*, (Ten Speed Press, 2012).

Dalby, A, *Dangerous Tastes: The Story of Spices*, (University of California Press, USA, 2000)

Davey, R, *The Pageant of London*, (Methuen & Co., London, 1906) 387.

De Chelus, D., *The Natural History of Chocolate,* (J.Roberts, London, 1724).

de Chesnay, M (ed) *Sex Trafficking: A Clinical Guide for Nurses,* (Springer publishing, 2012)

Del Castillo, B, *The Memoirs of the Conquistador Bernal Diaz Del Castillo*, Vol 1, (J Hatchard & Son, London, 1844)

de Montespan, Madame La Marquise, *Memoirs of Madame La Marquise de Montespan, Volume 1*, (L.C. Page & Company, Boston, 1899).

Desaulniers, M, *The Trellis Cook Book,* (Simon & Schuster, New York, London, Toronto, Sidney, Tokyo, Singapre, 1992)

Deutschmann, E, *The Home Confectioner*, (New York, 1915)

Dickens, C, *A Tale of Two Cities* (Chapman & Hall, London, 1868)

Dillinger, T, Barriga, P, Escarcega, S, Jimenez, M, Lowe, Diana, Grivetti, L, *Food of the Gods: Cure for Humanity? A Cultural History of the medicinal and Ritual Use of Chocolate*, (American Society for Nutritional Sciences, 2000).

Douglas Jerrold's Shilling Magazine. v. 1, (London, 1845)

Duff, C, *Ireland and the Irish*, (Putnam, New York, 1953)

Eales, M, *Mrs Mary Eales's Receipts,* (J.Brindley, London, 1733).

Elizabeth, M, *My Candy Secrets*, (Frederick A.Stokes, New York, 1919)

Esquivel, L, *Like Water for Chocolate,* (Black Swan, London, 1993)

Farmer, F. M, *The Boston Cooking School Cook Book,* (Little Brown and Co., Boston, 1911)

Fleck, H, Fernandez, L, Munves, E, *Exploring Home and Family Living,* (Prentice-Hall, New Jersey, 1959)

Forbes Irvine, A, *Report of the Trial of Madeleine Smith,* (T&T Clark, Edinburgh, 1857)

Francatelli, C.E., *The Cook's Guide and Housekeeper's & Butler's Assistant*, (1862)

Frederick, J.G., *The Pennsylvania Dutch and Their Cookery*, (The Business Boures, New York, 1935)

Frost, A, *Utterly Unbelieveable WWII in Facts*, (Penguin, 2019).

Gaul, E, Berolzheimer, R (ed), *The Candy Book*, (Consolidated Book Publishers, Chicago. 1954).

Georgescu, I, *Carpathia: Food from the Heart of Romania,* (Frances Lincoln, 2020)

Gerhard, P, *Pirates of the Pacific, 1575-1742*, (University of Nebraska Press, 1990)

Glasse, H, *The Art of Cookery Made Plain and Easy*, (J. Rivington& sons, London, 1788)

Goldoni, C The *Coffee House*, (Marsilio Publishers, 1998)

Goncourt, E, Goncourt, J *Madame Du Barry*, (J.Long, London, 1914)

Gouffe, J, *The Royal Cookery Book*, (Sampson Low, Son & Marston, London, 1869)

Gould, R, *The Corruption of the Times by Money: A Satyr*, (Matthew Wotton, London, 1693)

Grivetti, L.E., Shapiro, Y,(ed), *Chocolate: History, Culture and Heritage,* (John Wiley and Sons, Uni of California, 2000)

Guittard, A, *Guittard Chocolate Cookbook, Chronicle Books,* (San Francisco 2015)

Hackenesch, S, *Chocolate and Blackness: A Cultural History*, (Campus Verlag, Frankfurt/New York, 2017)

Hagman, B, *The Gluten-Free Gourmet Makes Dessert*, (Henry Holt and Company, New York, 2003).

Hale, S.J., *Mrs. Hale's New Cook Book*, (T.B Peterson and Brothers, Philadelphia, 1857)

Hall, H, *The Vertues of Chocolate East-India Drink*, (Oxford, 1660)

Hall, R, Burgess, C, *The First Soviet Cosmonaut Team*, (Springer 2009)

Harris, J, *Chocolate*, (Thorndike Press, 1999)

Harris, J, Warde, F, *The French Kitchen: A Cookbook*, (Random House, London, 2002)

Hasse, D, *The Greenwood Encyclopaedia of Folktales*, (Greenwood Publishing Group, 2017)

Hershey Community Archives *"Ration D Bars –"*Hersheyarchives.org.

Higginbotham, P, *The Workhouse. The Story of an Institution.* Online at Workhouses.org.uk/Dewsbury

Higgs, C, *Chocolate Islands: Cocoa, Slavery and Colonial Africa*, (Ohio University Press, 2012)

Historic Royal Palaces Enterprises Limited, *Chocolate Fit for a Queen*, (Random House, 2015)

Hough, P.M., *Dutch Life in Town and Country,* (G.P Putnam's Sons, New York, 1902)

House, J, Jeffrey, R, Findlay,D, *Square Mile of Murder: Horrific Glasgow Killings.* (Black and White Publishing, 2002).

Howard, B, Bruce, A, Duncan, A, Semmes, J, *Tight Lines and a Happy Landing : Anticosti, July, 1937.* (Reese Press, Baltimore, 1937)

Hughes, W, *The American Physician,* (William Crook, London 1672).

Jaine T (ed), *Oxford Symposium on Food and Cookery, 1984 & 1985*, (Prospect Books, 1986) 159.

Jeffers, H.P., *Roosevelt the Explorer*, (Taylor Trade Publishing, 2002).

Joyce, J, *Ulysses*, (General Press, 2016).

Kay, E, *Dining with the Georgians*, (Amberley Publishing, Stroud, 2014).

Kisluk-Grosheide, D, Rondot, B (ed), *Visitors to Versailles: From Louis XIV to the French Revolution,* (The Metropolitan Museum of Art, New York. USA and London)

Krakauer, J, *Into thin Air: A Personal Account of the Mount Everest Disaster*, (Pan Books, New York, Canada and Great Britain, 1997)

Kuritz, P, *The Making of Theatre History*, (Pearson College division, 1988)

Kurlansky, M, *The Basque History of the World*, (Vintage books, London, 2000)

Kushen, R, Schwartz, H, Mikva, A, *Prison Conditions in the Soviet Union*, (Human Rights Watch, USA, 1991)

Latosinska, J.N., Latosinska, M (ed), *The Question of Caffeine,* (InTech, Croatia, 2017) 5.

Le Blanc, R.D., *Bonbons and Bolsheviks: The Stigmatization of Chocolate in Revolutionary Russia*, (University of New Hampshire, 2018)

Leake J, *Medical Instructions Towards the Prevention and Cure of Chronic Diseases Peculiar to Women*, (Baldwin, London, 1787).

LeMoine, J.M, *The Chronicles of the St Lawrence*, (Montreal, 1878)

Library of Congress, Historic American Newspapers, *Virginia Argus*, (6 February 1814).

Library of Congress, Historic American Newspapers, *The Centre Reporter*, (27 April 1876).

Life Magazine, (November 1952)

Life Magazine, (1939)

London Evening Standard, (Monday 17 August 1846).

Loomis, S, Du Barry, (Lippincott, 1959)

Loveman, K. (2013). The Introduction of Chocolate into England: Retailers, Researchers, and Consumers, 1640–1730. Journal of Social History 47(1), 27-46. Oxford University Press.

Loveman, K. (2013). *The Introduction of Chocolate into England: Retailers, Researchers, and Consumers, 1640–1730.* Journal of Social History 47(1), 27-46. Oxford University Press.

Lummis, C.F., *The Landmark Club Cook Book: a California Collection of the Choicest Recipes from Everywhere,* (The Out West company, Los Angeles, 1903)

Mackay, C London *Memoirs of Extraordinary Popular Delusions and Madness of Crowds* (London, 1852)

Macky, J, *Journey Through England,* (J. Roberts, 1714)

Mathur, S, *Indian Sweets* (Ocean Books, New Delhi, 2000)

Matt Gozun, *Jeffrey Dahmer: Twenty Years Later,* The Marquette Wire, Feb 28, 2012 Accessed from marquettewire.org/3807972/tribune/tribune-featured/dahmer-closer-look/

Matthews,K, *Great Blueberry Recipes*, (Storey Publishing, U.S.A, 1997)

Mayhew, M *London Labour and the London Poor*, volume 1, (1861)

McGrath, J.F, *War Diary of 354ᵗʰ Infantry*, (J. Lintz, U.S.A, 1920)

McGregor, A, *Frank Hurley: A Photographer's Life,* (National Library of Australia, 2019)

Meade, L.T., *A Sweet Girl Graduate*, (1ˢᵗ World Publishing, 2004)

Meder, T, *The Flying Dutchman and Other folktales from the Netherlands*, (Greenwood Publishing Group, 2008)

Mercier, J, *The Temptation of Chocolate*, (Lannoo Uitgeverij, 2008)

Mercier, J, *The Temptation of Chocolate*, (Racine, 2008)

Monlau, P.F, *Higiene de Matrimonio: El Libro de los Casados*, (The Book of Marriage Hygiene), (1881)

Montague, C, *Pirates and Privateers: A Swashbuckling Compendium of Seafaring Scoundrels*, (Chartwell Books, 2017)

Moody, H, *Mrs William Vaughn Moody's Cook-Book*, (C.Sribner's Sons, New York, 1931)

Mrs. Ben Issacs, *The New Orleans Federation of Clubs Cook Book*, (New Orleans, 1917)

Neil, M,H, *Candies and Bonbons and How to Make Them*, (D.McKay, Philadelphia, 1913)

Neil, H, *The True Story of the Cook and Peary Discovery of the North Pole,* (The Educational Co., Chicago, 1909).

Nevinson, H, *A Modern Slavery*, (Wentworth Press, 2016)

Norton, Marcy, Sacred Gifts, Profane Pleasures: A History of Tobacco and Chocolate....

Notes and Queries, (Oxford University Press, 1869)

Nott, J, *The Cooks and Confectioners Dictionary*, (C.Rivington, London, 1723).

O'Neil, D.S, *Fix the Pumps: The History of the Soda Fountain*, (2010, Art of Drink.com)

Ohler, Norman, *Blitzed: Drugs in Nazi Germany*. (Penguin, 2016).

Orange Coast Magazine, (U.S.A.,March 2006)

Orange Coast Magazine, (U.S.A., December 1987)

Ordahl Kupperman, K, *Roanoke: The Abandoned Colony*, (Rowan & Littlefield, United States and Plymouth, UK, 2007)

Ordinary's Account, 21 April 1714, The Old Bailey *Old Bailey Proceedings Online* (www.oldbaileyonline.org, version 8.0, 17 July 2020), *Ordinary of Newgate's Account*, April 1714 (OA17140421).

Otterman, *Handcuffed for selling Churros: Inside the World of illegal food vendors*, The New York Times, 12 November 2019

Parascandola, J, *King of Poisons: A History of Arsenic*, (Potomac Books, Washington D.C., 2012).

Pare, J, *Company's Coming Cookies*, (Company's Coming Publishing Limited, Canada, 1988)

Parks, T, *The Works of British Poets*, (J. Sharpe, London, 1818).

Parloa, M, *Miss Parloa's New Cook Book and Marketing Guide*, (Applewood Books, U.S.A, 2008)

Parrott, T,M (ed,) *The Rape of the Lock and Other Poems*, (1906)

Patterson, R, *A Kitchen Witch's World of Magical Food,* (Moon Books, 2015)

Pepys, S, *Delphi Complete Works of Samuel Pepys (Illustrated)*, (Delphi Classics, Hastings, 2015)

Printz, D,R, *On The Chocolate Trail*, (Jewish Lights Publishing, U.S.A., 2013)

Prior, M, *The Poetical Works of Matthew Prior*, (William Pickering, London, 1835).

Prison Discipline Society, *Annual Report of the Board of managers of the Prison Discipline, volumes 1-6.*, (T. R Marvin, Boston Massachusettes,1830).

Psychopedia, (Blackhous Applications, 2014).

Puri, R. K, Puri, R., *Natural Aphrodisiacs: Myth or Reality*, (Xlibris Corporation, USA, 2011)

Radford, R.A, *The Economic Organization of a P.O.W. Camp,* (Economica, 1945)

Rawley, J. A, Behrendt, S. D, *The Transatlantic Slave Trade: A History*, (University of Nebraska Press, U.S.A, London, 1981)

Read, P, *Alive*, (Open Road Media, New York, 2016).

Reed, T, *The Whole Duty of a Woman*, (London, 1737)

Redfield, R, *Chan Kom a Maya Village*, (University of Chicago Press, 1962).

Reilly, N, *Ukrainian Cuisine with an American Touch and Ingredients*, (Xlibris corporation, U.S.A, 2010)

Reitain, E, *Is God A Delusion?*, (John Wiley & Sons, 2011).

Richards, P, *Candy for Desert*, (The Hotel Monthly Press, Chicago, 1919)

Rowntree's Little Cookbook of 'Elect Recipes, (Rowntree's, York, Circa 1930).

Roy, S, *Business Biographies: Shaken not Stirred*, (IUniverse, Inc. USA, 2011).

Ruiz de Alarcon, H, *Treatise on the Heathen Superstitions that Today Live Among the Indians Native to this New Spain, 1629,* (University of Oklahoma Press, 1984)

Ryalls, C.W, (ed) *Transactions of The National Association for the Promotion of Social Science,* (Longman's, Green and Co.,1877)

Sahgal,N, *Prison and Chocolate cake* (Harper perennial, 2007)

Sammarco, A., *The Baker Chocolate Company: A Sweet History* (The History Press, U.S.A. 2009).

Sandler, M, *Flying Over the U.S.A: Airplanes in American Life*, (Oxford University Press, New York, 2004).

Saunders, N, J, *The Peoples of the Caribbean: An Encyclopedia of Archaeology and Traditional Culture,* (A.B.C. Clio, California, Colorado and Oxford, England. 2005)

Scott, R.F., *Captain Scott's Last Expedition*, (Oxford University Press, 2008).

Sinclair, S, Cadbury Bros, Ltd., *Cadbury's Practical Recipes,* (*Partridge & Love Ltd., Bristol,* 1955)

Smith, J, McKay, C (ed), *The Streets of London*, (R. Bentley, London, 1854)

Smith, Mary G, *Temperance Cook Book*, (Mercury Book and Job Print House, California, 1887)

Smith, M, D., (ed), *Sex and Sexuality in Early America*, (New York University Press, New York and London, 1998).

Stevenson, R, *The First Dated Mention of the Sarabande,* Journal of the American Musicological Society, volume 5, 1952.

Stewarton, L.G., *The Secret History of the Court and Cabinet of St Cloud, 1806,* (J.Murray, 1806)

Stirling, A.,(ed), *A Belle of the Fifties. Memoirs of Mrs. Clay of Alalabama, Covering Social and Political Life in Washington and the South, 1853-66,* (Doubleday, Page and Company, 1905)

Strother, E, *Criticon Febrium, or A Critical Essay on Fevers*, (Charles Rivington, London 1718).

Strother, E, *Materia medica or A new description of the virtues and effects of all drugs or simple medicines*, (Charles Rivington, London, 1729)

Stubbe, H, *The Indian Nectar, Or a Discourse Concerning Chocolata,* (Andrew Crook, London, 1662).

Sukley, B, *Pennsylvania Made*, (Rowman and Littlefield, 2016)

Testa, D.W., (ed) *Government Leaders, Military Rulers and political Activists*. (Routledge, London 2014).

Thackeray, W.M, *The Four Georges* (Smith, Elder & Co., London)

The Collected Works of Samuel Taylor Coleridge, Volume 1: Lectures (Princeton University Press, 2015)

The Magazine of Domestic Economy, Volume 4, (W.S. Orr & Co., London, 1839)

The Magazine of Science, and School of Arts, Volume 5, (1844)

The Medical Times and Gazette: A Journal of Medical Science, Volume 1, (John Churchill and Sons, London, 1869).

The Village Improvement Society, *A Book for the Cook : Old Fashioned Receipts for new Fashioned Kitchens,* (Greenfield, Connecticut, 1899)

Toblerone Cookbook: 40 Fabulous Baking Treats, (Kyle Books, 2020).

Treadwell, T, Vernon, M, *Last Suppers: Famous Final Meals from Death Row*, (CreateSpace Independent Publishing Platform, USA, 2011).

Trusler, J, *CHAP. XXIII. Review of the Manners and Customs of the Italians in general, particularly in their private Life, their Games and Pastimes*, (London 1788)

Vanetti, D, *The Querulous Cook; Haute Cuisine in the American Manner,* Macmillan, New York, 1963)

Visioli, F, *Chocolate and Health*, (Springer, 2012)

Wairy, L.C., *Memoirs of Constant – First Valet de Chambre to the Emperor, Volume 2*, (Pickle Partners Publishing, 2011).

Walsh, J, H, *The English Cookery Book*, (G.Routledge and Company, London, 1859)

Wheatley, H.B., *Hogarth's London: Pictures of the Manners of the Eighteenth Century*, (Constable and Company, London 1909).

Williams, V, *Celebrating Life Customs around the World: From Baby Showers to Funerals*, (ABC-CLIO, U.S.A., 2016)

Wingate Chemical Company, *The Wingate Almanac*, (1903).

Wood, A, *Home-made Candies*, (Buffalo, 1904)

Wyman, A.L., (ed) *Los Angeles Times Prize Cook Book,* (Times-Mirror Print and Binding House, Los Angeles, 1923).

Wyman, A.L., *Chef Wyman's Daily Health Menus*, (Wyman Food Service, Los Angeles, 1927)

Website References

[*Attested copies from the Register of the Court of Admiralty. S.P. Dom., Car. II.* 291, *No.* 148.] 'Charles II: July 1671', in *Calendar of State Papers Domestic: Charles II, 1671*, ed. F H Blackburne Daniell (London, 1895), pp. 352-408. *British History Online* http://www.british-history.ac.uk/cal-state-papers/domestic/chas2/1671/pp352-408

Abstracts of the Creditors for the year 1750, George III Financial Papers, 1759, Royal Collection Trust https://gpp.rct.uk/Record.aspx?src=CalmView.Catalog&id=GIII_FIN%2f2%2f3%2f9&pos=4,

Akbar, A, 'Aztec ruler Moctezuma Unmasked', *The Independent,* Mon 13 April, 2009, https://www.independent.co.uk/arts-entertainment/art/features/aztec-ruler-moctezuma-unmasked-1668030.html

'America and West Indies: January 1714', in *Calendar of State Papers Colonial, America and West Indies: Volume 27, 1712-1714*, ed. Cecil Headlam (London, 1926), pp. 284-295. *British History Online* http://www.british-history.ac.uk/cal-state-papers/colonial/america-west-indies/vol27/pp284-295

Beata's Bakery, Wuzetka cake, https://wypiekibeaty.com.pl/ciasto-wuzetka/,

Blake, I, *So that's Why American chocolate tastes so horrible,* Mail Online, 2017, https://www.dailymail.co.uk/femail/food/article-4155658/The-real-reason-American-chocolate-tastes-terrible.html

Carlson, M., *Twelve. A Poema in a new translation*, KU ScholarWorks, https://kuscholarworks.ku.edu/handle/1808/6598?show=full,

Choat, I, *A Chocolate tour of London: a taste of the past*, The Guardian, 23 December, 2013. https://www.theguardian.com/travel/2013/dec/23/chocolate-tour-of-london,

Chocolate in Norway – Now and then, online at 2017https://sunnygandara.com/chocolate-in-norway-now-and-then/

Chocolate Mousse Murderer *Mail Online*, 27 February, 2008. Online at https://www.dailymail.co.uk/news/article-520312/Chocolate-mousse-murderer-Middle-aged-man-kills-parents-lacing-pudding-poison-wouldnt-let-leave-home.html

Clark, September 17, 1806, *Journals of the Lewis & Clark Expedition*, https://lewisandclarkjournals.unl.edu/item/lc.jrn.1806-09-17#lc.jrn.1806-09-17.01

Cookpad, Suzi Q Cakes with Cream Filling, https://cookpad.com/uk/recipes/7285321-suzy-q-cakes-with-cream-filling,

Cox, N, Dannehl, K, 'Checker - Chypre', in *Dictionary of Traded Goods and Commodities 1550-1820* (Wolverhampton, 2007), *British History Online* http://www.british-history.ac.uk/no-series/traded-goods-dictionary/1550-1820/checker-chypre

Elit Chocolate, Recipes, Chocolate Cheesecake, http://www.elit-chocolate.com/recipies/cheese-cake/

'Entry Book: July 1688, 1-10', in *Calendar of Treasury Books, Volume 8, 1685-1689*, ed. William A Shaw (London, 1923), pp. 1974-1993. *British History Online* http://www.british-history.ac.uk/cal-treasury-books/vol8/pp1974-1993

Favy, Japan, *Choco Banana: Only at Summer Festivals in Japan*, available from https://favy-jp.com/topics/644,

Haigh's Chocolate, Recipes, available from https://www.haighschocolates.com.au/recipes/haighs-celebration-chocolate-mousse-cake,

https://www.mirror.co.uk/news/world-news/scott-expedition-cake-almost-edible-10969916

https://www.nzherald.co.nz/business/news/article.cfm?c_id=3&objectid=12301483

https://www.rbth.com/russian-kitchen/329408-birds-milk-soviet-cake,

Inside US$31.5 billion Ferrero Rocher heir Giovanni Ferrero's family tragedies, News.com.au, 18 January,2020

Kitching, C, *Scott expedition cake 'almost' edible after being found near South Pole 100 years after explorer's ill-fated voyage,* 11 August, 2017, The Daily Mail,

Library of Congress newspaper archives. https://chroniclingamerica.loc.gov/

Marquesa de Chocolate, Venezuelatuya.com https://www.venezuelatuya.com/cocina/marquesa_chocolate.htm,

Martyris, N, *Amelia Earhart's Travel Menu Relied on 3 Rules and People's Generosity*, July 8, 2017, https://www.npr.org/sections/thesalt/2017/07/08/536024928/amelia-earharts-travel-menu-relied-on-three-rules-and-peoples-generosity?t=1601381978599

May 16, 2018, https://www.insider.com/serial-killers-last-meals-2018-5

Menier Chocolate, recipes, available from : https://www.menier.co.uk/wp-content/uploads/2017/02/Tender-Curried-Lamb-Stew.pdf

Mignon Chocolate, https://mignonchocolate.com/about-us/

Milwaukee Public Lib, *Milwaukee Journal*, 1983, Online at https://www.mpl.org/special_collections/images/index.php?slug=historic-recipe-file

Ordinary's Account, 3 November, 1725, Ref: t17251013-25, Old Bailey, https://www.oldbaileyonline.org/browse.jsp?id=t17251013-25&div=t17251013-25&terms=Foster_Snow#highlight

'Pall Mall, South Side, Past Buildings: Ozinda's Chocolate House', in *Survey of London: Volumes 29 and 30, St James Westminster, Part 1*, ed. F H W Sheppard (London, 1960), p. 384. *British History Online* http://www.british-history.ac.uk/survey-london/vols29-30/pt1/p384

Park, M, CNN Health News Jan 8, 2010, *Soda Fountains contained fecal bacteria, study found.* http://edition.cnn.com/2010/HEALTH/01/08/soda.fountain.bacteria/index.html

Rabbi Debbie Prinz, Jewish Journal, *On the Trail of Chocolate*, May 14, 2014, available from https://jewishjournal.com/culture/food/129134/on-the-trail-of-chocolate/

Rowling, J.K., *Dementors and Chocolate*, Wizarding World https://www.wizardingworld.com/writing-by-jk-rowling/dementors-and-chocolate,

Siddique, H, *Charlie and the Chocolate Factory hero 'was originally black'*. The Guardian. Wednesday 13 September, 2017, https://www.theguardian.com/books/2017/sep/13/charlie-and-the-chocolate-factory-hero-originally-black-roald-dahl

Smith, Nasha, *What 9 Serial Killers Were Served for Their Last Meal*

'St. James's Street', in *Survey of London: Volumes 29 and 30, St James Westminster, Part 1*, ed. F H W Sheppard (London, 1960), pp. 431-432. *British History Online* http://www.british-history.ac.uk/survey-london/vols29-30/pt1/pp431-432

'St. James's Street, West Side, Past Buildings', in *Survey of London: Volumes 29 and 30, St James Westminster, Part 1*, ed. F H W Sheppard (London, 1960), pp. 459-471. *British History Online* http://www.british-history.ac.uk/survey-london/vols29-30/pt1/pp459-471

Tan, W, *Cadbury loses fight for colour purple* The Sunday Morning Herald, April 11, 2008, https://www.smh.com.au/national/cadbury-loses-fight-for-colour-purple-20080411-25gw.html

Tewari, S, *Paid to Poo: Combating open defecation in India* BBC News 30 August 2015 https://www.bbc.co.uk/news/health-33980904

Than, C, *The Rich and Flavourable History of Chocolate in Space*, 10 February, 2015 available at https://www.smithsonianmag.com/science-nature/rich-and-flavorful-history-chocolate-space-180954160/

The American Druggist and Pharmaceutical Record, Volume 25, (American Druggist Publishing Company New York, 1894) 201.

The Independent, *Nestle pays $14.6m into Swiss banks' Holocaust settlement* Monday 28 August,2000,https://web.archive.org/web/20150703053430/http://www.independent.co.uk/news/business/news/nestle-pays-146m-into-swiss-banks-holocaust-settlement-711755.html

The Recipe for Nougat, Arnaud-Soubeyran, https://www.nougatsoubeyran.com/en/the-recipe-of-nougat/

The Smell of Chocolate, Hebrew Songs, http://www.hebrewsongs.com/song-reachshelshokolad.htm

Uhlig, R, *How Edmund Hillary conquered Everest,* 12 January, 2008, The Telegraph. https://www.telegraph.co.uk/news/uknews/1575348/How-Edmund-Hillary-conquered-Everest.html,

United Press International, *Chocolate Possibly Contaminated by Chernobyl Radiation*, April 5, 1988, https://www.upi.com/Archives/1988/04/05/Chocolate-possibly-contaminated-by-Chernobyl-radiation/3538576216000/

Van Houtens Chocolate, *Grace's Guide to British Industrial History*, https://www.gracesguide.co.uk/Van_Houtens_Chocolate,

Wilkie, J, *Select Trials for murder, robbery, burglary, rapes, sodomy, coining, forgery, piracy and other offences and misdemeanours at the Sessions-House in the Old Bailey*, (London, 1764).

Endnotes

Introduction

1. D'Anghiera's, P. W., *The Decades of the Newe Worlde or West India Conteynyng the Nauigations and Conquestes of the Spanyardes* (Edward Sutton publishers, London, 1555).
2. Del Castillo, B, *The memoirs of the Conquistador Bernal Diaz Del Castillo*, Vol 1, (J Hatchard & Son, London, 1844)
3. Testa, D. W., (ed) *Government Leaders, Military Rulers and political Activists* (Routledge, London, 2014).
4. Akbar, A, 'Aztec ruler Moctezuma Unmasked', *The Independent*, Monday, 13 April 2009, https://www.independent.co.uk/arts-entertainment/art/features/aztec-ruler-moctezuma-unmasked-1668030.html, (accessed 27/09/2020).
5. Mercier, J, *The Temptation of Chocolate*, (Lannoo Uitgeverij, 2008)
6. *Chocolate in Norway – Now and then,* online at https://sunnygandara.com/chocolate-in-Norway-now-and-then/ (accessed, 15/10/2020).
7. British Newspaper Archive, *Stamford Mercury* (Wednesday 8 March 1721).
8. Cox, N, Dannehl, K, 'Checker – Chypre', in *Dictionary of Traded Goods and Commodities 1550-1820* (Wolverhampton, 2007), *British History Online* http://www.british-history.ac.uk/no-series/traded-goods-dictionary/1550-1820/checker-chypre [accessed 16 May 2020].
9. Nott, J, *The Cooks and Confectioners Dictionary*, (C. Rivington, London, 1723).
10. Ordinary's Account, 21 April 1714, The Old Bailey *Old Bailey Proceedings Online* (www.oldbaileyonline.org, version 8.0, 17 July 2020), *Ordinary of Newgate's Account*, April 1714 (OA17140421).
11. British Newspaper Archive, *Liverpool Echo* (Thursday 8 June 1995).

12. Higginbotham, P, *The Workhouse. The Story of an Institution*. Online at Workhouses.org.uk/Dewsbury (accessed 27/07/2020).
13. Kushen, R, Schwartz, H, Mikva, A, *Prison Conditions in the Soviet Union* (Human Rights Watch, USA, 1991, p20).
14. Prison Discipline Society *Annual Report of the Board of managers of the Prison Discipline, volumes 1-6*, (T. R Marvin, Boston, Massachusetts, 1830).
15. Nott, J, *The Cooks and Confectioners Dictionary*, (C. Rivington, London, 1723).

Chapter 1: Killers, Cargo and Cajolery: Chocolate at its Darkest

1. 'Entry Book: July 1688, 1-10', in *Calendar of Treasury Books, Volume 8, 1685-1689*, ed. William A Shaw (London, 1923), pp. 1974-1993. *British History Online* http://www.british-history.ac.uk/cal-treasury-books/vol8/pp1974-1993 [accessed 16 May 2020].
2. Rawley, J. A, Behrendt, S. D, *The Transatlantic Slave Trade: A History*, (University of Nebraska Press, U.S.A, London, 1981) 124.
3. Higgs, C, *Chocolate Islands: Cocoa, Slavery and Colonial Africa*, (Ohio University Press, Ohio, 2012) 9
4. 'America and West Indies: January 1714', in *Calendar of State Papers Colonial, America and West Indies: Volume 27, 1712-1714*, ed. Cecil Headlam (London, 1926), pp. 284-295. *British History Online* http://www.british-history.ac.uk/cal-state-papers/colonial/america-west-indies/vol27/pp284-295 [accessed 16 May 2020].
5. [*Attested copies from the Register of the Court of Admiralty. S.P. Dom., Car. II. 291, No. 148.*] 'Charles II: July 1671', in *Calendar of State Papers Domestic: Charles II, 1671*, ed. F H Blackburne Daniell (London, 1895), pp. 352-408. *British History Online* http://www.british-history.ac.uk/cal-state-papers/domestic/chas2/1671/pp352-408 [accessed 16 May 2020].
6. Ball, J, *Angola's Colossal Lie: Forced Labor on a Sugar Plantation,1913-1977*, (Brill, Boston, 2015) 33.
7. Nevinson, H, *A Modern Slavery*, (Wentworth Press, 2016) 188.
8. Ibid. 194
9. Nevinson, H, *A Modern Slavery*, (Harper & Brothers, 1906) 191.

10. Ball, J, *Angola's Colossal Lie: Forced Labor on a Sugar Plantation,1913-1977*, (Brill, Boston, 2015) 34

11. de Chesnay, M (ed) *Sex Trafficking: A Clinical Guide for Nurses*, (Springer publishing, 2012) 47

12. British Newspaper Archive, *Newcastle Courant*, (Saturday 16 August 1746).

13. Gerhard, P, *Pirates of the Pacific, 1575-1742*. (University of Nebraska Press, 1990) 84-85.

14. Montague, C, *Pirates and Privateers: A Swashbuckling Compendium of Seafaring Scoundrels*, (Chartwell Books, 2017) 14.

15. Grivetti, L.E., Shapiro, Y,(ed) *Chocolate: History, Culture and Heritage*, (John Wiley and Sons, Uni of California, 2000) 1970.

16. Cabell, C, *Captain Kidd: The Hunt for the Truth,* (Pen & Sword Maritime, Yorkshire, 2011).

17. Hughes, W, *The American Physician*, (William Crook, London 1672).

18. Chocolate Mousse Murderer *Mail Online,* 27 February 2008. Online at https://www.dailymail.co.uk/news/article-520312/Chocolate-mousse-murderer-Middle-aged-man-kills-parents-lacing-pudding-poison-wouldnt-let-leave-home.html, (accessed 11/10/2020).

19. British Newspaper Archive, *Sunday World*, (Dublin) (Sunday 04 August 2002).

20. British Newspaper Archive *Western Times*, (Saturday 24 May 1890).

21. British Newspaper Archive *Northern Whig*, (Friday 08 April 1898).

22. British Newspaper Archive *The Bridgeport Evening Farmer*, (16 September 1913.

23. Chronicling America. Historic American Newspapers. Lib of Congress, *New York Tribune* (12 January 1911).

24. British Newspaper Archive *Belfast Telegraph*, (Tuesday 20 October 1925).

25. British Newspaper Archive *The Scotsman*, (Thursday 15 July, 1920).

26. British Newspaper Archive *Berwickshire News and General Advertiser*, (Tuesday 26 December 1871).

27. Gouffe, J, The Royal Cookery Book, (Sampson Low, Son & Marston, London, 1869) 557.

28. British Newspaper Archive *Aberdeen Herald and General Advertiser* (Saturday, 11 July, 1857).

29. Forbes Irvine, A, *Report of the trial of Madeleine Smith*, (T&T Clark, Edinburgh, 1857) 109.

30. Parascandola, *King of Poisons: A History of Arsenic*, (Potomac Books, Washington D.C., 2012).

31. House, Jeffrey, R, Findlay, *Square Mile of Murder: Horrific Glasgow Killings*, (Black and White Publishing, 2002).

32. Hale, S.J., *Mrs. Hale's New Cook Book*, (T.B Peterson and Brothers, Philadelphia, 1857) 441

33. Chronicling America. Historic American Newspapers. Lib of Congress. *New York Evening Post*, (1750).

34. MacKay London *Memoirs of Extraordinary Popular Delusions and Madness of Crowds*, (London, 1852) 206-208.

35. Ibid. 213-14.

36. British Newspaper Archive, *Portsmouth Evening News*, (Tuesday 21 December 1926).

37. British Newspaper Archive *Northampton Chronicle and Echo*, (Tuesday 14 November 1911).

38. British Newspaper Archive, *Illustrated Police News*, (Thursday 24 January 1918).

39. British Newspaper Archive, *Aberdeen Evening Express*, (Wednesday 10 September, 1986).

40. British Newspaper Archive, *Western Mail*, (Tuesday 18 February 1913).

41. Buttar, P, *Russia's Last Gasp: The Eastern Front 1916-17*, (Bloomsbury Publishing, 2016).

42. https://www.rbth.com/russian-kitchen/329408-birds-milk-soviet-cake, (accessed 18/10/2020).

43. Afoakwa, E.O., *Chocolate Science and Technology*, (Wiley-Blackwell, Chichester, 2011).

44. Puri, R. K, Puri, R., *Natural Aphrodisiacs: Myth or Reality*, (Xlibris Corporation, USA, 2011) 6.

45. Cadbury, R, *Cocoa: All About It*, (S. Low, Marston, Ltd, 1896).

46. Stewarton, L.G., *The Secret History of the Court and Cabinet of St Cloud, 1806,* (J.Murray, 1806) 58-59

47. Hackenesch, S, *Chocolate and Blackness: A Cultural History,* (Campus Verlag, Frankfurt/New York, 2017) 89

48. Grivetti, L.E., Shapiro, Y,(ed) *Chocolate: History, Culture and Heritage,* (John Wiley and Sons, Uni of California, 2000) 670

49. Mercier, J, *The Temptation of Chocolate*, (Racine, 2008) 66.

50. Bashor, W, *Marie Antoinette's Darkest Days: Prisoner No.280 in the Conciergerie*, (Rowman and Littlefield, New York and London) 2016.

51. Loomis, S, *Du Barry*, (Lippincott, 1959) 12.

52. Kisluk-Grosheide, D, Rondot, B (ed) *Visitors to Versailles: From Louis XIV to the French Revolution*, (The Metropolitan Museum of Art, New York. USA and London) 27

53. Arnot, R, *Memoirs of the Comtesse du Barry*, (Dustan Society, 1903) 21.

54. Goncourt, E, Goncourt, J *Madame Du Barry*, (J.Long, London, 1914) 374.

55. Casanova, G, *The Memoirs of Casanova*, (Musaicum Books, 2017)

56. Casanova, G, *The Complete Memoirs of Casanova, the Story of My Life, (*Benediction Classics, 2013*).*

57. Ibid.

58. Grivetti, L.E., Shapiro, Y, (ed) *Chocolate: History, Culture and Heritage*, (John Wiley and Sons, Uni of California, 2000)

59. Matt Gozun, *Jeffrey Dahmer: Twenty Years Later,* The Marquette Wire, Feb 28, 2012 Accessed from marquettewire.org/3807972/tribune/tribune-featured/dahmer-closer-look/ accessed on, 17/06/2020

60. Milwaukee Public Lib, *Milwaukee Journal*, 1983, Online at https://www.mpl.org/special_collections/images/index.php?slug=historic-recipe-file accessed, 12/10/2020.

61. Ibid.

62. Smith, Nasha, *What 9 Serial Killers Were Served for Their Last Meal* May 16, 2018, https://www.insider.com/serial-killers-last-meals-2018-5 accessed 17/06/2020.

63. Desaulniers, M, *The Trellis Cook Book,* (Simon & Schuster, New York, London, Toronto, Sidney, Tokyo, Singapre, 1992) 264

64. Treadwell, T, Vernon, M, *Last Suppers: Famous Final Meals from Death Row*, (Create Space Independent Publishing Platform, USA, 2011)

65. Wyman, A.L., *Chef Wyman's Daily Health Menus*, (Wyman Food Service, Los Angeles, 1927) 241.

66. Parloa, M *Miss Parloa's New Cook Book and Marketing Guide*, (Applewood Books, U.S.A, 2008) 330.

67. Hall, R, Burgess, C, *The First Soviet Cosmonaut Team*, (Springer 2009) 176.

68. Than, C, *The Rich and Flavourable History of Chocolate in Space*, 10 February, 2015 available at https://www.smithsonianmag.com/science-nature/rich-and-flavorful-history-chocolate-space-180954160/ accessed 20/09/2020

69. Read, P, *Alive*, (Open Road Media, New York, 2016).

70. *Douglas Jerrold's shilling magazine. v. 1*, (London,1845) 374.

71. United Press International, *Chocolate Possibly Contaminated by Chernobyl Radiation*, April 5, 1988, https://www.upi.com/Archives/1988/04/05/Chocolate-possibly-contaminated-by-Chernobyl-radiation/3538576216000/ Accessed, 04/08/2020.

72. Williams, V, *Celebrating Life Customs around the World: From Baby Showers to Funerals*, (ABC-CLIO, U.S.A.,2016) 278.

73. Favy, Japan, *Choco Banana: Only at Summer Festivals in Japan*, available from https://favy-jp.com/topics/644, accessed 04/09/2020

74. D'imperio, Chuck, *A Taste of Upstate New York: The People and The Stories Behind 40 Food Favorites*, (Syracuse University Press, U.S.A.,2015) 235

75. Pare, J, *Company's Coming Cookies*, (Company's Coming Publishing Limited, Canada,

Chapter 2: Potions, Perilous Passages and Political Conflict: The Milkier Elements of Chocolate

1. Ohler, Norman, *Blitzed: Drugs in Nazi Germany*, (Penguin, 2016).

2. Schiller, Annie, *German National Cookery for English Kitchens,* (Chapman and Hall, London 1873) 193.

3. British Newspaper Archive, *Hampshire Advertiser*, (Wednesday 20 December 1899).

4. American Home Economics Association, *Journal of Home Economics, Volume 44, Issue 7,* 1952 p.481

5. Radford, R.A, *The Economic Organization of a P.O.W. Camp,* (Economica, 1945)

6. Printz, D,R, *On The Chocolate Trail*, (Jewish Lights Publishing, U.S.A., 2013) 70.

7. The Independent, *Nestle pays $14.6m into Swiss banks' Holocaust settlement* Monday 28 August, 2000, https://web.archive.org/web/20150703053430/http://www.independent.co.uk/news/business/news/nestle-pays-146m-into-swiss-banks-holocaust-settlement-711755.html accessed on 09/09/2020.

8. British Newspaper Archive, *Daily Record*, (Thursday 15 October 1914).

9. British Newspaper Archive *Weekly's Freeman's Journal*, (Saturday 18 February 1922).

10. Frost, A, *Utterly Unbelievable WWII in Facts,* (Penguin, 2019).

11. Jaine T (ed) *Oxford Symposium on Food and Cookery, 1984 & 1985*, (Prospect Books, 1986) 159.

12. McGrath, J.F, *War Diary of 354th Infantry*,(J.Lintz, U.S.A, 1920) 56.

13. Barnard, C, I, *Paris War Days: Diary of an American,* (Library of Alexandria, 1914).

14. Stirling, A., (ed), *A Belle of the Fifties. Memoirs of Mrs. Clay of Alalabama, covering social and political life in Washington and the South, 1853-66.* (Doubleday, Page and Company, 1905) 225.

15. Hershey Community Archives *"Ration D Bars –"*Hersheyarchives.org. Accessed 10/09/2020

16. *Life Magazine*, (November, 1952) 11

17. Le Blanc, R.D., *Bonbons and Bolsheviks: The Stigmatization of Chocolate in Revolutionary Russia*, (University of New Hampshire, 2018).

18. Carlson, M., *Twelve. A Poem in a New Translation*, KU ScholarWorks, https://kuscholarworks.ku.edu/handle/1808/6598?show=full, (accessed 06/08/2020).

19. Mignon Chocolate, https://mignonchocolate.com/about-us/ (accessed 09/08/2020)

20. Reilly, N, *Ukrainian Cuisine with an American Touch and Ingredients*, (Xlibris corporation, U.S.A, 2010) 558

21. Wairy, L.C., *Memoirs of Constant – First Valet de Chambre to the Emperor, Volume 2,* (Pickle Partners Publishing, 2011).

22. Beata's Bakery, Wuzetka cake, available from https://wypiekibeaty.com.pl/ciasto-wuzetka/, (accessed 08/10/2020).

23. Dillinger, T, Barriga, P, Escarcega, S, Jimenez, M, Lowe, Diana, Grivetti, L, *Food of the Gods: Cure for Humanity? A Cultural History of the medicinal and Ritual Use of Chocolate*, (American Society for Nutritional Sciences, 2000).

24. *Norton, Marcy, Sacred Gifts, profane Pleasures: A History of Tobacco and Chocolate...*
25. Grivetti, L.E., Shapiro, Y, (ed) *Chocolate: History, Culture and Heritage*, (John Wiley and Sons, Uni of California, 2000) 1844
26. Ibid. 63
27. Loveman, K. (2013). The Introduction of Chocolate into England: Retailers, Researchers, and Consumers, 1640–1730. Journal of Social History 47(1), 27-46. Oxford University Press.
28. Stubbe, H, *The Indian Nectar, Or a Discourse Concerning Chocolata* (Andrew Crook,London, 1662).
29. Ibid.
30. Colmenero de Ledesma, A, (Translated by Capt. James Wadsworth), *Chocolate, Or, An Indian Drinke*, (John Dakins,London 1652).
31. Loveman, K.(2013). *The Introduction of Chocolate into England: Retailers, Researchers, and Consumers, 1640–1730.* Journal of Social History 47(1), 27-46. Oxford University Press.
32. Ibid.
33. Strother, E, *Materia medica or A new description of the virtues and effects of all drugs or simple medicines*, (Charles Rivington, London, 1729) 316.
34. Leake J, *Medical Instructions Towards the Prevention and Cure of Chronic Diseases Peculiar to Women,* (Baldwin, London, 1787).
35. Hall, H, *The Vertues of Chocolate East-India Drink,* (Oxford, 1660)
36. Pepys, S, *Delphi Complete Works of Samuel Pepys (Illustrated)*, (Delphi Classics, Hastings, 2015)
37. Arbuthnot, J, *An Essay Concerning the Nature of Ailments*, (London, 1731)
38. De Chelus, D., *The Natural History of Chocolate,* (J.Roberts, London, 1724).
39. *The Medical Times and Gazette: A Journal of Medical Science, Volume II,* (John Churchill and Sons, London, 1869).
40. British Newspaper Archive, *Daily Mirror*, (Monday, 20 May 1929).
41. Wingate Chemical Company, *The Wingate Almanac*, (1903).
42. Visioli, F, *Chocolate and Health*, (Springer, 2012) 11.
43. Beals, R,L *Cherán: a Sierra Tarascan Village*, (U.S. Government, Washington, 1946) 167

44. British Newspaper Archive *Cornish and Devon Post*, (Saturday 11 January 1908).

45. Mrs. Ben Issacs, *The New Orleans Federation of Clubs Cook Book*, (New Orleans, 1917).

46. McGregor, A, *Frank Hurley: A Photographer's Life,* (National Library of Australia, 2019) 62.

47. Scott, R.F., *Captain Scott's Last Expedition*, (Oxford University Press, 2008).

48. Kitching, C, *Scott expedition cake 'almost' edible after being found near South Pole 100 years after explorer's ill-fated voyage,* 11 August, 2017, The Daily Mail, https://www.mirror.co.uk/news/world-news/scott-expedition-cake-almost-edible-10969916 (accessed, 14/09/2020)

49. Farmer, F.M, *The Boston Cooking School Cook Book,* (Little Brown and Co., Boston, 1911) 512-513.

50. Ibid. 528.

51. Jeffers, H.P., *Roosevelt the Explorer* (Taylor Trade Publishing, 2002).

52. Clark, September 17, 1806, *Journals of the Lewis & Clark Expedition*, https://lewisandclarkjournals.unl.edu/item/lc.jrn.1806-09-17#lc.jrn.1806-09-17.01 (accessed, 28 September 2020).

53. Clarke, C.G., *The Men of the Lewis and Clark Expedition*, (University of Nebraska Press, 2002) 317.

54. Moody, H, *Mrs William Vaughn Moody's Cook-Book*, (C.Sribner's Sons, New York, 1931) 276.

55. Neil, H, *The True Story of the Cook and Peary Discovery of the North Pole,* (The Educational Co., Chicago, 1909).

56. Blake, E. Vale, *Arctic Experiences*, (Marston, Low & Searle, London, 1874).

57. Martyris, N, *Amelia Earhart's Travel Menu Relied on 3 Rules and People's Generosity*, July 8, 2017, https://www.npr.org/sections/thesalt/2017/07/08/536024928/amelia-earharts-travel-menu-relied-on-three-rules-and-peoples-generosity?t=1601381978599 (accessed 29/09/2020)

58. Burke, J, *Amelia Earhart: Flying Solo,* (Quarto Publishing Group, U.S.A, 2017).

59. Sandler, M, *Flying Over the U.S.A: Airplanes in American Life*, (Oxford University Press, New York, 2004).

60. Claire, M, *The Modern Cook Book for the Busy Woman*, (Greenberg, New York, 1932).
61. Uhlig, R, *How Edmund Hillary Conquered Everest,* 12 January, 2008, The Telegraph. https://www.telegraph.co.uk/news/uknews/1575348/How-Edmund-Hillary-conquered-Everest.html, accessed 25/06/2020
62. Krakauer, J, *Into thin Air: A Personal Account of the Mount Everest Disaster*, (Pan Books, New York, Canada and Great Britain, 1997) 117.
63. Gaul, E, Berolzheimer, R (ed) *The Candy Book*, (Consolidated Book Publishers, Chicago. 1954).
64. Trusler, J, *CHAP. XXIII. Review of the Manners and Customs of the Italians in general, particularly in their private Life, their Games and Pastimes.* (London 1788) 220.
65. Berdan, F, Anawalt, F, *Codex Mendoza: Four Volume set*, (University of California Press, 1992).
66. Redfield, R, *Chan Kom a Maya Village*, (University of Chicago Press, 1962).
67. Ruiz de Alarcon, H, *Treatise on the Heathen Superstitions that Today Live Among the Indians Native to this New Spain, 1629,* (University of Oklahoma Press, 1984) 132.
68. Ibid.
69. Wyman A.L., (ed) *Los Angeles Times Prize Cook Book,* (Times-Mirror Print and Binding House, Los Angeles, 1923).
70. Patterson, R, *A Kitchen Witch's World of Magical Food,* (Moon Books, 2015)
71. Bainton, R, *The Mammoth Book of Superstition: From Rabbits' Feet to Friday the 13th,* (Hatchette UK, London, 2016).
72. Matthews, K, *Great Blueberry Recipes*, (Storey Publishing, U.S.A, 1997) 7.
73. Reitain, E *Is God A Delusion?*, (John Wiley & Sons, 2011).
74. *Orange Coast Magazine*, (U.S.A., March, 2006) 108-109.
75. *Orange Coast Magazine*,(U.S.A., December 1987) 311.
76. de Montespan, Madame La Marquise, *Memoirs of Madame La Marquise de Montespan, Volume 1*, (L.C. Page & Company, Boston, 1899).
77. *Psychopedia,* (Blackhous Applications, 2014).
78. Brown, N, I, *Recipes from old hundred: 200 Years of New England Cooking*, (M.Barrows and Company, U.S.A.,1939) 181.

Chapter 3: Money, Markets and Merchandise: Chocolate at its Sickly Sweetest

1. Library of Congress, Historic American Newspapers, *The Centre Reporter*, (27 April 1876).
2. British Newspaper Archive, *Eastbourne Gazette*, (Wednesday, 29 May 1867).
3. British Newspaper Archive, *Bell's Weekly Messenger*, (Saturday 02 August, 1862).
4. *The Magazine of Domestic Economy, Volume 4*, (W.S. Orr & Co., London, 1839)
5. Duff, C, *Ireland and the Irish*, (Putnam, New York, 1953) 170.
6. British Newspaper Archive, *Newcastle Daily Chronicle*, (Wednesday 26 November 1919).
7. British Newspaper Archive, *Newcastle Daily Chronicle*, (Friday 12 December 1919).
8. British Newspaper Archive, *Whitby Gazette*, (Saturday 06 June 1863).
9. British Newspaper Archive, *Globe*, (Saturday, 24 April 1920).
10. British Newspaper Archive, *Sheffield Evening Telegraph*, (Friday 08 May 1914).
11. British Newspaper Archive, *Leeds Mercury*, (Friday 02 March 1934).
12. British Newspaper Archive, *Bucks Herald,* (Friday 27 February 1948).
13. British Newspaper Archive, *Leeds Times*, (Saturday 21 March, 1846).
14. British Newspaper Archive, *Newcastle Courant*, (Saturday 14 October, 1721.
15. British Newspaper Archive, *Nottingham Evening Post*, (Friday 09 February, 1894).
16. Ryalls, C.W, (ed) *Transactions of The National Association for the Promotion of Social Science*, (Longman's, Green and Co.,1877) 383.
17. British Newspaper Archive, *Manchester Courier and Lancashire general advertiser*, (Saturday 29 January 1881).
18. Burnett, J, *Liquid Pleasures: A Social History of Drinks in Modern Britain*, (Routledge, 2012) 87.
19. Smith, Mary G., *Temperance cook book*, Mercury Book and Job Print. House, California, 1887. 207.

20. D'Arcy,B, *Chocolagrams: The Secret Language of Chocolates*, (Chocolate Boat Press, 2016) 50-51.
21. *Toblerone Cookbook: 40 Fabulous Baking Treats*, (Kyle Books, 2020).
22. Bellin, M *Modern Kosher Meals*, (Bloch Publishing Company, 1934) 95.
23. D'Antonio, M, *Hershey: Milton S.Hershey's Extraordinary Life of Wealth, Empire and Utopian Dreams,* (Simon & Schuster, New York, 2006).
24. Blake, I *So that's Why American chocolate tastes so horrible,* Mail Online, 2017, https://www.dailymail.co.uk/femail/food/article-4155658/The-real-reason-American-chocolate-tastes-terrible.html (accessed 02/10/2020).
25. Hagman, B, *The Gluten-Free Gourmet Makes Dessert*, (Henry Holt and Company, New York, 2003).
26. Binda,V, *The Dynamics of Big Business: Structure, Strategy and Impact in Italy and Spain*, (Routledge, 2013) 116.
27. *Inside US$31.5 billion Ferrero Rocher heir Giovanni Ferrero's family tragedies,* News.com.au, 18 January, 2020 https://www.nzherald.co.nz/business/news/article.cfm?c_id=3&objectid=12301483 (accessed 06/10/2020)
28. Ibid.
29. Elizabeth, M, *My Candy Secrets*, (Frederick A.Stokes, New York, 1919) 70.
30. Higgs, C, *Chocolate Islands: Cocoa, Slavery and Colonial Africa*, (Ohio University Press, 2012) 9.
31. Sinclair, S, Cadbury Bros, Ltd., *Cadbury's Practical Recipes, (Partridge & Love Ltd., Bristol,* 1955) 11.
32. Latosinska, J.N., Latosinska, M (ed) *The Question of Caffeine*, (InTech, Croatia, 2017) 5.
33. Van Houtens Chocolate, *Grace's Guide to British Industrial History*, https://www.gracesguide.co.uk/Van_Houtens_Chocolate, (accessed 02/10/2020).
34. Frederick, J.G., *The Pennsylvania Dutch and Their Cookery*, (The Business Boures, New York, 1935) 357.
35. British Newspaper Archive, *Yorkshire Evening Post*, (Saturday 18 July 1891).
36. British Newspaper Archive, *Truth*, (Thursday 20 December 1888).
37. Francatelli, C.E., *The Cook's Guide and Housekeeper's & Butler's Assistant*, (1862)

38. Chrystal, P, Dickinson, J., *History of Chocolate in York*, (Remember When, Yorkshire, 2012).

39. British Newspaper Archive, *Shepton Mallet Journal*, (Friday 27 July, 1923).

40. British Newspaper Archive, *West Sussex County Times*, (Friday 01 October, 1943)

41. British Newspaper Archive, West Sussex County Times, Friday 27 April, 1945.

42. Deutschmann, E, *The Home Confectioner*, (New York, 1915) 8-10.

43. Rabbi Debbie Prinz, Jewish journal *On the Trail of Chocolate*, May 14, 2014, available from https://jewishjournal.com/culture/food/129134/on-the-trail-of-chocolate/Accessed, 05/10/2020.

44. Neil, M,H, *Candies and Bonbons and How to Make Them*, (D.McKay, Philadelphia, 1913) 74.

45. Troy, S, *Business Biographies: Shaken not Stirred*, (IUniverse, Inc. USA, 2011).

46. Richards, P *Candy for Dessert*, (The Hotel Monthly Press, Chicago, 1919) 23.

47. British Newspaper Archive, *Western Daily Press*, Saturday 23 November 1935.

48. British Newspaper Archive, *Hull Daily*, Saturday 07 December, 1935.

49. Elizabeth,M *My Candy Secrets*, (Frederick A. Stokes, New York, 1919)

50. Tan, W, *Cadbury loses fight for colour purple* The Sunday Morning Herald, April 11, 2008, https://www.smh.com.au/national/cadbury-loses-fight-for-colour-purple-20080411-25gw.html (accessed 02/10/2020)

51. Haigh's Chocolate, Recipes, available from https://www.haighschocolates.com.au/recipes/haighs-celebration-chocolate-mousse-cake, (accessed 13/10/2020).

52. Chalmers, C, *French San Francisco*, (Arcadia Publishing, 2007) 73.

53. Guittard, A, *Guittard Chocolate Cookbook, Chronicle Books,* (San Francisco 2015) 9.

54. Lummis, C.F., *The Landmark Club Cook Book: a California Collection of the Choicest Recipes from Everywhere,* (The Out West company, Los Angeles, 1903)160.

55. *Rowntree's Little Cookbook of 'Elect Recipes,* (Rowntree's, York, Circa 1930).

56. Howard, B, Bruce, A, Duncan, A, Semmes, J, *Tight Lines and a Happy Landing : Anticosti, July, 1937,* (Reese Press, Baltimore, 1937).

57. Allen, E.W, *The New Monthly Magazine Volume 124*, (1862).
58. LeMoine, J.M, *The Chronicles of the St Lawrence*, (Montreal, 1878) 89.
59. Menier Chocolate, recipes, available from : https://www.menier. co.uk/wp-content/uploads/2017/02/Tender-Curried-Lamb-Stew.pdf (accessed 12/10/2020).
60. Sukley, B, *Pennsylvania Made*, (Rowman and Littlefield, 2016) 19.
61. Macky, J, *Journey Through England*, (J.Roberts, 1714).
62. British Newspaper Archive, *Falkirk Herald*, (Wednesday 27 April, 1887).
63. British Newspaper Archive, *Hampshire Chronicle*, (Saturday 05 September 1846).
64. London Evening Standard, (Monday 17 August 1846).
65. Kay, E, *Dining with the Georgians*, (Amberley Publishing, Stroud, 2014).
66. Smith, J, McKay, C (ed) *The Streets of London*, (R.Bentley, London, 1854) 158.
67. British Newspaper Archive, *Evening Herald (Dublin)*, (Saturday 14 January, 2006).
68. Wheatley, H.B., *Hogarth's London: pictures of the manners of the eighteenth century*, (Constable and Company, London 1909).
69. Davey, R, *The Pageant of London*, (Methuen & Co., London, 1906) 387.
70. Dalby, A, *Dangerous Tastes: The Story of Spices*, (University of California Press, USA, 2000) 147.
71. 'St. James's Street', in *Survey of London: Volumes 29 and 30, St James Westminster, Part 1*, ed. F H W Sheppard (London, 1960), pp. 431-432. *British History Online* http://www.british-history.ac.uk/ survey-london/vols29-30/pt1/pp431-432 [accessed 15 April 2020].
72. 'St. James's Street, West Side, Past Buildings', in *Survey of London: Volumes 29 and 30, St James Westminster, Part 1*, ed. F H W Sheppard (London, 1960), pp. 459-471. *British History Online* http://www. british-history.ac.uk/survey-london/vols29-30/pt1/pp459-471 [accessed 16 May 2020].
73. Ibid.
74. Choat, I, *A Chocolate tour of London: a taste of the past*, The Guardian, 23 December, 2013. https://www.theguardian.com/ travel/2013/dec/23/chocolate-tour-of-london, (accessed 15/10/2020)

75. British Newspaper Archive, *Derby Mercury*, (Thursday 08 February, 1733).

76. 'Pall Mall, South Side, Past Buildings: Ozinda's Chocolate House', in *Survey of London: Volumes 29 and 30, St James Westminster, Part 1*, ed. F H W Sheppard (London, 1960), p. 384. *British History Online* http://www.british-history.ac.uk/survey-london/vols29-30/pt1/p384 [accessed 15 April 2020].

77. Smith, M,D., (ed) *Sex and Sexuality in Early America*, (New York University Press, New York and London, 1998).

78. Stubbe, H, *The Indian Nectar, Or a Discourse Concerning Chocolata,* (Andrew Crook, London, 1662).180

79. *Notes and Queries*, (Oxford University Press, 1869) 244.

80. Aslet, C *The Story of Greenwich*, (Harvard University Press, 1999) 255.

81. British Newspaper Archive, *Sussex Advertiser*, (Monday 03 November 1760).

82. Abstracts of the Creditors for the year 1750, George III Financial Papers, 1759, Royal Collection Trust https://gpp.rct.uk/Record.aspx?src=CalmView.Catalog&id=GIII_FIN%2f2%2f3%2f9&pos=4, (accessed 07/10/20).

83. Historic Royal Palaces Enterprises Limited, *Chocolate Fit for a Queen*, (Random House, 2015).

84. Ordinary's Account, 3 November, 1725, Ref: t17251013-25, Old Bailey, https://www.oldbaileyonline.org/browse.jsp?id=t17251013-25&div=t17251013-25&terms=Foster_Snow#highlight, accessed 07/10/2020.

85. Wilkie, J, *Select Trials for murder, robbery, burglary, rapes, sodomy, coining, forgery, piracy and other offences and misdemeanours at the Sessions-House in the Old Bailey*, (London, 1764).

86. Library of Congress, Historic American Newspapers, *Virginia Argus*, (16 February 1814).

87. Kurlansky, M, *The Basque History of the World*, (Vintage books, London, 2000) 115.

88. Sarna, S, *Modern Jewish Baker: Callah, Babka, Bagels and More*, (The Countryman Press, 2017).

89. Chocolate Babka, June Xie, *delish* www.delish.com/cooking/recipe-ideas/a32648362/chocolate-babka-recipe (accessed, 26/10/2020)

Chapter 4: An Audience with Chocolate

1. Hasse, D, *The Greenwood Encyclopaedia of Folktales*, (Greenwood Publishing Group, 2017) 4.
2. Gould, R, *The Corruption of the Times by Money: A Satyr*. (Matthew Wotton, London, 1693) 14.
3. Prior, M, *The Poetical Works of Matthew Prior*, (William Pickering, London, 1835).
4. Parrott, T,M (ed), *The Rape of the Lock and other poems*, (1906).
5. Goldoni, C The *Coffee House*, (Marsilio Publishers, 1998)
6. Glasse, H, *The Art of Cookery Made Plain and Easy*, (J. Rivington & sons, London, 1788) 358.
7. Thackeray, W.M, *The Four Georges*, (Smith, Elder & Co., London) 48-52.
8. Briggs, R, *The English Art of Cookery,* (G.G.J. and J. Robinson, London 1788) 439.
9. Meade, L.T., *A Sweet Girl Graduate*, (1st World Publishing, 2004) 35-36.
10. Civitello, L, *Cuisine and Culture: A History of Food and People,* (John Wiley & Sons, 2008) 232.
11. The Village Improvement Society, *A Book for the Cook : Old Fashioned Receipts for new Fashioned Kitchens,* (Greenfield, Connecticut, 1899)
12. Sammarco, A, *The Baker Chocolate Company: A Sweet History*, (The History Press, U.S.A. 2009).
13. *The Collected Works of Samuel Taylor Coleridge, Volume 1: Lectures*, (Princeton University Press, 2015) 236.
14. Dickens, C, *A Tale of Two Cities* (Chapman & Hall, London, 1868) 118
15. Walsh, J,H, *The English Cookery Book*, (G.Routledge and Company, London, 1859) 249.
16. Joyce, J, *Ulysses*, (General Press, 2016).
17. Sahgal, N, *Prison and Chocolate cake*, (Harper Perennial, 2007) 21.
18. Mathur, S, *Indian Sweets*, (Ocean Books, New Delhi, 2000)
19. Meder, T, *The Flying Dutchman and Other folktales from the Netherlands*, (Greenwood Publishing Group, 2008) 20-21.

20. Hough, P.M., *Dutch Life in Town and Country,* (G.P Putnam's Sons, New York, 1902) 109-110.
21. Rowling, J.K., *Dementors and Chocolate*, Wizarding World https://www.wizardingworld.com/writing-by-jk-rowling/dementors-and-chocolate, (accessed 13/10/20)
22. Blyton, E, *Five Get Into Trouble*, (Hatchette UK, 2014).
23. *Life Magazine*, (1939) 81.
24. Esquivel, L, *Like Water for Chocolate,* (Black Swan, London, 1993) 152.
25. Wood, A, *Home-made Candies*, (Buffalo, 1904) 9.
26. Siddique, H, *Charlie and the Chocolate Factory hero 'was originally black'*. The Guardian. Wednesday 13 September, 2017, https://www.theguardian.com/books/2017/sep/13/charlie-and-the-chocolate-factory-hero-originally-black-roald-dahl (accessed, 09/09/2020).
27. Dahl, S *Very Fond of Food: A Year in Recipes*, (Ten Speed Press, 2012).
28. Harris, J, *Chocolat* (Thorndike Press, 1999) 36.
29. Harris, J, Warde,F, *The French Kitchen: A Cookbook*, (Random House, London, 2002) 220.
30. Georgescu, I, *Carpathia: Food from the heart of Romania,* (Frances Lincoln, 2020)
31. Vanetti, D, *The Querulous Cook; Haute Cuisine in the American, Manner.* Macmillan, New York, 1963) 273.
32. Sharon Otterman, *Handcuffed for selling Churros: Inside the World of illegal food vendors*, The New York Times, November 12, 2019 (accessed 12/10/2020)
33. Kuritz, P, *The Making of Theatre History*, (Pearson College division, 1988) 228.
34. British Newspaper Archive, *Lancashire Evening Post* (Thursday 27 May 1920).
35. British Newspaper Archive, *Daily Herald*, (Thursday 10 June 1920).
36. British Newspaper Archive, *Pall Mall Gazette*, (Monday 15 August 1921).
37. British Newspaper Archive, *Hastings and St. Leonards Observer*, (Saturday 20 September, 1919).
38. British Newspaper Archive, *Millom Gazette*, (Friday 12 September 1913).

39. British Newspaper Archive, *Uxbridge & W. Drayton Gazette* (Friday 29 August, 1930).

40. British Newspaper Archive, *Pall Mall Gazette*, (Saturday 01 July 1916).

41. British Newspaper Archive, *Daily Mirror*, (Saturday 19 February, 1938).

42. British Newspaper Archive, *The Editor's Box*, (Wednesday 06 November 1929).

43. *Rowntree's Little Cookbook of 'Elect Recipes,* (Rowntree's, York, Circa 1930).

44. Cookpad, Suzi Q Cakes with Cream Filling, https://cookpad.com/uk/recipes/7285321-suzy-q-cakes-with-cream-filling, (accessed 14/10/2020).

45. Saunders, N,J, *The Peoples of the Caribbean: An Encyclopedia of Archaeology and Traditional Culture*, (A.B.C. Clio, California, Colorado and Oxford, England. 2005) 65.

46. Stevenson, R, *The First Dated Mention of the Sarabande,* Journal of the American Musicological Society, volume 5, 1952, 29-31.

47. Coomansingh, J, *Cocoa Woman: A Narrative About Cocoa Estate Culture in the British West Indies*, (Xlibris, 2016).

48. Aleman-Fernandez,C.E., *Corpus Christi and Saint John The Baptist: A History of Art in an African-Venezuelan Community*, (ProQuest, United States, 1990).

49. Marquesa de Chocolate, Venezuelatuya.com https://www.venezuela tuya.com/cocina/marquesa_chocolate.htm, (accessed on 18/09/2020).

50. *The American Druggist and Pharmaceutical Record*, Volume 25, (American Druggist Publishing Company New York, 1894) 201.

51. O'Neil, D,S, *Fix the Pumps: The History of the Soda Fountain*, (2010, Art of Drink.com) 34.

52. Park,M,CNN Health News Jan 8,2010, *Soda Fountains contained fecal bacteria, study found.* http://edition.cnn.com/2010/HEALTH/01/08/soda.fountain.bacteria/index.html (accessed 02/10/2020)

53. Ordahl Kupperman, K, *Roanoke: The Abandoned Colony*, (Rowan & Littlefield, United States and Plymouth, UK, 2007).

54. Fleck, H, Fernandez, L, Munves, E,, *Exploring Home and Family Living,* (Prentice-Hall, New Jersey, 1959) 126.

55. *The Magazine of Science, and School of Arts*, Volume 5, (1844) 349.

56. The Recipe for Nougat, Arnaud-Soubeyran, https://www.nougatsoub eyran.com/en/the-recipe-of-nougat/ (accessed 15/10/2020).
57. *The Smell of Chocolate*, Hebrew Songs, http://www.hebrewsongs. com/song-reachshelshokolad.htm (accessed 20/10/2020).
58. Elit Chocolate, Recipes, Chocolate Cheesecake, http://www.elit-chocolate.com/recipies/cheese-cake/ (accessed 16/10/2020).
59. Anna Jones, Sea Salted Chocolate and Lemon Mousse, Fairtrade Foundation, Recipes, https://www.fairtrade.org.uk/media-centre/ blog/anna-jones-sea-salted-chocolate-and-lemon-mousse/ (accessed, 27/10/2020)